LYSIAS
FIVE SPEECHES

LYSIAS
FIVE SPEECHES
Speeches 10, 12, 14, 19 and 22

EDITED WITH INTRODUCTION
AND NOTES BY
E.S. SHUCKBURGH

PUBLISHED BY BRISTOL CLASSICAL PRESS
GENERAL EDITOR: JOHN H. BETTS

(BY ARRANGEMENT WITH MACMILLAN & CO. LTD)

Cover illustration: Head of Lysias (from a Roman copy of a Greek bust, Capitoline Museum, Rome).

First published in 1882 by Macmillan & Co. Ltd

This edition published in 1979, with permission, by
Bristol Classical Press
an imprint of
Gerald Duckworth & Co. Ltd
The Old Piano Factory
48 Hoxton Square, London N1 6PB

Reprinted 1994

A catalogue record for this book is available from the British Library

ISBN 0-906515-44-0

Printed in Great Britain by
Booksprint, Bristol

CONTENTS

Preface v

Introduction:

Life of Lysias 1
Works 13
Style 15
Lysias and Athenian Life and History 19

Text:

10 (IV) Against Theomnestus (384-3 BC) 23
12 (V) Against Eratosthenes (403 BC) 31
14 (VII) Against Alcibiades (395 BC) 60
19 (X) On Aristophanes' Property (after 388-7 BC) 76
22 (XI) Against the Corn Dealers (prob. after 387 BC) 95

Notes:

10 (IV) 104
12 (V) 114
14 (VII) 137
19 (X) 150
22 (XI) 167

Appendices:

I The Thirty 173
II 'Ατιμία 184
III Money 186
IV Life of Lysias (from Preface to 2nd edition) 186
V The Dicasts' Oath 191
VI Additional Notes and References 192

PREFACE

This edition is primarily intended to serve the needs of students studying these five speeches of Lysias for 'A' Level School Certificate Examinations. As no comparable edition of Lysias is at present in print, it may also serve to introduce other students to an orator whose clarity of thought, purity (and relative simplicity) of language make him ideal for reading at an early stage, and whose subject-matter gives a fascinating insight into the history and everyday life of Athens at the close of and just after the Peloponnesian War. The reproduction of an Introduction, Text and Notes first published in 1882 is hardly ideal for the modern student, but E.S. Shuckburgh's work has served for many years and may continue to do so until such time as a more up-to-date edition of some of the speeches can be prepared.

In preparing this edition we have retained Shuckburgh's Introduction, the Text of and Notes on five speeches, and four of his five Appendices. For the original Appendix IV which contained the list of Lysias' speeches from Harpocration's Lexicon, we have substituted some addenda to the Introduction which Shuckburgh included as part of his Preface to the Second Edition (1892). We have also added a sixth Appendix of our own. It was inevitable, in extracting five speeches from Shuckburgh's original sixteen, that the remaining parts of the book would contain cross-references to the omitted parts and, as Shuckburgh almost always quoted his own (Roman) numbering of the speeches with line numbers in his own edition, the references to speeches no longer included in our edition became unintelligible to a reader who was able to refer only to an edition (O.C.T., Loeb) which retained the usual numbering (speech and paragraph) of the *Corpus Lysiacum*. Of Shuckburgh's idiosyncratic references, those to the five speeches included in this volume have been left as they stood (Roman speech number and line number); those to the other speeches have been omitted where they seemed to add little but a verbal parallel or have been marked with an asterisk in the margin. The asterisk invites the reader to turn to Appendix VI where he will find the reference translated into the usual *Corpus Lysiacum* numbering and will, in most cases where it seemed relevant, also find the gist of Shuckburgh's original note, given at the point referred to.

J.H.B., Bristol

INTRODUCTION.

§ 1.—Life of Lysias.[1]

It seems to have been one of Pericles' ideas, as a means of realising his great conception of Athens as a centre and capital of Hellas, to attract to her men of wealth and character wherever he found them. "Men, not walls or ships of war, make a city,"[2] was a principle on which he knew how to act. The high reputation which he enjoyed made it possible for him to do much to accomplish his object. Among those whom he induced to remove to Athens was a certain Cephalus of Syracuse. He was a man of great

[1] *For the facts of the life of Lysias, besides his own story in the κατ' Ἐρατοσθένους, we are indebted (1) to Dionysius of Halicarnassus (about the time of the Christian Era); (2) to the author of the* Lives of the Ten Orators, *attributed probably falsely to Plutarch. (Edit. by A. Westermann, 1833.) The work of the former is rather a dissertation on his style than a biography, a few lines only being devoted to the outline of his life. The latter is somewhat fuller in a biographical sense. An epitome of these lives is found in Suidas (11th cent.* A.D.*), and a dissertation on his style in Photius (9th cent.* A.D.*) There is a graphic description of one incident in his life in his own speech against Eratosthenes (Orat. v. of this edition), and a sketch of his father in Plato's* Republic, *and criticisms on his intellectual position in the* Phædrus. *There is a Latin life of him also by the English scholar, John Taylor.*

[2] *Thucyd. 8, 77, 7.*

wealth,[3] obtained very likely by the manufacture of arms, which in itself would be likely to be useful at Athens.[4] He lived as a metic in the Peiræus, and appears to have attained a great age, and to have been remarkable for the grace with which he bore his years. A pleasant picture of family life is given in the opening scene of Plato's *Republic*, with the central figure of the old Cephalus sitting with his sacrificial wreath on his head, having just conducted or been present at a sacrifice in the αὐλή of his son Polemarchus' house at the Bendideia or festival of Bendis.[5] It was a holiday in Peiræus, and his two other sons, Lysias and Euthydemus, were there to keep it with their aged father, and other guests from the Asty besides. Socrates was struck with the venerable appearance, the cheerfulness, and intellectual activity of Cephalus, and his expressions of surprise and admiration form the prelude to the Dialogue. We may gladly believe that the picture drawn by Plato is not wholly imaginary.[6]

Cephalus appears to have survived to about B.C. 443. Some fifteen years probably after his arrival in Athens, his son Lysias was born, in the year of Philocles (458-7 B.C).[7] His father's wealth made it natural for the boy to mix with the sons of the leading men of the city, and accordingly he attended the best schools in Athens till he was about fifteen

[3] πλούτῳ διαφέροντα, *X Or.* διὰ τὸ πολλὴν οὐσίαν κεκτῆσθαι, *Plat. Rep. 330.*

[4] *Another account stated that he was* banished *from Syracuse on the usurpation of Gelo. But this (B.C. 491-478) is too early. From v. l. 28 we learn that he lived thirty years at Athens; he must therefore have come about B.C. 473.*

[5] *A Thracian goddess identified with Artemis. Hence the sacred enclosure round the temple of Artemis in Munychia was called the Bendideion.*

[6] *Plato, Repub. i. 328.*

[7] *X Or., 320 C. For a discussion of another view as to these dates, see Preface to Second Edition.*

years old (B.C. 444-3). His father being now dead, and he being no doubt under the guardianship of his elder brother, Polemarchus,[8] the latter seems to have been induced to join a party of colonists who were going out, with great expectations of land and wealth, to settle in the territory of Sybaris, and to found a new town on its ruins, to be called Thurii. To Italy, therefore, Lysias accompanied his brother, but seems at first to have devoted himself to the completion of his education under the Syracusan sophists, Tisias and Nicias.[9]

When this was done he obtained a house and an allotment of land at Thurii, and there the next thirty years of his life were spent. Of his life there we know nothing, but we may gather that he took an active part in the politics of the new colony,[10] which presents an interesting picture of the vicissitudes of an Hellenic settlement.

Sybaris, a town of which the wealth and luxury have passed into a proverb, was destroyed by the Crotonians in B.C. 510. Some fifty-seven years later (B.C. 452) an attempt was made to restore it, which was frustrated by the interference of Croton.[11] The inhabitants appealed to various Hellenic States for aid. The prime mover in answering the application was Pericles, who persuaded many able men, among them the

[8] *In vit. X Or. his younger brothers are called Eudidus and Brachyllus. The former should be changed to* Euthydemus. *See Plat. Rep. l. c. The latter Blass infers from [Dem.] Neær., § 22, to have been* brother-in-law *to Lysias. It is not a very certain, though probable, inference.*

[9] *X Or., 321 D. The name Nicias is not known, and has been supposed to have crept into the text as a corruption (dittography) of Tisias. Perhaps we should read* Corax.

[10] *Dr. Thompson's* Introduction to the Phædrus, *p. xxviii.*

[11] *The inhabitants removed to Laus and Scidrus, and there remained. It was their children and grandchildren that attempted the Restoration.—Her. vi. 21.*

historian Herodotus, to take part in the colony.[12] The Athenian contingent was led by Lampon, and started in ten ships. Notice at the same time was sent to various cities of the Peloponnesus. An oracle of Apollo was obtained, ordering them to found a city where they should "drink water from a measure and eat barley-cake without measure;" and the Peloponnesians having met the Athenians at Sybaris, they made a joint search for the place. They supposed themselves to have found it near a fountain, *Thyria*, which had a metal pipe which the country folk called a medimnus.[13] Here, accordingly, in conjunction with the Sybarites, they commenced building their city. In was laid out in a peculiarly regular manner, with four broad streets running parallel to each other, crossed by three diagonal streets. There seem to have been difficulties from the first. To begin with, the Sybarites claimed annoying privileges over the new-comers. They claimed the chief offices; precedence for their women in religious ceremonies; and the possession of land allotments nearest the town. This led to bloody intestine quarrels, which ended, if we may trust Diodorus, in the almost entire extermination of the old Sybarite people, and the consequent enrolment of fresh colonists from all parts of Hellas, who were to be on an equal footing with the older settlers. The colony rose in wealth with

[12] *B.C. 443 in the spring. See Rawlinson's Herod., vol. i. p. 19, note. Diodorus (xii. 9) makes it occur in B.C. 446.*

[13] *Diodor. xii. 9. These consultations and interpretations of oracles are doubtless due to Lampon, who was a mantis; see Plut. Per. 6: and Arist. Av. 521, where the Scholiast explains that he was χρησμόλογος καὶ μάντις, hence the disrespectful mention of θουριομάντεις in Nub. 332. An anecdote, which seems to show that Pericles had no high opinion of him, is quoted in Aristot. Rhet. 3, 18. Diodorus mentions Lampon and Xenocritus as joint founders. Plut. (Nic. 5) says that the leader was Hieron.*

astonishing rapidity, made terms with Croton,—the old enemy of Sybaris,—and established a democratical form of government after the model, it is said, of Charondas of Catana, whom Diodorus wrongly assumes to have personally superintended the business, but who appears to have lived at least 160 years earlier.[14] But the seeds of discord were even then germinating, and the new settlers soon quarrelled with each other, as bitterly as they had done with the original Sybarites. Part of the constitutional arrangements had been the division of the citizens into ten tribes, not according to their place of residence, but to their nations. Thus three were made up of all those who came from the Peloponnesus; three of the more northern Dorian States, as their names imply, Bœotia, Amphictuòn, Doris. The other four were Ionic—Ias, Athenais, Eubois, Nesiotis.[15] The names sufficiently indicate that the old distinction of Ionian and Dorian, such a fruitful source of discord in Hellas, was maintained in the colony. With this distinction came also the rival theories of government, the oligarchic and the democratic. This opposition was brought into prominence some thirty years later by the presence of an Athenian fleet blockading the harbour of the Dorian Syracuse, and the subsequent arrival of a squadron of relief from Sparta.

So long as the contest at Syracuse was undecided, the political state of Thurii remained outwardly unchanged, the favourers of democracy being as yet able to retain their position. But that the other

[14] *Bentley* (Phalaris, *364-5*) *shows that the Thurian constitution was founded on the laws, not of Charondas, but probably of Zaleucus. See also Rawlinson, Her. i. p. 19, note.*

[15] *Diod. xii. 10. Rawlinson's Herod. vol. i. p. 19, note.*

party was possessed of considerable influence was shown by the fact that it was at Thurii that Alcibiades, and those recalled to Athens with him, managed to effect their escape, no doubt by the connivance of the anti-Attic party; Alcibiades himself lying in concealment there for a short time before crossing to the Peloponnesus.[16]

The Oligarchic party, however, were for a time worsted, and in B.C. 413 banished. Demosthenes, when bringing over the second fleet, found on his arrival in Italy that this *coup d'état* had just been completed, and was able to use Thurii as a base of operations while negotiating with the other Italian towns,[17] and obtained from it a contingent of 700 hoplites and 300 javelin men.[18] Finally, Dionysius says that, the failure of the Athenian expedition to Syracuse becoming undoubted, the Oligarchic party returned. There was a revolution, and the leaders of the Democratic party were in their turn banished. Among these was Lysias, who thereupon returned to Athens, where, with a short interruption, he remained for the rest of his life.[19]

He arrived in Athens in the year of Callias (B.C. 412-11); he had left it in the year of Praxiteles (B.C. 444-3). The thirty-two years of his absence had been momentous ones in the fortunes of Athens. He had left the city in the height of her power. Signs of discontent at her supremacy had indeed not been wanting. Bœotia had thrown off the yoke (B.C. 447). The Spartans had invaded the Attic

[16] *Thucyd. vi. 61, 6-7.*

[17] *Thucyd. vii. 33, 4-5,* καὶ καταλαμβάνουσι νεωστὶ στάσει τοὺς τῶν Ἀθηναίων ἐναντίους ἐκπεπτωκότας. *Demosthenes had probably heard of the state of things, for he made almost direct for Thurii.*

[18] *Thucyd. vii. 35.*

[19] *Dionys. Vit. Lys., cp. X Or. 'Lysias.'*

soil; and Samos had revolted (B.C. 445). But the former danger had been averted by the diplomacy of Pericles, and the rebellious Samians had been reduced by his promptitude: Athens was still the leading state in Hellas. But in the interval of his absence the Peloponnesian war had dragged its slow length along; and though there had been reverses on both sides, it was now growing evident that Athens must fall. Her territory had been repeatedly ravaged; war, plague, and revolting subjects, had thinned the number of her citizens and drained her exchequer. For many miles round the city the traces of the war must have been miserably apparent in ruined homesteads, vineyards and olive groves burnt or cut down. The soil was bare and hardened by the constant tramp of cavalry; the farms and olive presses were deserted and ruinous.[20] The enemy were in constant occupation of Decelea.

Inside the city, however, there were no signs of decay; the docks and fortifications of the Peiræus were intact; the long walls and the city walls still seemed to promise safety and perpetuity to the State. The harbour was thronged with corn ships*; the theatre was crowded at the great festivals; the law courts were busy; the supreme ecclesia, however negligently attended on ordinary occasions, was thronged with excited citizens when any grave matter was pending, and still passed haughty and imperious decrees. There had been, too, in these thirty-two years, an extraordinary outburst of literary activity. In them the masterpieces of Herodotus and of Sophocles, Euripides, and Aristophanes, had been produced, and many other works which are now lost

[20] *See Lysias, Orat.* 7. § 7-8; *cp. Thucyd.* 7, 27, 5, ἵπποι ἀπεχωλοῦντο ἐν γῇ ἀποκρότῳ. * *Xen. Hell.* 1, 1, 35.

to us. Some of the most famous sophists of the day had visited Athens and gathered round them an eager crowd of listeners. Socrates, amidst fame and obloquy, had been stimulating the youth of the city by an influence which, if not literary, was the cause of literature; and the young Plato, in his eighteenth year when Lysias returned, was learning from the lips of his master lessons which his transcendent powers were destined to mould into world-wide influences. We cannot doubt that Lysias, though absent from Athens, had shared to the full in the intellectual feast which she had been preparing for the world; and that he must have looked upon a return to her as to the metropolis of literature and philosophy,[21] —glad to escape from the vexations of provincial politics and the narrowness of provincial life.

Politics at Athens, however, were as unsettled as those he left at Thurii. When he arrived the Four Hundred were enjoying their brief supremacy. But there does not seem to have been any danger to a metic, who had no share in politics, and who did not even reside in the Asty. His elder brother, Polemarchus, either accompanied him, or more probably had preceded him in his return. The two brothers resided in the Peiræus,* and conducted together a manufactory of armour, and appear to have been possessed of considerable wealth. The circumstances of the time would be likely to make their business a profitable one, and the public events of their seven years' residence there do not seem to have interfered with their quiet prosperity. The Spartans might be

[21] *So Pericles calls Athens* τῆς Ἑλλάδος παίδευσις, *Thucyd. 2, 41, 1: and Isocrates says of her that* τὸ τῶν Ἑλλήνων ὄνομα πεποίηκε μηκέτι τοῦ γένους ἀλλὰ τῆς διανοίας δοκεῖν εἶναι. *Panegyr. § 51.*

* *See Preface to Second Edition.*

beaten at Cyzicus, or the Athenians at Notium; generals might be impeached for misconduct at Arginusæ; Alcibiades be welcomed with chaplets and hymns, or be deposed from his command amidst popular execrations;—in any case the armourer would be driving a good trade, and the metic's tax was a light evil compared to the dangers of citizens in these troublous times.[22]

But evil days were coming upon them. The disaster at Ægospotami (405 B.C.) was followed by the starving out of the city and its surrender to Lysander, by the overthrow of the constitution and the setting up of the Thirty (404 B.C.) The year of anarchy (year of Pythodorus 404-3) was a terrible one for many. Still an unoffending and industrious metic, meddling not at all in politics, might hope to be unmolested by anything worse than increased public burdens. But the Thirty were in dire want of money, and in an evil moment two of their number suggested that there were many metics, unprotected by the new constitution, residing in Athens and the Peiræus, who possessed great wealth, and might plausibly be represented as disaffected to the Government. Let them be arrested and put to death on the charge of disaffection, and their wealth be confiscated to the State. This suggestion, in spite of the protest of Theramenes, which cost him his life, was eagerly adopted. Ten were to be first selected, not all rich, lest the object of the tyrants should be too apparent.[23] In the first fatal list were the names

[22] *Lysias does not seem to have engaged in any active service, as metics in times of difficulty occasionally did. A man of his name is mentioned as in command of ships in B.C. 406, Xen. Hell. 1, 6, 30, and as one of the six generals executed after Arginusæ, id. 1, 7, 2.*

* [23] *Xen. Hell. 2, 3, 21. Lysias, vi. l. 48.*

of Lysias and his brother Polemarchus. What fol lowed we know from his own indignant narrative.

The party of the Tyrants to whom the task fell came with their attendants suddenly to Lysias' house. He, in complete unconsciousness, was entertaining a party of guests, who fled precipitately, leaving Lysias in the hands of the Tyrants. He was committed to the charge of Peison, while the others went to the workshop and took an inventory of the slaves working in it. Lysias was at once fully aware of the desperate nature of his danger and the only means of averting it. He offered Peison a talent to let him go. Peison consented, but followed him when he went to his money chest, and finding there a considerably larger sum, took the whole, but seems to have meant to carry out his bargain as to letting Lysias slip. But as they were leaving the house they met two others of the Thirty, to whom Peison explained that he was on his way to the house of Polemarchus. These two offered to take charge of Lysias, which Peison was afraid to decline. He was accordingly taken for custody to the house of Damnippus, where others arrested in a similar manner were being guarded. Damnippus was a personal friend, and by his connivance Lysias took advantage of a back door, and escaped to the house of a ship captain, Archeneos, where he might be sure of securing some passage. Here he lay hid till he had ascertained that Polemarchus had been arrested and put in prison, and that night he effected his escape to Megara.[24]

Here he appears to have remained quietly for some months, and though his property in the Peiræus had been seized, he seems to have still possessed

[24] *Lysias, v. ll. 40-111.*

some means, perhaps from money invested in foreign towns, or goods warehoused abroad. For no sooner had the expedition of Thrasybulus to Phylè (Sept. 404 B.C.) given the Democrats new hopes, than he threw himself into their cause with energy, and supported it with liberality. He supplied Thrasybulus with 2000 drachmæ, and persuaded his friend Thrasydæus of Elis, always an opponent of Sparta [Xen. Hell. 3, 2, 2], to give or lend two talents. He supplied 200 shields, and in conjunction with Hermon raised over 300 men.[25]

Accordingly, when the party of Thrasybulus was triumphant and in possession of Athens, a decree was passed by the ecclesia, on the proposition of Thrasybulus, conferring on him the full Athenian citizenship. The first use which he made of his new privileges was to impeach Eratosthenes, one of the two tyrants who remained in the city, for the murder of his brother Polemarchus. The tyrants had been expressly exempted from the amnesty made between the party of Thrasybulus and the party of the city; but Lysias, if he ever really delivered his speech, seems to have been unsuccessful in obtaining his condemnation, and he himself soon lost the power of conducting an impeachment, which could only be done by a citizen. His enfranchisement had been passed at the end of the so-called year of anarchy, and had not had the previous sanction of the senate, which had not as yet been properly appointed; and when the ordinary constitution was re-established with the beginning of the year of Euclides (*i.e.* Midsummer 403 B.C.), one Archinus brought in a γραφὴ

[25] *Vit. X Or. 835. Prof. Mahaffy seems to regard this passage as taken from Lysias' own speech περὶ τῶν ἰδίων εὐεργεσιῶν, Hist. Gr. Lit. 1, p. 140. It may be so.*

παρανόμων against Thrasybulus, and the decree was quashed.[26] Lysias thenceforward had to be content with the status of an Isoteles, the highest grade to which a naturalised resident could attain, and differing from that of a full citizen probably in little except the right of holding offices, of speaking and voting in the ecclesia, and therefore of acting as prosecutor in impeachments.[27]

But the reputation obtained by his speech delivered against Eratosthenes seems to have put in his way a new means of acquiring wealth—namely, by the exercise of the profession of speech-writer. If the *Phædrus* of Plato is not wholly dramatic, he appears, in the interval of his residence at Athens before the Revolution, to have acquired some reputation for his compositions, and a supposed essay by him on love forms the text of that dialogue. But his inclination for philosophy or sophistic writings must now be considered as superseded by the more practical and remunerative pursuit.[28] In this his activity must have been very great. The Pseudo-Plutarch asserts that as many as 425 speeches had been attributed to him, of which Dionysius admitted 230 as genuine. It is evident, at any rate, from the quotations of Harpocration, that we have but a small fragment of the work left by him.[29] He died in B.C. 378, thus

26 *Archinus seems to have made several such charges against Thrasybulus, who, no doubt, in the then unsettled state of things, must have more than once laid himself open to the charge. See Æschines, c. Ctes., § 195. The irregularity in this case was that the decree was an ἀπροβούλευτον ψήφισμα.*

27 *Boeckh, pp. 540, 541. Hermann, Pol. Ant. § 116.*

28 *"There is no doubt that some discredit attached to this profession of a λογογράφος, at least sufficient to deter a man of wealth and good connections from engaging in it."—Dr. Thompson,* Phædrus, *Introd., p. xxvii.*

29 *Harpocration quotes from some ninety speeches attributed to Lysias.*

reaching the age of fourscore. Of the twenty-five last years of his life, beyond the fact that they were busily employed in his new profession, we know little or nothing. The Pseudo-Plutarch tells us that he married his niece, the daughter of Brachyllus,[30] a * connection legal at Athens [see Orat. xvi.]; and there seems to be the ghost of some scandal as to his connection with an hetæra, called by the Pseudo-Demosthenes (c. Neæram, 1351) Metaneira, and by Athenæus Lagis.[31] On the strength of a passage in one of his speeches (de pecun. Arist. § 19) he has been credited with a joint mission to Dionysius of Syracuse, but his name has probably no right to appear in the text. We cannot doubt, however, that he must have been somewhat more than a mere spectator of the events which from 394 B.C. to the time of his death gradually raised Athens from her degradation to something like her old power on the seas. Nor, while engaged in the calling of a speech-writer, does he seem to have forsaken the philosophical studies and friendships of earlier times, for he is said to have composed a defence of Socrates. That his earlier writings had attracted great attention is shown by Plato, who puts into the mouth of Phædrus the description of him as δεινότατος τῶν νῦν γράφειν, while lamenting his turning from the lofty pursuit of philosophy to that of the professional speech-writer: in which passage Plato no doubt puts into the mouth of a contemporary the criticism of a later date.

§ 2.—Works.

The Pseudo-Plutarch mentions three classes of writings left by Lysias:—

[30] *See note 8.*

[31] *Athenæus, xvii. 592 l.*

(1.) Public speeches, *i.e.* speeches delivered, or meant to be delivered, in his own person before the ecclesia. Of these he mentions two—(1) A defence of his citizenship against the decree of Archinus.[32] (2) A speech against the Thirty, by which he seems to mean the κατ' Ἐρατοσθένους. The short time during which Lysias enjoyed, if he may be said to have ever enjoyed, full citizenship accounts for the small number of these speeches.

(2.) Speeches written for others in public or in private causes. It was in these that Lysias enjoyed the greatest success and reputation, having only twice, it is said, lost a case. It is not possible to decide even approximately their number. Probably many of those which he composed survived their delivery a very short time. When in subsequent times collections were made of his speeches, many were attributed to him which he did not compose.

As we have seen, of the 425 assigned to him, more than half were rejected by Dionysius. Of this half only thirty-four have survived to our time, and of them no inconsiderable proportion are ousted from their place of honour by modern criticism.

(3.) Besides these he composed rhetorical treatises, public addresses, letters, panegyrics, funeral orations, erotics. A specimen of a funeral speech appears as Or. ii. in editions of his works, but its genuineness is denied. Of erotics, the speech in the *Phædrus* (Plato, Phaedr. 230-236) may perhaps be a genuine production of his, or a close imitation of some of his compositions.

[32] *Perhaps the lost speech περὶ τῶν ἰδίων εὐεργεσιῶν.*

§ 3.—The Style of Lysias.

There are two points of view from which we may regard a writer's style, the historical and the critical. As to the first, the interest attaching to the writings of Lysias arises from the consideration of the place he holds in the development of Attic prose. The treatises of the old philosophers, the history of Herodotus, though read and admired at Athens, were in a foreign dialect. Thucydides, with all his splendour, betrays the awkwardness of a man using a tool not yet thoroughly adapted to the work it is to do.[33] But Attic life had developed with marvellous rapidity in the fifth century B.C., and with this enlarged life came constant and pressing needs for the artistic and trained use of language. Every day brought some occasion for clear or persuasive statements. The demand created the supply. What Lysias did hundreds did also. Composition ceased to be an affair for the few; it was the daily need of the many. It is in such circumstances that really great work is produced; and from the multitude of mediocre or passable workmen the genius will surely emerge. The peculiar needs of the time irresistibly moulded the language used. The audience to be persuaded was a mixed one. Before all things, a man to be successful must be intelligible to persons of ordinary intelligence. If he indulged in long digressions he would weary. If he used high-flown language he would be laughed at. If he contradicted himself, if he told his story ill, if he confused names and dates and facts, he would miss the objects of his speech—

[33] *For an opposite view as to the style of Thucydides, see Mahaffy, Hist. of Gr. Lit. ii. pp. 110-111.*

persuasion and conviction. The audience, however, which he addressed, though a mixed one, had been long accustomed to listen to the oratory of the Tragedians; they had learnt to admire the gorgeous word-painting of Æschylus, the pure taste of Sophocles, the simplicity and pathos of Euripides. They would, therefore, be easily disgusted at language too bald, at a style showing lack of ear for rhythm or culture, at dulness and absence of emotion.

The critical view of Lysias' style will show how far he answered to these demands.

We may notice, then, that he conspicuously tells a story well. His facts are well arranged, their connection clearly shown, and their significance not left doubtful. The language in which he tells it is simple without being vulgar, and clear without being bald or inartistic. The meaning is generally to be caught at a glance. Very rarely in him are found long or involved sentences, words used in a recondite sense, or words employed at all not in common use among all educated persons of his time. And though his object is nearly always to tell a simple story simply, he is saved from being dull,—first by his dramatic faculty, by which he managed to adapt the speech which he wrote to the character of the person who delivered it, of which the speeches "for Mantitheus" and "for the Cripple" are good instances; and secondly, by his power of occasionally rising above the placid stream of his narrative or argument to real passion. Of this his denunciations of the Thirty in the Eratosthenes may serve as one instance, and the account of the interview of the mother of the orphans with her father, in the last speech in this edition, as another and very striking one.

Among ancient writers on oratory a very high

place has always been assigned to Lysias. The qualities which they admired in him were his simplicity and purity of style, his power of clear statement, and freedom from superfluous ornamentation.

Cicero, B.C. 104-43.

Cicero calls him *disertissimus*, and selects as his distinctive merit *subtilitas*. He is *subtilis, elegans, prope orator perfectus*, Demosthenes being the standard of absolute perfection. And though he attained to such refinement of style and such subtilty and almost cunning in seeing and stating his points, he had also nervous strength and force (*lacerti*). He is *venustissimus* and *politissimus*, though generally not *amplus* or *grandis*. This, however, was from deliberate purpose, as the causes he usually pleaded required the former qualities rather than the latter.[34]

Dionysius of Halicarnassus, circ. A.D. 18.

Dionysius has left us an elaborate criticism of Lysias' style. He selects as his points of praise: (1) his lucidity and the purity of his Attic;[35] (2) the homeliness and simplicity of his language, while he yet contrives to dignify his subject. This he contrasts with the vulgarity and extravagance (φορτικὴν καὶ ὑπέρογκον κατασκευήν) of Gorgias;[36] (3) his clearness of statement as well as language;[37] (4) his condensed and terse style;[38] (5) his graphic power—the power, that is, of conveying clear ideas to others;[39] (6) his

[34] *Cicero de Orat. 118*; ib. *316*; *Brut. 17*; ib. *31*; *Orat. 15*; ib. *16*; *de opt. gen. Or. 3*.

[35] *Vit. Lys.*, καθαρὸς τὴν ἑρμηνείαν καὶ τῆς Ἀττικῆς γλώττης ἄριστος κανών.

[36] ib. διὰ τῶν κυρίων τε καὶ κοινῶν καὶ ἐν μέσῳ κειμένων ὀνομάτων κτλ.

[37] ib. σαφήνεια . . . οὐ μόνον ἐν τοῖς ὀνόμασι ἀλλὰ καὶ ἐν τοῖς πράγμασι.

[38] ib. ἡ συστρέφουσα τὰ νοήματα καὶ στρογγύλως ἐκφέρουσα λέξις.

[39] ib. δύναμίς τις ὑπὸ τὰς αἰσθήσεις ἄγουσα τὰ λεγόμενα.

dramatic faculty (ἠθοποιΐα), or power of suiting words and sentiments to the individuals for whom the speeches are composed;[40] (7) his power of adapting his style to the subject and the hearers, and to the necessities of the case, adopting, for instance, quite different styles for the law court, the ecclesia, and the national assembly (πανήγυρις). Thus, too, in the various parts of a speech he varies his style. In the *exordium* it is quiet and didactic (καθεστηκυῖα καὶ ἠθική); in the *narrative* convincing and concise (πιθανὴ καὶ ἀπερίεργος); in the *demonstration* terse and condensed (στρογγύλη καὶ πυκνή); when he enlarges and appeals to the emotions (παθαινομένῳ) it is solemn and genuine (σεμνὴ καὶ ἀληθινή); in his summing up it is analytic and brief.[41] (8) Besides these there is that indefinable and nameless something, which, like the bloom of personal beauty, harmony in music, or felicity in poetry, cannot be easily or exactly expressed, but may perhaps be partially represented by the word "charm" or "grace" (χάρις).

Quintilian, A.D. 42-118.

Quintilian speaks of his dramatic faculty, his simplicity and freedom from affectation, his easy and elegant style, his gracefulness and model Attic.[42]

[40] *Vit. Lys.*, τὰ προσήκοντα ἑκάστοις ἀποδοῦναι πάθη τε καὶ ἔργα. *For examples of this see especially Orations viii. and xiii.*

[41] *The last two sections are embraced in the* peroratio. *The four parts of a speech are thus taken, viz. the* exordium, narratio, demonstratio, peroratio. *By calling his style in his summing up "analytic"* (διαλελυμένη), *he seems to refer to his distinct separation of the various heads of his argument in a recapitulation. For a good specimen see Or.* 7. *§ 42-3.*

[42] *Quint. iii. 8; ix. 4; x. 1; xii. 10. He, however, seems to think him wanting in greatness,* puro tamen fonti quam magno flumini proprior.

Gellius quotes Favorinus as saying that no word can be taken from Plato without injury to his literary perfection, none from Lysias without injury to his meaning.[43] A. Gellius, circ. A.D. 140.

The upshot of these criticisms seems to be that Lysias is to be regarded as furnishing a model of correct language, and as being the type of a business-like speaker, who kept steadily in view as his first object that he should enlighten and convince his hearers, and this without loss of literary grace or general interest. Many critics, Plutarch tells us, were fond of comparing the style of the elder Cato with that of Lysias.[44] Plutarch himself dissents from the judgment; but that it should have been formed at all is an illustration of the impression made generally on readers by Lysias.

§ 4.—Value of Lysias as illustrating Athenian Life and History.

Lysias, as a model of style, and as illustrating a special phase in the development of Greek prose writing, has thus much interest. But there is another kind of interest in his work. The subjects with which he has to deal were closely connected, either with historical events or with the everyday life of his time. In the case of historical events his contribution to our knowledge possesses the advantages which contemporary *allusions* must ever have over formal history. And in the matter of the illustration of common life we feel that he deals with his topics

43 *A. Gellius, Noctes, 2, 5.*

44 *Plutarch, Cato, vii. Cf. Cicero, Brutus, 16, 63,* sed ille Græcus ab omni laude felicior. *Though he acknowledges* nonnulla similitudo *between them.*

without exaggeration or ulterior design. Accordingly, in reading his speeches, we catch many clear glimpses of Athenian life and habits, of Hellenic politics and sentiment, worth a good many pages of Xenophon and whole books of Diodorus. We shall find illustrated the cheapness of Athenian life [45] to remind us of Pericles' boast φιλοκαλοῦμεν μετ' εὐτελείας. We shall learn the prices of provisions, of land and houses, of animals and tombs.[46] We shall hear of the simplicity of their houses and furniture;[47] of the sacredness of the duty of performing funeral rites;[48] of the mourning robes of their women;[49] of the duties of children to parents; of the father, brother, or guardian, to daughters, sisters, or wards.[50] We may see the Athenian citizen in his daily lounge in the Agora, or hanging about the law courts on the chance of some amusing scene or speech.[51] We may go on the Corn Exchange and watch the brokers trying to evade the law, and eagerly catching at or spreading rumours that may lower or raise the price of their goods.[52] Or we may stroll into the barbers' or perfumers' shops, or the banker's stall, and listen to the gossip of the town, and in some secret chamber see some young spendthrift stake his last drachma on the fall of the dice.[53] Penetrating deeper into social relations, we get light upon the connection of master and slave; the discredit of the position of the latter even when emancipated; the difficulties of escape, or in proving an emancipation once obtained. We have a picture of the vicissitude of landownership in Attica;[55] of an elementary "poor law;"[56] of the

* [45] *xvi. 165, 245.* [46] *xvi. 165, 171, 176.*
* [47] *x. l. 200.* [48] *v. l. 680; vi. l. 311; x. l. 41; xvi. 60.*
* [49] *vi. l. 276.* [50] *vi. l. 313; x. l. 404.* [51] *iv. l. 70; x. l. 65.*
[52] *xi. § 14-15.* [53] *iii. l. 29; xii. l. 15; xiii. l. 147.*
* [55] *ii. § 4-8.* [56] *Or. xiii.*

rush of all the neighbours to help themselves from the abandoned house on a confiscated estate.[57] In Hellenic politics we have vividly illustrated the endless shifts and turns of public feeling; the rapid combinations of States, and their as rapid dissolution; and especially the importance of the part played by individual enterprise and speculation in the various expeditions and wars which arose from time to time between the Hellenic States.[58] Nor is it a small contribution which Lysias makes to the fulness of our understanding of an interesting period of the history of Athens; that, namely, from her fall in B.C. 405 to her partial revival in B.C. 394-390; nor to our power of rightly appreciating the career and character of some of her most eminent citizens—Alcibiades, Theramenes, Conon, Thrasybulus.

57 *x. § 31.*

58 *See the cases of Alcibiades, Conon, and Thrasybulus, and especially the account of the last expedition of Thrasybulus in Or. 28.*

ORATION IV. [10.]

For the Prosecution, against Theomnestus on a Charge of Slander.

§ 1. *Many of you were present when Theomnestus accused me of killing my father. For this slander I appeal to you to punish him.*

Μαρτύρων μὲν οὐκ ἀπορίαν μοι ἔσεσθαι
δοκῶ, ὦ ἄνδρες δικασταί· πολλοὺς γὰρ ὑμῶν
ὁρῶ δικάζοντας τῶν τότε παρόντων, ὅτε Λυσίθεος
Θεόμνηστον εἰσήγγελλε τὰ ὅπλα ἀποβεβληκότα,
οὐκ ἐξὸν αὐτῷ, δημηγορεῖν· ἐν ἐκείνῳ γὰρ τῷ
ἀγῶνι τὸν πατέρα μ' ἔφασκεν ἀπεκτονέναι τὸν
ἐμαυτοῦ. ἐγὼ δ', εἰ μὲν τὸν ἑαυτοῦ με ἀπεκτονέναι 2
ᾐτιᾶτο, συγγνώμην ἂν εἶχον αὐτῷ τῶν εἰρημένων
(φαῦλον γὰρ αὐτὸν καὶ οὐδενὸς ἄξιον ἡγούμην)·
οὐδ' εἴ τι ἄλλο τῶν ἀπορρήτων ἤκουσα, οὐκ ἂν
ἐπεξῆλθον αὐτῷ (ἀνελεύθερον γὰρ καὶ λίαν
φιλόδικον εἶναι νομίζω κακηγορίας δικάζεσθαι)·
νυνὶ δὲ αἰσχρόν μοι εἶναι δοκεῖ περὶ τοῦ πατρός, 3
οὕτω πολλοῦ ἀξίου γεγενημένου καὶ ὑμῖν καὶ τῇ
πόλει, μὴ τιμωρήσασθαι τὸν ταῦτ' εἰρηκότα. καὶ
παρ' ὑμῶν εἰδέναι βούλομαι πότερον δώσει δίκην,
ἢ τούτῳ μόνῳ Ἀθηναίων ἐξαίρετόν ἐστι καὶ ποιεῖν
καὶ λέγειν παρὰ τοὺς νόμους ὅ τι ἂν βούληται.

§ 2. *I was only thirteen when my father was killed, and I had every motive to wish him to live, for my elder brother seized his property, and as my guardian deprived me of all share in it.*

4 Ἐμοὶ γάρ, ὦ ἄνδρες δικασταί, ἔτη ἐστι[1]
τριάκοντα τρία, ἐξ ὅτου δ' ὑμεῖς κατεληλύθατε
εἰκοστὸν τουτί. φαίνομαι οὖν τρισκαιδεκέτης
ὢν ὅτε ὁ πατὴρ ὑπὸ τῶν τριάκοντα ἀπέθνησκε.
ταύτην δὲ ἔχων τὴν ἡλικίαν οὔτε τί[2] ἐστιν
ὀλιγαρχία ἠπιστάμην, οὔτε ἂν ἐκείνῳ ἀδικουμέ-
5 νῳ ἐδυνάμην βοηθῆσαι. καὶ μὲν δὴ οὐκ ὀρθῶς
τῶν χρημάτων ἕνεκα ἐπεβούλευσα ἂν αὐτῷ· ὁ
γὰρ πρεσβύτερος ἀδελφὸς Πανταλέων ἅπαντα
παρέλαβε, καὶ ἐπιτροπεύσας ἡμᾶς τῶν πατρῴων
ἀπεστέρησεν, ὥστε πολλῶν ἕνεκα, ὦ ἄνδρες
δικασταί, προσῆκέ μοι αὐτὸν βούλεσθαι ζῆν.
ἀνάγκη μὲν οὖν περὶ αὐτῶν μνησθῆναι, οὐδὲν δὲ δεῖ
πολλῶν λόγων· σχεδὸν ἐπίστασθε ἅπαντες ὅτι
ἀληθῆ λέγω. ὅμως δὲ μάρτυρας αὐτῶν παρέξομαι.

EVIDENCE OF ABOVE FACTS PUT IN.

§ 3. *My opponent will not controvert these facts, but will plead that what he said was that I "killed" my father, whereas the law forbids one to call another a "homicide." But this quibble will not hold good, and in fact the terms he used are those employed in trials of murder in the Areopagus. And he himself once prosecuted Theon for saying of him that he "ἐρριφέναι τὴν ἀσπίδα," though in the law the word used is "ἀποβεβληκέναι."*

6 Ἴσως τοίνυν, ὦ ἄνδρες δικασταί, περὶ τούτων
μὲν οὐδὲν ἀπολογήσεται, ἐρεῖ δὲ πρὸς ὑμᾶς
ἅπερ ἐτόλμα λέγειν καὶ πρὸς τὸν διαιτητήν, ὡς
οὐκ ἔστι τῶν ἀπορρήτων, ἐάν τίς τιν' εἴπῃ τὸν
πατέρα ἀπεκτονέναι· τὸν γὰρ νόμον οὐ ταῦτ'

[1] ἐστι ego dedi. al. εἰσί.
[2] MSS. οὔτ' εἰ ἔστιν. *Madv.* et alii correxerunt.

ἀπαγορεύειν, ἀλλ' ἀνδροφόνον οὐκ ἐᾶν λέγειν.
ἐγὼ δ' οἶμαι δεῖν ὑμᾶς, ὦ ἄνδρες δικασταί, οὐ 7
περὶ τῶν ὀνομάτων διαφέρεσθαι ἀλλὰ τῆς τούτων
διανοίας, καὶ πάντας εἰδέναι ὅτι, ὅσοι ἀπεκτόνασί
τινας, καὶ ἀνδροφόνοι τῶν αὐτῶν εἰσι, καὶ ὅσοι
ἀνδροφόνοι εἰσί, καὶ ἀπεκτόνασί τινας. πολὺ
γὰρ ἂν ἔργον ἦν τῷ νομοθέτῃ ἅπαντα τὰ ὀνόματα
γράφειν, ὅσα τὴν αὐτὴν δύναμιν ἔχει· ἀλλὰ περὶ
ἑνὸς εἰπὼν περὶ πάντων ἐδήλωσεν. οὐ γὰρ 8
δήπου, ὦ Θεόμνηστε, εἰ μέν τίς σ' εἴποι πα-
τραλοίαν ἢ μητραλοίαν, ἠξίους ἂν αὐτὸν ὀφλεῖν
σοι δίκην, εἰ δέ τις εἴποι ὡς τὴν τεκοῦσαν ἢ τὸν
φύσαντα ἔτυπτες, ᾤου ἂν αὐτὸν ἀζήμιον δεῖν
εἶναι ὡς οὐδὲν τῶν ἀπορρήτων εἰρηκότα. ἡδέως 9
γὰρ ἄν σου πυθοίμην (περὶ τοῦτο γὰρ δεινὸς
εἶ καὶ μεμελέτηκας καὶ ποιεῖν καὶ λέγειν)· εἴ τίς
σε εἴποι ῥῖψαι τὴν ἀσπίδα, ἐν δὲ τῷ νόμῳ εἴρητο,
ἐάν τις φάσκῃ ἀποβεβληκέναι, ὑπόδικον εἶναι,
οὐκ ἂν ἐδικάζου αὐτῷ, ἀλλ' ἐξήρκει ἄν σοι
ἐρριφέναι τὴν ἀσπίδα λέγοντι "οὐδέν μοι μέλει·[3]
οὐδὲ γὰρ τὸ αὐτό ἐστι ῥῖψαι καὶ ἀποβεβληκέναι;"
ἀλλ' οὐδ' ἂν τῶν ἕνδεκα γενόμενος ἀποδέξαιο, 10
εἴ τις ἀπάγοι τινὰ φάσκων θοἰμάτιον ἀποδεδύσθαι
ἢ τὸν χιτωνίσκον ἐκδεδύσθαι, ἀλλ' ἀφείης ἂν τὸν
αὐτὸν τρόπον, ὅτι οὐ λωποδύτης ὀνομάζεται.
οὐδ' εἴ τις παῖδα ἐξαγαγὼν ληφθείη, οὐκ ἂν
φάσκοις αὐτὸν ἀνδραποδιστὴν εἶναι, εἴπερ μαχῇ
τοῖς ὀνόμασιν, ἀλλὰ μὴ τοῖς ἔργοις τὸν νοῦν
προσέξεις, ὧν ἕνεκα τὰ ὀνόματα πάντες τίθενται.

[3] MS. *οὐδέν σοι μέλει.* Correxit *Scheibe* pro λέγοντι. *Francken* vult ἀκούοντι.

11 Ἔτι τοίνυν σκέψασθε, ὦ ἄνδρες δικασταί·
οὑτοσὶ γάρ μοι δοκεῖ ὑπὸ ῥᾳθυμίας καὶ μαλακίας
οὐδ' εἰς Ἄρειον πάγον ἀναβεβηκέναι. πάντες
γὰρ ἐπίστασθε ὅτι ἐν ἐκείνῳ τῷ χωρίῳ, ὅταν τὰς
τοῦ φόνου δίκας δικάζωνται, οὐ διὰ τούτου τοῦ
ὀνόματος τὰς διωμοσίας ποιοῦνται, ἀλλὰ δι'
οὗπερ ἐγὼ κακῶς ἀκήκοα· ὁ μὲν γὰρ διώκων
ὡς ἔκτεινε διόμνυται, ὁ δὲ φεύγων ὡς οὐκ
12 ἔκτεινεν. οὐκοῦν ἄτοπον ἂν εἴη [ἀφεῖναι][4] τὸν
δόξαντα κτεῖναι φάσκοντα ἀνδροφόνον εἶναι, ὅτι
ὁ διώκων, ὡς ἔκτεινε, τὸν φεύγοντα διωμόσατο.
τί γὰρ ταῦτα, ὧν οὗτος ἐρεῖ, διαφέρει; καὶ
αὐτὸς μὲν Θέωνι κακηγορίας ἐδικάσω εἰπόντι σε
ἐρριφέναι τὴν ἀσπίδα. καίτοι περὶ μὲν τοῦ
ῥῖψαι οὐδὲν ἐν τῷ νόμῳ εἴρηται, ἐὰν δέ τις εἴπῃ
ἀποβεβληκέναι τὴν ἀσπίδα, πεντακοσίας δραχμὰς
13 ὀφείλειν κελεύει. οὐκ οὖν δεινόν, εἰ ὅταν μὲν
δέῃ σὲ* κακῶς ἀκούσαντα τοὺς ἐχθροὺς τιμωρεῖσθαι, οὕτω τοὺς νόμους ὥσπερ ἐγὼ νῦν λαμβάνειν,
ὅταν δ' ἕτερον παρὰ τοὺς νόμους εἴπῃς κακῶς,
οὐκ ἀξιοῖς δοῦναι δίκην; πότερον οὕτω σὺ
δεινὸς εἶ ὥστε, ὅπως ἂν βούλῃ, οἷός τ' εἶ χρῆσθαι
τοῖς νόμοις, ἢ τοσοῦτον δύνασαι ὥστε οὐδέποτε
οἴει τοὺς ἀδικουμένους ὑπὸ σοῦ τιμωρίας τεύ-
14 ξεσθαι; εἶτ' οὐκ αἰσχύνῃ οὕτως ἀνοήτως δια-
κείμενος, ὥστε οὐκ ἐξ ὧν εὖ πεποίηκας τὴν πόλιν,
ἀλλ' ἐξ ὧν ἀδικῶν οὐ δέδωκας δίκην, οἴει δεῖν
πλεονεκτεῖν; καί μοι ἀνάγνωθι τὸν νόμον.

[4] ἀφεῖναι hic scribere vult *Scheibe*. Al. ἀποφεύγειν post κτεῖναι interponunt. * *W.* δοκῇ σοι . . ἀκούσαντι.

LAW PUT IN, WHICH MAKES THE ACCUSATION OF THROWING AWAY ONE'S SHIELD SLANDER.

§ 4. *I will now quote old laws still in force though the actual expressions are obsolete and not in use.*

Ἐγὼ τοίνυν, ὦ ἄνδρες δικασταί, ὑμᾶς μὲν 15
πάντας εἰδέναι ἡγοῦμαι ὅτι ἐγὼ μὲν ὀρθῶς λέγω, τοῦτον δὲ οὕτω σκαιὸν εἶναι ὥστε οὐ δύνασθαι μαθεῖν τὰ λεγόμενα. βούλομαι οὖν αὐτὸν καὶ ἐξ ἑτέρων νόμων περὶ τούτων διδάξαι, ἄν πως ἀλλὰ νῦν ἐπὶ τοῦ βήματος παιδευθῇ καὶ τὸ λοιπὸν ἡμῖν μὴ παρέχῃ πράγματα. καί μοι ἀνάγνωθι τούτους τοὺς νόμους τοὺς Σόλωνος τοὺς παλαιούς.

ΝΟΜΟΣ. ΔΕΔΕΣΘΑΙ Δ' ΕΝ ΤΗΙ ΠΟΔΟΚΑΚΚΗΙ 16
ʽΗΜΕΡΑΣ ΠΕΝΤΕ ΤΟΝ ΠΟΔΑ, ΕΑΝ ΠΡΟΣΤΙΜΗΣΗΙ ʽΗ ʽΗΛΙΑΙΑ.

ʽΗ ΠΟΔΟΚΑΚΚΗ ταὐτό ἐστιν, ὦ Θεόμνηστε, ὃ νῦν καλεῖται ἐν τῷ ξύλῳ δεδέσθαι. εἰ οὖν ὁ δεθεὶς ἐξελθὼν ἐν ταῖς εὐθύναις τῶν ἕνδεκα κατηγοροίη ὅτι οὐκ ἐν τῇ ΠΟΔΟΚΑΚΚΗΙ ἐδέδετο ἀλλ' ἐν τῷ ξύλῳ, οὐκ ἂν ἠλίθιον αὐτὸν νομίζοιεν; λέγε ἕτερον νόμον.

ΝΟΜΟΣ. ʼΕΠΕΓΓΥΑΝ Δ' ΕΠΙΟΡΚΗΣΑΝΤΑ ΤΟΝ 17
ΑΠΟΛΛΩ ΔΕΔΙΟΤΑ ΔΕ ΔΙΚΗΣ ʽΕΝΕΚΑ ΔΡΑΣΚΑΖΕΙΝ.

Τοῦτο τὸ ΕΠΙΟΡΚΗΣΑΝΤΑ ὀμόσαντά ἐστι, τὸ δὲ ΔΡΑΣΚΑΖΕΙΝ, ὃ νῦν ἀποδιδράσκειν ὀνομάζομεν.

ʽΟΣΤΙΣ ΔΕ ΑΠΙΛΛΕΙ ΤΗΙ ΘΥΡΑΙ, ΕΝΔΟΝ ΤΟΥ ΚΛΕΠΤΟΥ ΟΝΤΟΣ.

Τὸ ΑΠΙΛΛΕΙΝ τὸ ἀποκλείειν νομίζεται, καὶ μηδὲν διὰ τοῦτο διαφέρου.

18 Το ΑΡΓΥΡΙΟΝ ΣΤΑΣΙΜΟΝ ΕΙΝΑΙ ΕΦ' 'ΟΠΟΣΩΙ ΑΝ ΒΟΥΛΗΤΑΙ 'Ο ΔΑΝΕΙΖΩΝ.

Τὸ ΣΤΑΣΙΜΟΝ τοῦτό ἐστιν, ὦ βέλτιστε, οὐ ζυγῷ ἱστάναι ἀλλὰ τόκον πράττεσθαι ὁπόσον ἂν βούληται. ἐπανάγνωθι τουτουὶ τοῦ νόμου τὸ τελευταῖον.

19 'ΟΣΑΙ ΔΕ ΠΕΦΑΣΜΕΝΩΣ ΠΟΛΟΥΝΤΑΙ,

καὶ

ΟΙΚΗΟΣ ΚΑΙ ΔΟΥΛΗΣ ΤΗΝ ΒΛΑΒΗΝ ΕΙΝΑΙ ΟΦΕΙΛΕΙΝ.

Προσέχετε τὸν νοῦν. τὸ μὲν ΠΕΦΑΣΜΕΝΩΣ
ἐστὶ φανερῶς, ΠΟΛΕΙΣΘΑΙ δὲ βαδίζειν, τὸ δὲ
ΟΙΚΗΟΣ θεράποντος. πολλὰ δὲ τοιαῦτα καὶ ἄλλα
20 ἐστίν, ὦ ἄνδρες δικασταί. ἀλλ' εἰ μὴ σιδηροῦς
ἐστιν, οἴομαι αὐτὸν ἔννουν γεγονέναι[5] ὅτι τὰ μὲν
πράγματα ταὐτά ἐστι νῦν τε καὶ πάλαι, τῶν
δὲ ὀνομάτων ἐνίοις οὐ τοῖς αὐτοῖς χρώμεθα νῦν
τε καὶ πρότερον.

§ 5. *He will probably confess his defeat by his silence. But if not, consider how much more serious to me it is to be condemned of parricide, as I shall be if I lose this suit, than to him to have been convicted of throwing away his shield: and yet he obtained satisfaction for that charge. Besides, the untruth of the charge against me is patent; and the cruelty of the charge is enhanced by the eminent and patriotic character of my father, contrasted with the notorious cowardice of my assailant.*

δηλώσει δέ· οἰχήσεται γὰρ ἀπιὼν ἀπὸ τοῦ
21 βήματος σιωπῇ. εἰ δὲ μή, δέομαι ὑμῶν, ὦ
ἄνδρες δικασταί, τὰ δίκαια ψηφίσασθαι, ἐνθυμουμένους ὅτι πολὺ μεῖζον κακόν ἐστιν ἀκοῦσαί
τινα τὸν πατέρα ἀπεκτονέναι ἢ τὴν ἀσπίδα

5 *Cobet* scribit νῦν γ' ἐγνωκέναι.

ἀποβεβληκέναι. ἐγὼ γοῦν δεξαίμην ἂν πάσας
τὰς ἀσπίδας ἐρριφέναι ἢ τοιαύτην γνώμην ἔχειν
περὶ τὸν πατέρα. οὗτος οὖν ἔνοχος μὲν ὢν τῇ 22
αἰτίᾳ, ἐλάττονος δὲ οὔσης αὐτῷ τῆς συμφορᾶς,
οὐ μόνον ὑφ᾽ ὑμῶν ἠλεήθη, ἀλλὰ καὶ τὸν μαρ-
τυρήσαντα ἠτίμωσεν. ἐγὼ δὲ ἑωρακὼς μὲν ἐκεῖνο
τοῦτον ποιήσαντα ὃ καὶ ὑμεῖς ἴστε, αὐτὸς δὲ
σώσας τὴν ἀσπίδα, ἀκηκοὼς δὲ οὕτως ἄνομον
καὶ δεινὸν πρᾶγμα, μεγίστης δὲ οὔσης μοι τῆς
συμφορᾶς, εἰ ἀποφεύξεται, τούτῳ δ᾽ οὐδενὸς
ἀξίας, εἰ κακηγορίας ἁλώσεται, οὐκ ἄρα δίκην
παρ᾽ αὐτοῦ λήψομαι; τίνος ὄντος ἐμοὶ πρὸς
ὑμᾶς ἐγκλήματος; πότερον ὅτι δικαίως ἀκήκοα; 23
ἀλλ᾽ οὐδ᾽ ἂν αὐτοὶ φήσαιτε. ἀλλ᾽ ὅτι βελτίων
καὶ ἐκ βελτιόνων ὁ φεύγων ἐμοῦ; ἀλλ᾽ οὐδ᾽ ἂν
αὐτὸς ἀξιώσειεν. ἀλλ᾽ ὅτι ἀποβεβληκὼς τὰ
ὅπλα δικάζομαι κακηγορίας τῷ σώσαντι; ἀλλ᾽
οὐχ οὗτος ὁ λόγος ἐν τῇ πόλει κατεσκέδασται.
ἀναμνήσθητε δὲ ὅτι μεγάλην καὶ καλὴν ἐκείνην 24
δωρεὰν αὐτῷ δεδώκατε· ἐν ᾗ[6] τίς οὐκ ἂν ἐλεήσειε
Διονύσιον, τοιαύτῃ μὲν συμφορᾷ περιπεπτωκότα,
ἄνδρα δὲ ἄριστον ἐν τοῖς κινδύνοις γεγενημένον,
ἀπιόντα δὲ ἀπὸ τοῦ δικαστηρίου λέγοντα ὅτι 25
δυστυχεστάτην ἐκείνην εἴημεν στρατείαν ἐστρα-
τευμένοι, ἐν ᾗ πολλοὶ μὲν ἡμῶν ἀπέθανον, οἱ δὲ
σώσαντες τὰ ὅπλα ὑπὸ τῶν ἀποβαλόντων ψευ-
δομαρτυριῶν ἑαλώκασι, κρεῖττον δὲ ἦν αὐτῷ τότε
ἀποθανεῖν ἢ οἴκαδ᾽ ἐλθόντι τοιαύτῃ τύχῃ χρῆσθαι; μὴ τοίνυν ἀκούσαντα Θεόμνηστον κακῶς 26
τὰ προσήκοντα ἐλεεῖτε, μηδ᾽ ὑβρίζοντί τε καὶ

[6] Pro *ἐκείνην δωρεὰν* *Francken* conj. *νίκην*, et pro *ἐν ᾗ* aut *ἐν ᾧ* (*Emperius*) aut *ᾗ*.

λέγοντι παρὰ τοὺς νόμους συγγνώμην ἔχετε.
τίς γὰρ ἂν ἐμοὶ μείζων ταύτης γένοιτο συμφορά,
περὶ τοιούτου πατρὸς οὕτως αἰσχρὰς αἰτίας
27 ἀκηκοότι; ὃς πολλάκις μὲν ἐστρατήγησε, πολλοὺς δὲ καὶ ἄλλους κινδύνους μεθ' ὑμῶν ἐκινδύ-
νευσε· καὶ οὔτε τοῖς πολεμίοις τὸ ἐκείνου σῶμα
ὑποχείριον ἐγένετο, οὔτε τοῖς πολίταις οὐδεμίαν
πώποτε ὦφλεν εὐθύνην, ἔτη δὲ γεγονὼς ἑπτὰ καὶ
ἑξήκοντα ἐν ὀλιγαρχίᾳ δι' εὔνοιαν τοῦ ὑμετέρου
28 πλήθους ἀπέθανεν. ἆρ' ἄξιον ὀργισθῆναι τῷ
εἰρηκότι καὶ βοηθῆσαι τῷ πατρί, ὡς καὶ ἐκείνου
κακῶς ἀκηκοότος; τί γὰρ ἂν τούτου ἀνιαρότερον
γένοιτο αὐτῷ, ἢ τεθνάναι μὲν ὑπὸ τῶν ἐχθρῶν,
αἰτίαν δ' ἔχειν ὑπὸ τῶν παίδων ἀνῃρῆσθαι;[7] οὗ
ἔτι καὶ νῦν, ὦ ἄνδρες δικασταί, τῆς ἀρετῆς τὰ
μνημεῖα πρὸς τοῖς ὑμετέροις ἱεροῖς[7] ἀνάκειται,
τὰ δὲ τούτου καὶ τοῦ τούτου πατρὸς τῆς κακίας
πρὸς τοῖς τῶν πολεμίων· οὕτω σύμφυτος αὐτοῖς
29 ἡ δειλία. καὶ μὲν δή, ὦ ἄνδρες δικασταί, ὅσῳ
μείζους εἰσὶ καὶ νεανίαι τὰς ὄψεις, τοσούτῳ
μᾶλλον ὀργῆς ἄξιοί εἰσι· δῆλον γὰρ ὅτι τοῖς μὲν
σώμασι δύνανται, ταῖς δὲ ψυχαῖς οὐκ ἰσχύουσιν.[8]

§ 6. *If he pleads that his words were spoken in the anger of a moment, I reply that the law does not recognise that excuse. And remember, that on gaining this suit really depends my being cleared of a charge of parricide.*

30 Ἀκούω δ' αὐτόν, ὦ ἄνδρες δικασταί, ἐπὶ
τοῦτον τὸν λόγον τρέψεσθαι, ὡς ὀργισθεὶς εἴρηκε

[7] ἀνῃρῆσθαι . . ἱεροῖς addunt *Scheibe et al.* ex oratione [xi.] quæ hujus epitome est.

[8] ταῖς δὲ ψυχαῖς Westermann pro τὰς δὲ ψυχὰς οὐκ ἔχουσι.

ταῦτα ἐμοῦ μαρτυρήσαντος τὴν αὐτὴν μαρτυρίαν
Διονυσίῳ. ὑμεῖς δ' ἐνθυμεῖσθε, ὦ ἄνδρες δικασταί,
ὅτι ὁ νομοθέτης οὐδεμίαν ὀργῇ συγγνώμην δίδω-
σιν, ἀλλὰ ζημιοῖ τὸν λέγοντα, ἐὰν μὴ ἀποφαίνῃ
ὡς ἔστιν ἀληθῆ τὰ εἰρημένα. ἐγὼ δὲ δὶς ἤδη
περὶ τούτου μεμαρτύρηκα· οὐ γάρ πω ᾔδειν ὅτι
ὑμεῖς τοὺς μὲν ἰδόντας τιμωρεῖσθε, τοῖς δὲ ἀπο-
βαλοῦσι συγγνώμην ἔχετε. περὶ μὲν οὖν 31
τούτων οὐκ οἶδ' ὅ τι δεῖ πλείω λέγειν· ἐγὼ δ'
ὑμῶν δέομαι καταψηφίσασθαι Θεομνήστου, ἐνθυμουμένους ὅτι οὐκ ἂν γένοιτο τούτου μείζων
ἀγών μοι. νῦν γὰρ διώκω μὲν κακηγορίας, τῇ
δ' αὐτῇ ψήφῳ φόνου φεύγω τοῦ πατρός, ὃς μόνος,
ἐπειδὴ τάχιστα ἐδοκιμάσθην, ἐπεξῆλθον τοῖς
τριάκοντα ἐν Ἀρείῳ πάγῳ. ὧν μεμνημένοι καὶ 32
ἐμοὶ καὶ τῷ πατρὶ βοηθήσατε καὶ τοῖς νόμοις
τοῖς κειμένοις καὶ τοῖς ὅρκοις οἷς ὀμωμόκατε.

ORATION V. [12.]

For the Prosecution; against Eratosthenes, who had been One of the Thirty, for the Murder of Polemarchus.

§ 1. *There is no want of matter for speech. Rather, there is too much for the time allowed me. My only fear is that from inexperience I may fail to do justice to the cause.*

Οὐκ ἄρξασθαί μοι δοκεῖ ἄπορον εἶναι, ὦ ἄνδρες δικασταί, τῆς κατηγορίας, ἀλλὰ παύσασθαι λέγοντι· τοιαῦτα αὐτοῖς τὸ μέγεθος καὶ τοσαῦτα

τὸ πλῆθος εἴργασται, ὥστε μήτ᾽ ἂν ψευδόμενον
δεινότερα τῶν ὑπαρχόντων κατηγορῆσαι, μήτε
τἀληθῆ βουλόμενον εἰπεῖν ἅπαντα δύνασθαι, ἀλλ᾽
ἀνάγκη ἢ τὸν κατήγορον ἀπειπεῖν ἢ τὸν χρόνον
2 ἐπιλιπεῖν. τοὐναντίον δέ μοι δοκοῦμεν πείσεσθαι
ἢ ἐν τῷ πρὸ τοῦ χρόνῳ. πρότερον μὲν γὰρ ἔδει
τὴν ἔχθραν τοὺς κατηγοροῦντας ἐπιδεῖξαι, ἥτις
εἴη πρὸς τοὺς φεύγοντας· νυνὶ δὲ παρὰ τῶν
φευγόντων χρὴ πυνθάνεσθαι ἥτις ἦν αὐτοῖς πρὸς
τὴν πόλιν ἔχθρα, ἀνθ᾽ ὅτου τοιαῦτα ἐτόλμησαν
εἰς αὐτὴν ἐξαμαρτάνειν. οὐ μέντοι ὡς οὐκ ἔχων
οἰκείας ἔχθρας καὶ συμφορὰς τοὺς λόγους ποιοῦ-
μαι, ἀλλ᾽ ὡς ἅπασι πολλῆς ἀφθονίας οὔσης ὑπὲρ
τῶν ἰδίων ἢ ὑπὲρ τῶν δημοσίων ὀργίζεσθαι.
3 ἐγὼ μὲν οὖν, ὦ ἄνδρες δικασταί, οὔτ᾽ ἐμαυτοῦ
πώποτε οὔτε ἀλλότρια πράγματα πράξας νῦν
ἠνάγκασμαι ὑπὸ τῶν γεγενημένων τούτου κατηγορεῖν, ὥστε πολλάκις εἰς πολλὴν ἀθυμίαν
κατέστην, μὴ διὰ τὴν ἀπειρίαν ἀναξίως καὶ
ἀδυνάτως ὑπὲρ τοῦ ἀδελφοῦ καὶ ἐμαυτοῦ τὴν κατηγορίαν ποιήσωμαι·[1] ὅμως δὲ πειράσομαι ὑμᾶς
ἐξ ἀρχῆς ὡς ἂν δύνωμαι δι᾽ ἐλαχίστων διδάξαι.

§ 2. *My family were settlers in Athens, and lived there harmlessly and unmolested until the usurpation of the Thirty, who, on the instigation of Theognis and Pison, resolved to enrich their revenues by the murder and confiscation of certain aliens. I and my brother were among the first victims. I managed to escape to Megara. But Polemarchus, my brother, was executed without trial, and*

[1] ποιήσομαι, Codex x.

all our goods were confiscated. Our fate was that of many others.

Οὑμὸς πατὴρ Κέφαλος ἐπείσθη μὲν ὑπὸ 4
Περικλέους εἰς ταύτην τὴν γῆν ἀφικέσθαι, ἔτη
δὲ τριάκοντα ᾤκησε, καὶ οὐδενὶ πώποτε οὔτε
ἡμεῖς οὔτε ἐκεῖνος δίκην οὔτε ἐδικασάμεθα οὔτε
ἐφύγομεν, ἀλλ' οὕτως ᾠκοῦμεν δημοκρατούμενοι
ὥστε μήτε εἰς τοὺς ἄλλους ἐξαμαρτάνειν μήτε
ὑπὸ τῶν ἄλλων ἀδικεῖσθαι. ἐπειδὴ δ' οἱ τριά- 5
κοντα πονηροὶ καὶ συκοφάνται ὄντες εἰς τὴν
ἀρχὴν κατέστησαν, φάσκοντες χρῆναι τῶν
ἀδίκων καθαρὰν ποιῆσαι τὴν πόλιν καὶ τοὺς
λοιποὺς πολίτας ἐπ' ἀρετὴν καὶ δικαιοσύνην
τραπέσθαι, τοιαῦτα λέγοντες οὐ τοιαῦτα ποιεῖν
ἐτόλμων, ὡς ἐγὼ περὶ τῶν ἐμαυτοῦ πρῶτον εἰπὼν
καὶ περὶ τῶν ὑμετέρων ἀναμνῆσαι πειράσομαι.
Θέογνις γὰρ καὶ Πείσων ἔλεγον ἐν τοῖς τριάκοντα 6
περὶ τῶν μετοίκων, ὡς εἶέν τινες τῇ πολιτείᾳ
ἀχθόμενοι· καλλίστην οὖν εἶναι πρόφασιν τιμωρεῖσθαι μὲν δοκεῖν, τῷ δ' ἔργῳ χρηματίζεσθαι·
πάντως δὲ τὴν μὲν πόλιν πένεσθαι, τὴν δ' ἀρχὴν
δεῖσθαι χρημάτων. καὶ τοὺς ἀκούοντας οὐ 7
χαλεπῶς ἔπειθον· ἀποκτιννύναι μὲν γὰρ ἀνθρώπους περὶ οὐδενὸς ἡγοῦντο, λαμβάνειν δὲ χρήματα
περὶ πολλοῦ ἐποιοῦντο. ἔδοξεν οὖν αὐτοῖς δέκα
συλλαβεῖν, τούτων δὲ δύο πένητας, ἵνα αὐτοῖς ᾖ
πρὸς τοὺς ἄλλους ἀπολογία, ὡς οὐ χρημάτων
ἕνεκα ταῦτα πέπρακται, ἀλλὰ συμφέροντα τῇ
πολιτείᾳ γεγένηται, ὥσπερ τι τῶν ἄλλων εὐλόγως
πεποιηκότες. διαλαβόντες δὲ τὰς οἰκίας ἐβάδιζον· 8

καὶ ἐμὲ μὲν ξένους ἑστιῶντα κατέλαβον, οὓς
ἐξελάσαντες Πείσωνί με παραδιδόασιν· οἱ δὲ
ἄλλοι εἰς τὸ ἐργαστήριον ἐλθόντες τὰ ἀνδράποδα
ἀπεγράφοντο. ἐγὼ δὲ Πείσωνα μὲν ἠρώτων εἰ
9 βούλοιτό με σῶσαι χρήματα λαβών· ὁ δ'
ἔφασκεν, εἰ πολλὰ εἴη. εἶπον οὖν ὅτι τάλαντον
ἀργυρίου ἕτοιμος εἴην δοῦναι· ὁ δ' ὡμολόγησε
ταῦτα ποιήσειν. ἠπιστάμην μὲν οὖν ὅτι οὔτε
θεοὺς οὔτ' ἀνθρώπους νομίζει ὅμως δ' ἐκ τῶν
παρόντων ἐδόκει μοι ἀναγκαιότατον εἶναι πίστιν
10 παρ' αὐτοῦ λαβεῖν. ἐπειδὴ δὲ ὤμοσεν ἐξώλειαν
ἑαυτῷ καὶ τοῖς παισὶν ἐπαρώμενος, λαβὼν τὸ
τάλαντόν με σώσειν, εἰσελθὼν εἰς τὸ δωμάτιον
τὴν κιβωτὸν ἀνοίγνυμι· Πείσων δ' αἰσθόμενος
εἰσέρχεται, καὶ ἰδὼν τὰ ἐνόντα καλεῖ τῶν ὑπηρε-
τῶν δύο, καὶ τὰ ἐν τῇ κιβωτῷ λαβεῖν ἐκέλευσεν.
11 ἐπειδὴ δ' οὐχ ὅσον ὡμολόγησα εἶχεν, ὦ ἄνδρες
δικασταί, ἀλλὰ τρία τάλαντα ἀργυρίου καὶ τετρα-
κοσίους κυζικηνοὺς καὶ ἑκατὸν δαρεικοὺς καὶ
φιάλας ἀργυρᾶς τέτταρας, ἐδεόμην αὐτοῦ ἐφόδιά
μοι δοῦναι, ὁ δ' ἀγαπήσειν με ἔφασκεν, εἰ τὸ
12 σῶμα σώσω. ἐξιοῦσι δ' ἐμοὶ καὶ Πείσωνι
ἐπιτυγχάνει Μηλόβιός τε καὶ Μνησιθείδης ἐκ
τοῦ ἐργαστηρίου ἀπιόντες, καὶ καταλαμβάνουσι
πρὸς αὐταῖς ταῖς θύραις, καὶ ἐρωτῶσιν ὅποι βαδί-
ζοιμεν· ὁ δ' ἔφασκεν εἰς τοῦ ἀδελφοῦ τοῦ ἐμοῦ,
ἵνα καὶ τὰ ἐν ἐκείνῃ τῇ οἰκίᾳ σκέψηται. ἐκεῖνον
μὲν οὖν ἐκέλευον βαδίζειν, ἐμὲ δὲ μεθ' αὑτῶν
13 ἀκολουθεῖν εἰς Δαμνίππου. Πείσων δὲ προσ-
ελθὼν σιγᾶν μοι παρεκελεύετο καὶ θαρρεῖν,

ὡς ἥξων ἐκεῖσε. καταλαμβάνομεν δὲ αὐτόθι
Θέογνιν ἑτέρους φυλάττοντα· ᾧ παραδόντες ἐμὲ
πάλιν ᾤχοντο. ἐν τοιούτῳ δ' ὄντι μοι κινδυνεύειν ἐδόκει, ὡς τοῦ γε ἀποθανεῖν ὑπάρχοντος
ἤδη. καλέσας δὲ Δάμνιππον λέγω πρὸς αὐτὸν 14
τάδε, "ἐπιτήδειος μέν μοι τυγχάνεις ὤν, ἥκω δ'
εἰς τὴν σὴν οἰκίαν, ἀδικῶ δ' οὐδέν, χρημάτων
δ' ἕνεκα ἀπόλλυμαι. σὺ οὖν ταῦτα πάσχοντί
μοι πρόθυμος παράσχου τὴν σεαυτοῦ δύναμιν εἰς
τὴν ἐμὴν σωτηρίαν." ὁ δ' ὑπέσχετο ταῦτα
ποιήσειν. ἐδόκει δ' αὐτῷ βέλτιον εἶναι πρὸς
Θέογνιν μνησθῆναι· ἡγεῖτο γὰρ ἅπαν ποιήσειν
αὐτόν, εἴ τις ἀργύριον διδοίη. ἐκείνου δὲ δια- 15
λεγομένου Θεόγνιδι (ἔμπειρος γὰρ ὢν ἐτύγχανον
τῆς οἰκίας, καὶ ᾔδειν ὅτι ἀμφίθυρος εἴη) ἐδόκει
μοι ταύτῃ πειρᾶσθαι σωθῆναι, ἐνθυμουμένῳ ὅτι,
ἐὰν μὲν λάθω, σωθήσομαι, ἐὰν δὲ ληφθῶ, ἡγούμην
μέν, εἰ Θέογνις εἴη πεπεισμένος ὑπὸ τοῦ Δαμνίππου χρήματα λαβεῖν, οὐδὲν ἧττον ἀφεθήσεσθαι,
εἰ δὲ μή, ὁμοίως ἀποθανεῖσθαι. ταῦτα διανοηθεὶς 16
ἔφευγον, ἐκείνων ἐπὶ τῇ αὐλείῳ θύρᾳ τὴν φυλακὴν
ποιουμένων· τριῶν δὲ θυρῶν οὐσῶν, ἃς ἔδει με
διελθεῖν, ἅπασαι ἀνεῳγμέναι ἔτυχον. ἀφικόμενος
δὲ εἰς Ἀρχένεω τοῦ ναυκλήρου ἐκεῖνον πέμπω
εἰς ἄστυ, πευσόμενον περὶ τοῦ ἀδελφοῦ· ἥκων δὲ
ἔλεγεν ὅτι Ἐρατοσθένης αὐτὸν ἐν τῇ ὁδῷ λαβὼν
εἰς τὸ δεσμωτήριον ἀπαγάγοι. καὶ ἐγὼ μὲν τοι- 17
αῦτα πεπυσμένος τῆς ἐπιούσης νυκτὸς διέπλευσα
Μέγαράδε. Πολεμάρχῳ δὲ παρήγγειλαν οἱ
τριάκοντα τὸ ἐπ' ἐκείνων* εἰθισμένον παράγγελμα,

* ἐπ', MS. ὑπ' ἐκείνων.

πίνειν κώνειον, πρὶν τὴν αἰτίαν εἰπεῖν δι' ἥντινα
ἔμελλεν ἀποθανεῖσθαι· οὕτω πολλοῦ ἐδέησε κρι-
18 θῆναι καὶ ἀπολογήσασθαι. καὶ ἐπειδὴ ἀπεφέρετο
ἐκ τοῦ δεσμωτηρίου τεθνεώς, τριῶν ἡμῖν οἰκιῶν
οὐσῶν ἐξ οὐδεμιᾶς εἴασαν ἐξενεχθῆναι, ἀλλὰ κλεισίον μισθωσάμενοι προὔθεντο αὐτόν. καὶ πολλῶν
ὄντων ἱματίων αἰτοῦσιν οὐδὲν ἔδοσαν εἰς τὴν
ταφήν, ἀλλὰ τῶν φίλων ὁ μὲν ἱμάτιον ὁ δὲ
προσκεφάλαιον ὁ δὲ ὅ τι ἕκαστος ἔτυχεν ἔδωκεν
19 εἰς τὴν ἐκείνου ταφήν. καὶ ἔχοντες μὲν ἑπτακο-
σίας ἀσπίδας τῶν ἡμετέρων, ἔχοντες δὲ ἀργύριον
καὶ χρυσίον τοσοῦτον, χαλκὸν δὲ καὶ κόσμον καὶ
ἔπιπλα καὶ ἱμάτια γυναικεῖα ὅσα οὐδεπώποτε
ᾤοντο κτήσεσθαι, καὶ ἀνδράποδα εἴκοσι καὶ
ἑκατόν, ὧν τὰ μὲν βέλτιστα ἔλαβον, τὰ δὲ λοιπὰ
εἰς τὸ δημόσιον ἀπέδοσαν, εἰς τοσαύτην ἀπλη-
στίαν καὶ αἰσχροκέρδειαν ἀφίκοντο καὶ τοῦ
τρόπου τοῦ αὑτῶν ἀπόδειξιν ἐποιήσαντο· τῆς
γὰρ Πολεμάρχου γυναικὸς χρυσοῦς ἑλικτῆρας,
οὓς ἔχουσα ἐτύγχανεν, ὅτε τὸ πρῶτον ἦλθεν εἰς
τὴν οἰκίαν Μηλόβιος, ἐκ τῶν ὤτων ἐξείλετο.
20 καὶ οὐδὲ κατὰ τὸ ἐλάχιστον μέρος τῆς οὐσίας
ἐλέου παρ' αὐτῶν ἐτυγχάνομεν. ἀλλ' οὕτως εἰς
ἡμᾶς διὰ τὰ χρήματα ἐξημάρτανον, ὥσπερ οὐκ
ἂν ἕτεροι* μεγάλων ἀδικημάτων ὀργὴν ἔχοντες,
οὐ τούτων ἀξίους γε ὄντας τῇ πόλει, ἀλλα πάσας
τὰς χορηγίας χορηγήσαντας, πολλὰς δ' εἰσφορὰς
εἰσενεγκόντας, κοσμίους δ' ἡμᾶς αὐτοὺς παρέχον-
τας καὶ πᾶν τὸ προσταττόμενον ποιοῦντας, ἐχθρὸν
δ' οὐδένα κεκτημένους, πολλοὺς δ' Ἀθηναίων ἐκ

* οὐδ' *W. R.* ἐχθροὶ *Fritzsche.*

τῶν πολεμίων λυσαμένους· τοιούτων ἠξίωσαν
οὐχ ὁμοίως μετοικοῦντας ὥσπερ αὐτοὶ ἐπολιτεύοντο. οὗτοι γὰρ πολλοὺς μὲν τῶν πολιτῶν 21
εἰς τοὺς πολεμίους ἐξήλασαν, πολλοὺς δ' ἀδίκως
ἀποκτείναντες ἀτάφους ἐποίησαν, πολλοὺς δ'
ἐπιτίμους ὄντας ἀτίμους [τῆς πόλεως] κατέστησαν,
πολλῶν δὲ θυγατέρας μελλούσας ἐκδίδοσθαι
ἐκώλυσαν. καὶ εἰς τοσοῦτόν εἰσι τόλμης ἀφιγ- 22
μένοι ὥσθ' ἥκουσιν ἀπολογησόμενοι, καὶ λέγουσιν
ὡς οὐδὲν κακὸν οὐδ' αἰσχρὸν εἰργασμένοι εἰσίν.
ἐγὼ δ' ἐβουλόμην ἂν αὐτοὺς ἀληθῆ λέγειν· μετῆν
γὰρ ἂν καὶ ἐμοὶ τούτου τἀγαθοῦ οὐκ ἐλάχιστον
μέρος. νῦν δὲ οὔτε πρὸς τὴν πόλιν αὐτοῖς τοι- 23
αῦτα ὑπάρχει οὔτε πρὸς ἐμέ· τὸν ἀδελφὸν γάρ
μου, ὥσπερ καὶ πρότερον εἶπον, Ἐρατοσθένης
ἀπέκτεινεν οὔτε αὐτὸς ἰδίᾳ ἀδικούμενος οὔτε εἰς
τὴν πόλιν ὁρῶν ἐξαμαρτάνοντα, ἀλλὰ τῇ ἑαυτοῦ
παρανομίᾳ προθύμως ἐξυπηρετῶν.

§ 3. *I will show by an examination of Eratosthenes that he was the actual cause of our ill-treatment, though confessing that he thought it unjust.*

Ἀναβιβασάμενος δ' αὐτὸν βούλομαι ἐρέ- 24
σθαι, ὦ ἄνδρες δικασταί. τοιαύτην γὰρ γνώμην
ἔχω· ἐπὶ μὲν τῇ τούτου ὠφελείᾳ καὶ πρὸς ἕτερον
περὶ τούτου διαλέγεσθαι ἀσεβὲς εἶναι νομίζω,
ἐπὶ δὲ τῇ τούτου βλάβῃ καὶ πρὸς αὐτὸν τοῦτον
ὅσιον καὶ εὐσεβές. ἀνάβηθι οὖν μοι καὶ ἀπόκριναι, ὅ τι ἄν σε ἐρωτῶ. Ἀπήγαγες Πολέ- 25
μαρχον ἢ οὔ; Τὰ ὑπὸ τῶν ἀρχόντων προστα-

χθέντα δεδιὼς ἐποίουν. Ἦσθα δ' ἐν τῷ βουλευτηρίῳ, ὅτε οἱ λόγοι ἐγίνοντο περὶ ἡμῶν; Ἦν. Πότερον συνηγόρευες τοῖς κελεύουσιν ἀποκτεῖναι ἢ ἀντέλεγες; Ἀντέλεγον. Ἵνα μὴ ἀποθάνωμεν; Ἵνα μὴ ἀποθάνητε. Ἡγούμενος ἡμᾶς
26 ἄδικα πάσχειν ἢ δίκαια; Ἄδικα. Εἶτ', ὦ σχετλιώτατε πάντων, ἀντέλεγες μὲν ἵνα σώσειας, συνελάμβανες δὲ ἵνα ἀποκτείναις;[2] καὶ ὅτε μὲν τὸ πλῆθος ἦν ὑμῶν κύριον τῆς σωτηρίας τῆς ἡμετέρας, ἀντιλέγειν φῄς τοῖς βουλομένοις ἡμᾶς ἀπολέσαι, ἐπειδὴ δὲ ἐπὶ σοὶ μόνῳ ἐγένετο καὶ σῶσαι Πολέμαρχον καὶ μή, εἰς τὸ δεσμωτήριον ἀπήγαγες; εἶθ' ὅτι μέν, ὡς φῄς, ἀντειπὼν οὐδὲν ὠφέλησας, ἀξιοῖς χρηστὸς νομίζεσθαι, ὅτι δὲ συλλαβὼν ἀπέκτεινας, οὐκ οἴει[3] ἐμοὶ καὶ τουτοισὶ δοῦναι δίκην;

§ 4. *His plea that he spoke against our ill-treatment, and only acted under compulsion, will not hold. For, 1st, It cannot be allowed to one of the Thirty to plead that he was compelled by the Thirty to do as he did. 2dly, He could have easily allowed my brother to escape if he had wished it. 3dly, His only defence must be either that he did not arrest my brother, or did so justly. Your decision is anxiously waited for, and is most important.*

27 Καὶ μὴν οὐδὲ τοῦτο εἰκὸς αὐτῷ πιστεύειν, εἴπερ ἀληθῆ λέγει φάσκων ἀντειπεῖν, ὡς αὐτῷ προσετάχθη. οὐ γὰρ δή που ἐν τοῖς μετοίκοις πίστιν παρ' αὐτοῦ ἐλάμβανον. ἐπεί τοι τῷ

[2] ἀποκτείναις *Bekk.* conj.; MS. ἀποκτείνῃς *vel* ἀποκτείνοις.
[3] οἴει *Madvig* omitti vult. Adv. Crit., p. 175.

ἧττον εἰκὸς ἦν προσταχθῆναι ἢ ὅστις ἀντειπών
γε ἐτύγχανε καὶ γνώμην[4] ἀποδεδειγμένος;
τίνα γὰρ εἰκὸς ἦν ἧττον ταῦτα ὑπηρετῆσαι
ἢ τὸν ἀντειπόντα οἷς ἐκεῖνοι ἐβούλοντο πραχ-
θῆναι; ἔτι δὲ τοῖς μὲν ἄλλοις Ἀθηναίοις ἱκανή 28
μοι δοκεῖ πρόφασις εἶναι τῶν γεγενημένων εἰς
τοὺς τριάκοντα ἀναφέρειν τὴν αἰτίαν· αὐτοὺς δὲ
τοὺς τριάκοντα, ἐὰν εἰς σφᾶς αὐτοὺς ἀναφέρωσι,
πῶς ὑμᾶς εἰκὸς ἀποδέχεσθαι; εἰ μὲν γάρ τις ἦν 29
ἐν τῇ πόλει ἀρχὴ ἰσχυροτέρα [αὐτῆς], ὑφ᾽ ἧς αὐτῷ
προσετάττετο παρὰ τὸ δίκαιον ἀνθρώπους ἀπολλύναι, ἴσως ἂν εἰκότως αὐτῷ συγγνώμην εἴχετε·
νῦν δὲ παρὰ τοῦ ποτε καὶ λήψεσθε δίκην, εἴπερ
ἐξέσται τοῖς τριάκοντα λέγειν ὅτι τὰ ὑπὸ τῶν
τριάκοντα προσταχθέντα ἐποίουν; καὶ μὲν δὴ 30
οὐκ ἐν τῇ οἰκίᾳ ἀλλ᾽ ἐν τῇ ὁδῷ σώζειν τε αὐτὸν
καὶ τὰ τούτοις ἐψηφισμένα παρόν,[5] συλλαβὼν
ἀπήγαγεν. ὑμεῖς δὲ πάντες ὀργίζεσθε, ὅσοι εἰς
τὰς οἰκίας ἦλθον τὰς ὑμετέρας ζήτησιν ποιούμενοι
ἢ ὑμῶν ἢ τῶν ὑμετέρων τινός. καίτοι εἰ χρὴ 31
τοῖς διὰ τὴν ἑαυτῶν σωτηρίαν ἑτέρους ἀπολέσασι
συγγνώμην ἔχειν, ἐκείνοις ἂν δικαιότερον ἔχοιτε·
κίνδυνος γὰρ ἦν πεμφθεῖσι μὴ ἐλθεῖν καὶ καταλαβοῦσιν ἐξάρνοις γενέσθαι. τῷ δὲ Ἐρατοσθένει
ἐξῆν εἰπεῖν ὅτι οὐκ ἀπήντησεν, ἔπειτα ὅτι οὐκ
εἶδεν· ταῦτα γὰρ οὔτ᾽ ἔλεγχον οὔτε βάσανον
εἶχεν, ὥστε μηδ᾽ ὑπὸ τῶν ἐχθρῶν βουλομένων
οἷόν τ᾽ εἶναι ἐξελεγχθῆναι. χρῆν δέ σε, ὦ 32

[4] *Scheibe* ante γνώμην scripsit ἐναντίαν.

[5] σώζειν τε αὐτὸν . . . παρόν. *Sauppius* conj. pro σώζοντα αὐτὸν . . . , ὄν. feliciter. In l. 207 *Francken* ὠργίζεσθε, sed de ira adhuc fervescente loquitur orator.

'Ερατόσθενες, εἴπερ ἦσθα χρηστός, πολὺ μᾶλλον
τοῖς μέλλουσιν ἀδίκως ἀποθανεῖσθαι μηνυτὴν
γενέσθαι ἢ τοὺς ἀδίκως ἀπολουμένους συλλαμ-
βάνειν. νῦν δέ σου τὰ ἔργα φανερὰ γεγένηται
οὐχ ὡς ἀνιωμένου ἀλλ' ὡς ἡδομένου τοῖς γιγνο-
33 μένοις, ὥστε τούσδε ἐκ τῶν ἔργων χρὴ μᾶλλον ἢ
ἐκ τῶν λόγων τὴν ψῆφον φέρειν, ἃ ἴσασι γεγενη-
μένα τῶν τότε λεγομένων τεκμήρια λαμβάνοντας,
ἐπειδὴ μάρτυρας περὶ αὐτῶν οὐχ οἷόν τε παρα-
σχέσθαι. οὐ γὰρ μόνον ἡμῖν παρεῖναι οὐκ ἐξῆν,
ἀλλ' οὐδὲ παρ' αὐτοῖς εἶναι, ὥστ' ἐπὶ τούτοις
ἐστὶ πάντα τὰ κακὰ εἰργασμένοις τὴν πόλιν
34 πάντα τἀγαθὰ περὶ αὑτῶν λέγειν. τοῦτο μέντοι
οὐ φεύγω, ἀλλ' ὁμολογῶ σοι, εἰ βούλει, ἀντειπεῖν.
θαυμάζω δὲ τί ἂν ποτ' ἐποίησας[6] συνειπών,
ὁπότε ἀντειπεῖν φάσκων ἀπέκτεινας Πολέμαρχον.
φέρε δή, τί ἂν εἰ καὶ ἀδελφοὶ ὄντες ἐτύχετε αὐτοῦ
ἢ καὶ υἱεῖς; ἀπεψηφίσασθε; δεῖ γάρ, ὦ ἄνδρες
δικασταί, 'Ερατοσθένη δυοῖν θάτερον ἀποδεῖξαι,
ἢ ὡς οὐκ ἀπήγαγεν αὐτόν, ἢ ὡς δικαίως τοῦτ'
ἔπραξεν. οὗτος δὲ ὡμολόγηκεν ἀδίκως συλλαβεῖν, ὥστε ῥᾳδίαν ὑμῖν τὴν διαψήφισιν περὶ
35 αὑτοῦ πεποίηκε. καὶ μὲν δὴ πολλοὶ καὶ τῶν
ἀστῶν καὶ τῶν ξένων ἥκουσιν εἰσόμενοι τίνα
γνώμην περὶ τούτων ἕξετε. ὧν οἱ μὲν ὑμέτεροι
ὄντες πολῖται μαθόντες ἀπίασιν ὅτι ἢ δίκην
δώσουσιν ὧν ἂν ἐξαμάρτωσιν, ἢ πράξαντες μὲν
ὧν ἐφίενται τύραννοι τῆς πόλεως ἔσονται, δυσ-
τυχήσαντες δὲ τὸ ἴσον ὑμῖν ἕξουσιν· ὅσοι δὲ

[6] ἐποίησας, MSS. ποιήσαις. Sic etiam *Sauppius*.

ξένοι ἐπιδημοῦσιν, εἴσονται πότερον ἀδίκως τοὺς
τριάκοντα ἐκκηρύττουσιν ἐκ τῶν πόλεων ἢ δικαίως.
εἰ γὰρ δὴ αὐτοὶ οἱ κακῶς πεπονθότες λαβόντες
ἀφήσουσιν, ἦ που σφᾶς αὐτοὺς ἡγήσονται περι-
έργους ὑπὲρ ὑμῶν τιμωρουμένους.[7] οὐκ οὖν δεινὸν 36
εἰ τοὺς μὲν στρατηγούς, οἳ ἐνίκων ναυμαχοῦντες,
ὅτε διὰ χειμῶνα οὐχ οἷοί τ' ἔφασαν εἶναι τοὺς
ἐκ τῆς θαλάττης ἀνελέσθαι, θανάτῳ ἐζημιώσατε,
ἡγούμενοι χρῆναι τῇ τῶν τεθνεώτων ἀρετῇ παρ'
ἐκείνων δίκην λαβεῖν, τούτους δέ, οἳ ἰδιῶται μὲν
ὄντες καθ' ὅσον ἐδύναντο ἐποίησαν ἡττηθῆναι
ναυμαχοῦντες, ἐπειδὴ δὲ εἰς τὴν ἀρχὴν κατέστησαν, ὁμολογοῦσιν ἑκόντες πολλοὺς τῶν πολιτῶν
ἀκρίτους ἀποκτιννύναι, οὐκ ἄρα χρὴ αὐτοὺς καὶ
τοὺς παῖδας ὑφ' ὑμῶν ταῖς ἐσχάταις ζημίαις
κολάζεσθαι;

§ 5. *If he follows a very general custom of accused persons, and, without making a direct answer to the charges against him, appeals to his public services, you have only to contrast those services with the many disservices he has done the State. To show you the truth as to this, I will make certain statements about him, which I will confirm severally by evidence.*

Ἐγὼ τοίνυν, ὦ ἄνδρες δικασταί, ἠξίουν 37
ἱκανὰ εἶναι τὰ κατηγορημένα· μέχρι γὰρ τούτου νομίζω χρῆναι κατηγορεῖν ἕως ἂν θανάτου δόξῃ τῷ φεύγοντι ἄξια εἰργάσθαι· ταύτην γὰρ ἐσχάτην δίκην δυνάμεθα παρ' αὐτῶν λαβεῖν. ὥστ' οὐκ οἶδ' ὅ τι δεῖ πολλὰ κατηγορεῖν τοιούτων ἀνδρῶν,

[7] Al. κηδομένους, διατεινομένους, τηρουμένους. *Weidn.* ἐχθροὺς ὑπὲρ ὑμῶν γ' αἱρουμένους.

οἳ οὐδ' ὑπὲρ ἑνὸς ἑκάστου τῶν πεπραγμένων δὶς
38 ἀποθανόντες δίκην δοῦναι* δύναιντ' ἄν. οὐ γὰρ
δὴ οὐδὲ τοῦτο αὐτῷ προσήκει ποιῆσαι, ὅπερ ἐν
τῇδε τῇ πόλει εἰθισμένον ἐστί, πρὸς μὲν τὰ
κατηγορημένα μηδὲν ἀπολογεῖσθαι, περὶ δὲ σφῶν
αὐτῶν ἕτερα λέγοντες ἐνίοτε ἐξαπατῶσιν, ὑμῖν
ἀποδεικνύντες ὡς στρατιῶται ἀγαθοί εἰσιν, ἢ ὡς
πολλὰς τῶν πολεμίων ναῦς ἔλαβον τριηραρχή-
σαντες, ἢ πόλεις πολεμίας οὔσας φίλας ἐποίησαν·
39 ἐπεὶ κελεύετε αὐτὸν ἀποδεῖξαι ὅπου τοσούτους
τῶν πολεμίων ἀπέκτειναν ὅσους τῶν πολιτῶν, ἢ
ναῦς ὅπου τοσαύτας ἔλαβον ὅσας αὐτοὶ παρέδοσαν, ἢ πόλιν ἥν τινα τοιαύτην προσεκτήσαντο
40 οἵαν τὴν ὑμετέραν κατεδουλώσαντο. ἀλλὰ γὰρ
ὅπλα τῶν πολεμίων ἐσκύλευσαν τοσαῦτα ὅσα
περ ὑμῶν ἀφείλοντο; ἀλλὰ τείχη τοιαῦτα εἷλον
οἷα τὰ τῆς ἑαυτῶν πατρίδος κατέσκαψαν; οἵτινες
καὶ τὰ περὶ τὴν Ἀττικὴν φρούρια καθεῖλον, καὶ
ὑμῖν ἐδήλωσαν ὅτι οὐδὲ τὸν Πειραιᾶ Λακεδαιμονίων προσταττόντων περιεῖλον, ἀλλ' ὅτι ἑαυτοῖς
τὴν ἀρχὴν οὕτω βεβαιοτέραν ἐνόμιζον εἶναι.

(1.) *In the time of the Four Hundred he deserted his ship when serving in the Hellespont, to join the aristocratic faction in Athens.*

41 Πολλάκις οὖν ἐθαύμασα τῆς τόλμης τῶν
λεγόντων ὑπὲρ αὐτῶν, πλὴν ὅταν ἐνθυμηθῶ
ὅτι τῶν αὐτῶν ἐστιν αὐτούς τε πάντα κακὰ
42 ἐργάζεσθαι καὶ τοὺς τοιούτους ἐπαινεῖν. οὐ
γὰρ νῦν πρῶτον τῷ ὑμετέρῳ πλήθει τὰ ἐναντία

* δοῦναι ἀξίαν *Markl.*, *Rauch.*

ἔπραξεν, ἀλλὰ καὶ ἐπὶ τῶν τετρακοσίων ἐν τῷ στρατοπέδῳ ὀλιγαρχίαν καθιστὰς ἔφευγεν ἐξ Ἑλλησπόντου τριήραρχος καταλιπὼν τὴν ναῦν, μετὰ Ἰατροκλέους καὶ ἑτέρων, ὧν τὰ ὀνόματα οὐδὲν δέομαι λέγειν. ἀφικόμενος δὲ δεῦρο τἀναντία τοῖς βουλομένοις δημοκρατίαν εἶναι ἔπραττε. καὶ τούτων μάρτυρας ὑμῖν παρέξομαι.

WITNESSES TO THE CONDUCT OF ERATOSTHENES PREVIOUS TO THE BATTLE OF ÆGOSPOTAMI.

(2.) *He and Critias were two of the five who, after the disaster at Ægospotami, took the management of affairs into their hands, and acted in a spirit hostile to the democracy.*

Τὸν μὲν τοίνυν μεταξὺ βίον αὐτοῦ παρήσω· 43
ἐπειδὴ δὲ ἡ ναυμαχία καὶ ἡ συμφορὰ τῇ πόλει
ἐγένετο, δημοκρατίας ἔτι οὔσης, ὅθεν τῆς στάσεως
ἦρξαν, πέντε ἄνδρες ἔφοροι κατέστησαν ὑπὸ τῶν
καλουμένων ἑταίρων, συναγωγεῖς μὲν τῶν πολιτῶν,
ἄρχοντες δὲ τῶν συνωμοτῶν, ἐναντία δὲ τῷ
ὑμετέρῳ πλήθει πράττοντες· ὧν Ἐρατοσθένης
καὶ Κριτίας ἦσαν. οὗτοι δὲ φυλάρχους τε ἐπὶ 44
τὰς φυλακὰς κατέστησαν, καὶ ὅ τι δέοι χειροτονεῖ-
σθαι καὶ οὕστινας χρείη ἄρχειν παρήγγελλον, καὶ
εἴ τι ἄλλο πράττειν βούλοιντο, κύριοι ἦσαν·
οὕτως οὐχ ὑπὸ τῶν πολεμίων μόνον ἀλλὰ καὶ
ὑπὸ τούτων πολιτῶν ὄντων ἐπεβουλεύεσθε ὅπως
μήτ' ἀγαθὸν μηδὲν ψηφιεῖσθε[8] πολλῶν τε
ἐνδεεῖς ἔσεσθε. τοῦτο γὰρ καὶ ἠπίσταντο, ὅτι 45

[8] ψηφιεῖσθε Cob. MS. ψηφίζησθε Bekk. ψηφίσαισθε.

ἄλλως μὲν οὐχ οἷοί τε ἔσονται περιγενέσθαι,
κακῶς δὲ πραττόντων δυνήσονται· καὶ ὑμᾶς
ἡγοῦντο τῶν παρόντων κακῶν ἐπιθυμοῦντας
ἀπαλλαγῆναι περὶ τῶν μελλόντων οὐκ ἐνθυμή-
46 σεσθαι. ὡς τοίνυν τῶν ἐφόρων ἐγένετο, μάρτυρας
ὑμῖν παρέξομαι, οὐ τοὺς τότε συμπράττοντας (οὐ
γὰρ ἂν δυναίμην), ἀλλὰ τοὺς αὐτοῦ Ἐρατο-
47 σθένους ἀκούσαντας. καίτοι εἰ ἐσωφρόνουν
κατεμαρτύρουν ἂν αὐτῶν, καὶ τοὺς διδασκάλους
τῶν σφετέρων ἁμαρτημάτων σφόδρ᾽ ἂν ἐκόλαζον,
καὶ τοὺς ὅρκους, εἰ ἐσωφρόνουν, οὐκ ἂν ἐπὶ μὲν
τοῖς τῶν πολιτῶν κακοῖς πιστοὺς ἐνόμιζον, ἐπὶ
δὲ τοῖς τῆς πόλεως ἀγαθοῖς ῥᾳδίως παρέβαινον.
πρὸς μὲν οὖν τούτους τοσαῦτα λέγω, τοὺς δὲ
μάρτυράς μοι κάλει. καὶ ὑμεῖς ἀνάβητε.

WITNESSES TO THE CONDUCT OF ERATOSTHENES IN HELPING TO ESTABLISH THE THIRTY.

(3.) *While in office among the Thirty, he did nothing to rebut the lying accusations of the informers Batrachus and Æschylides, though he knew them to be false. Thus he both held office illegally and exercised it unjustly.*

48 Τῶν μὲν μαρτύρων ἀκηκόατε. τὸ δὲ τελευταῖον εἰς τὴν ἀρχὴν καταστὰς ἀγαθοῦ μὲν οὐδενὸς μετέσχεν, ἄλλων δὲ πολλῶν. καίτοι εἴπερ ἦν ἀνὴρ ἀγαθός, ἐχρῆν αὐτὸν πρῶτον μὲν μὴ παρανόμως ἄρχειν, ἔπειτα τῇ βουλῇ μηνυτὴν γίγνεσθαι περὶ τῶν εἰσαγγελιῶν ἁπασῶν, ὅτι ψευδεῖς εἶεν, καὶ Βάτραχος καὶ Αἰσχυλίδης οὐ τἀληθῆ μηνύουσιν,

ἀλλὰ τὰ ὑπὸ τῶν τριάκοντα πλασθέντα εἰσ-
αγγέλλουσι, συγκείμενα ἐπὶ τῇ τῶν πολιτῶν
βλάβῃ. καὶ μὲν δή, ὦ ἄνδρες δικασταί, ὅσοι 49
κακόνοι ἦσαν τῷ ὑμετέρῳ πλήθει, οὐδὲν ἔλαττον
εἶχον σιωπῶντες· ἕτεροι γὰρ ἦσαν οἱ λέγοντες
καὶ πράττοντες ὧν οὐχ οἷόν τ᾽ ἦν μείζω κακὰ
γενέσθαι τῇ πόλει. ὁπόσοι δ᾽ εὖνοί φασιν εἶναι,
πῶς οὐκ ἐνταῦθα ἔδειξαν, αὐτοί τε τὰ βέλτιστα
λέγοντες καὶ τοὺς ἐξαμαρτάνοντας ἀποτρέποντες;

(4.) *When the split occurred among the Thirty, he plainly showed that the course he took was prompted by no patriotic motives, but by jealousy of others who were more powerful or more successful in enriching themselves. He made no overtures to the party at Phyle, but assisted to put to death three hundred citizens at Salamis and Eleusis. Nor when the anti-Critias party, of which he was one, obtained power, did they make any effort to come to terms with the loyalists in Peiræus, but invoked the aid of Sparta against them. All this is notorious, but I will call evidence to prove it.*

Ἴσως δ᾽ ἂν ἔχοι εἰπεῖν ὅτι ἐδεδοίκει, καὶ ὑμῶν 50
τοῦτο ἐνίοις ἱκανὸν ἔσται. ὅπως τοίνυν μὴ
φανήσεται ἐν τῷ λόγῳ τοῖς τριάκοντα ἐναντιού-
μενος· εἰ δὲ μή, ἐνταυθοῖ δῆλος ἔσται ὅτι ἐκεῖνά
τε αὐτῷ ἤρεσκε, καὶ τοσοῦτον ἐδύνατο ὥστε
ἐναντιούμενος μηδὲν κακὸν παθεῖν ὑπ᾽ αὐτῶν.
χρῆν δ᾽ αὐτὸν ὑπὲρ τῆς ὑμετέρας σωτηρίας ταύτην τὴν προθυμίαν ἔχειν, ἀλλὰ μὴ ὑπὲρ Θηραμένους, ὃς εἰς ὑμᾶς πολλὰ ἐξήμαρτεν. ἀλλ᾽ 51
οὗτος τὴν μὲν πόλιν ἐχθρὰν ἐνόμιζεν εἶναι, τοὺς
δ᾽ ὑμετέρους ἐχθροὺς φίλους, ὡς ἀμφότερα ταῦτα

ἐγὼ πολλοῖς τεκμηρίοις παραστήσω, καὶ τὰς
πρὸς ἀλλήλους διαφορὰς οὐχ ὑπὲρ ὑμῶν ἀλλ'
ὑπὲρ ἑαυτῶν γιγνομένας, ὁπότεροι ταῦτα πράξουσι
52 καὶ τῆς πόλεως ἄρξουσι. εἰ γὰρ ὑπὲρ τῶν
ἀδικουμένων ἐστασίαζον, ποῦ κάλλιον ἂν ἦν ἀνδρὶ
ἄρχοντι, ἢ Θρασυβούλου Φυλὴν κατειληφότος,
τότ' ἐπιδείξασθαι τὴν αὑτοῦ εὔνοιαν; ὁ δ' ἀντὶ
τοῦ ἐπαγγείλασθαί τι ἢ πρᾶξαι ἀγαθὸν πρὸς
τοὺς ἐπὶ Φυλῇ, ἐλθὼν μετὰ τῶν συναρχόντων
εἰς Σαλαμῖνα καὶ Ἐλευσῖνάδε τριακοσίους τῶν
πολιτῶν ἀπήγαγεν εἰς τὸ δεσμωτήριον, καὶ μιᾷ
ψήφῳ αὐτῶν ἁπάντων θάνατον κατεψηφίσατο.
53 ἐπειδὴ δὲ εἰς τὸν Πειραιᾶ ἤλθομεν καὶ αἱ ταραχαὶ
γεγενημέναι ἦσαν καὶ περὶ τῶν διαλλαγῶν οἱ
λόγοι ἐγίνοντο, πολλὰς ἑκάτεροι ἐλπίδας εἴχομεν
πρὸς ἀλλήλους ἔσεσθαι ὡς ἀμφότεροι ἐδείξαμεν,[9]
οἱ μὲν γὰρ ἐκ Πειραιῶς κρείττους ὄντες εἴασαν
54 αὐτοὺς ἀπελθεῖν· οἱ δὲ εἰς τὸ ἄστυ ἐλθόντες τοὺς
μὲν τριάκοντα ἐξέβαλον πλὴν Φείδωνος καὶ
Ἐρατοσθένους, ἄρχοντας δὲ τοὺς ἐκείνοις ἐχθί-
στους εἵλοντο, ἡγούμενοι δικαίως ἂν ὑπὸ τῶν
αὐτῶν τούς τε τριάκοντα μισεῖσθαι καὶ τοὺς ἐν
55 Πειραιεῖ φιλεῖσθαι. τούτων τοίνυν Φείδων [ὁ
τῶν τριάκοντα] γενόμενος καὶ Ἱπποκλῆς καὶ
Ἐπιχάρης ὁ Λαμπτρεὺς καὶ ἕτεροι οἱ δοκοῦντες
εἶναι ἐναντιώτατοι Χαρικλεῖ καὶ Κριτίᾳ καὶ τῇ
ἐκείνων ἑταιρείᾳ ἐπειδὴ αὐτοὶ εἰς τὴν ἀρχὴν
κατέστησαν, πολὺ μείζω στάσιν καὶ πόλεμον
ἐπὶ τοὺς ἐν Πειραιεῖ τοῖς ἐξ ἄστεως ἐποίησαν·

[9] ἐδείξαμεν. Al. ἔδειξαν. MSS. ἔδοξαν. *Francken* conj. πρᾳοι πρὸς ἀλλήλους. *Weidn.* οἷς ἀμφότεροι ἐνέδοσαν.

ᾧ[10] καὶ φανερῶς ἐπεδείξαντο ὅτι οὐχ ὑπὲρ τῶν ἐν 56
Πειραιεῖ οὐδ' ὑπὲρ τῶν ἀδίκως ἀπολλυμένων
ἐστασίαζον, οὐδ' οἱ τεθνεῶτες αὐτοὺς ἐλύπουν,
οὐδ' οἱ μέλλοντες ἀποθανεῖσθαι, ἀλλ' οἱ μεῖζον
δυνάμενοι καὶ θᾶττον πλουτοῦντες. λαβόντες 57
γὰρ τὰς ἀρχὰς καὶ τὴν πόλιν ἀμφοτέροις ἐπολέ-
μουν, τοῖς τε τριάκοντα πάντα κακὰ εἰργασμένοις
καὶ ὑμῖν πάντα κακὰ πεπονθόσι. καίτοι τοῦτο
πᾶσι δῆλον ἦν, ὅτι εἰ μὲν ἐκεῖνοι ἀδίκως ἔφευγον,
ὑμεῖς δικαίως, εἰ δ' ὑμεῖς ἀδίκως, οἱ τριάκοντα
δικαίως· οὐ γὰρ δὴ ἑτέρων ἔργων αἰτίαν λαβόντες
ἐκ τῆς πόλεως ἐξέπεσον, ἀλλὰ τούτων. ὥστε 58
σφόδρα χρὴ ὀργίζεσθαι, ὅτι Φείδων αἱρεθεὶς
ὑμᾶς διαλλάξαι καὶ καταγαγεῖν τῶν αὐτῶν ἔργων
Ἐρατοσθένει μετεῖχε καὶ τῇ αὐτῇ γνώμῃ τοὺς
μὲν κρείττους αὐτῶν δι' ὑμᾶς κακῶς ποιεῖν
ἕτοιμος ἦν, ὑμῖν δὲ ἀδίκως φεύγουσιν οὐκ ἠθέλησεν
ἀποδοῦναι τὴν πόλιν, ἀλλ' ἐλθὼν εἰς Λακεδαίμονα
ἔπειθεν αὐτοὺς στρατεύεσθαι, διαβάλλων ὅτι
Βοιωτῶν ἡ πόλις ἔσται, καὶ ἄλλα λέγων οἷς ᾤετο
πείσειν μάλιστα. οὐ δυνάμενος δὲ τούτων τυχεῖν, 59
εἴτε καὶ τῶν ἱερῶν ἐμποδὼν ὄντων εἴτε καὶ αὐτῶν
οὐ βουλομένων, ἑκατὸν τάλαντα ἐδανείσατο, ἵνα
ἔχοι ἐπικούρους μισθοῦσθαι. καὶ Λύσανδρον
ἄρχοντα ᾐτήσατο, εὐνούστατον μὲν ὄντα τῇ
ὀλιγαρχίᾳ, κακονούστατον δὲ τῇ πόλει, μισοῦντα
δὲ μάλιστα τοὺς ἐν Πειραιεῖ. μισθωσάμενοι δὲ 60
πάντας ἀνθρώπους ἐπ' ὀλέθρῳ τῆς πόλεως, καὶ
πόλεις ἐπάγοντες, καὶ τελευτῶντες Λακεδαιμονίους

[10] *Scheibe* conj. οἷς. X. οἱ.

καὶ τῶν συμμάχων ὁπόσους ἐδύναντο πεῖσαι, οὐ διαλλάξαι ἀλλ' ἀπολέσαι παρεσκευάζοντο τὴν πόλιν εἰ μὴ δι' ἄνδρας ἀγαθούς, οἷς ὑμεῖς δηλώσατε παρὰ τῶν ἐχθρῶν δίκην λαβόντες, ὅτι καὶ ἐκείνοις
61 χάριν ἀποδώσετε. ταῦτα δὲ ἐπίστασθε μὲν καὶ αὐτοί, καὶ οἶδ' ὅτι οὐ δεῖ* μάρτυρας παρασχέσθαι· ὅμως δέ· ἐγώ τε γὰρ δέομαι ἀναπαύσασθαι, ὑμῶν τ' ἐνίοις ἥδιον ὡς πλείστων τοὺς αὐτοὺς λόγους ἀκούειν.

Witnesses as to the Conduct of Eratosthenes after the fall of Critias.

§ 6. *But he intends, I hear, to rest his defence on the fact that he acted in connection with Theramenes, who, as head of the Moderate party, deserved well of you. How far from the truth this is you will see if you consider the part taken by Theramenes throughout our troubles. (1) He it was who was the chief agent in the former revolution and in establishing the Four Hundred, and only helped to break up their rule from personal jealousy; (2) He, when blindly trusted by you after Ægospotami, really brought about the demolition of the walls, and the revolution and the interference of Lysander, and the establishment of the Thirty; (3) And finally, he was justly put to death by the Oligarchy to which he was unfaithful, as he might have been by the Democracy to which he had been equally false.*

The defendant then will gain nothing by sheltering himself under the name of Theramenes.

62 Φέρε δὴ καὶ περὶ Θηραμένους ὡς ἂν δύνωμαι διὰ βραχυτάτων διδάξω. δέομαι δ' ὑμῶν ἀκοῦσαι ὑπέρ τ' ἐμαυτοῦ καὶ τῆς πόλεως. καὶ μηδενὶ τοῦτο παραστῇ, ὡς Ἐρατοσθένους

* *W.* ὥστ' οὐκ οἶδ' ὅτι δεῖ. MS. om. οὐκ.

κινδυνεύοντος Θηραμένους κατηγορῶ· πυνθάνομαι
γὰρ ταῦτα ἀπολογήσεσθαι αὐτόν, ὅτι ἐκείνῳ
φίλος ἦν καὶ τῶν αὐτῶν ἔργων μετεῖχε. καίτοι 63
σφόδρ᾽ ἂν αὐτὸν οἶμαι μετὰ Θεμιστοκλέους πολι-
τευόμενον προσποιεῖσθαι πράττειν ὅπως οἰκοδο-
μηθήσεται τὰ τείχη, ὁπότε καὶ μετὰ Θηραμένους
ὅπως καθαιρεθήσεται. οὐ γάρ μοι δοκοῦσιν ἴσου
ἄξιοι γεγενῆσθαι· ὁ μὲν γὰρ Λακεδαιμονίων
ἀκόντων ᾠκοδόμησεν αὐτά, οὗτος δὲ τοὺς πολίτας
ἐξαπατήσας καθεῖλε. περιέστηκεν οὖν τῇ πόλει 64
τοὐναντίον ἢ ὡς εἰκὸς ἦν. ἄξιον μὲν γὰρ καὶ
τοὺς φίλους τοὺς Θηραμένους προσαπολωλέναι,
πλὴν εἴ τις ἐτύγχανεν ἐκείνῳ τἀναντία πράττων·
νῦν δὲ ὁρῶ τάς τε ἀπολογίας εἰς ἐκεῖνον ἀναφερομένας, τούς τ᾽ ἐκείνῳ συνόντας τιμᾶσθαι πειρω-
μένους, ὥσπερ πολλῶν ἀγαθῶν αἰτίου ἀλλ᾽ οὐ
μεγάλων κακῶν γεγενημένου. ὃς πρῶτον μὲν 65
τῆς προτέρας ὀλιγαρχίας αἰτιώτατος ἐγένετο,
πείσας ὑμᾶς τὴν ἐπὶ τῶν τετρακοσίων πολιτείαν
ἑλέσθαι. καὶ ὁ μὲν πατὴρ αὐτοῦ τῶν προβούλων
ὢν ταῦτ᾽ ἔπραττεν, αὐτὸς δὲ δοκῶν εὐνούστατος
εἶναι τοῖς πράγμασι στρατηγὸς ὑπ᾽ αὐτῶν ᾑρέθη.
καὶ ἕως μὲν ἐτιμᾶτο, πιστὸν ἑαυτὸν παρεῖχεν· 66
ἐπειδὴ δὲ Πείσανδρον μὲν καὶ Κάλλαισχρον καὶ
ἑτέρους ἑώρα προτέρους αὐτοῦ γινομένους, τὸ
δὲ ὑμέτερον πλῆθος οὐκέτι βουλόμενον τούτων
ἀκροᾶσθαι, τότ᾽ ἤδη διά τε τὸν πρὸς ἐκείνους
φθόνον καὶ τὸ παρ᾽ ὑμῶν δέος μετέσχε τῶν
᾽Αριστοκράτους ἔργων. βουλόμενος δὲ τῷ ὑμε- 67
τέρῳ πλήθει δοκεῖν πιστὸς εἶναι ᾽Αντιφῶντα καὶ

᾿Αρχεπτόλεμον φιλτάτους ὄντας αὐτῷ κατηγορῶν
ἀπέκτεινεν, εἰς τοσοῦτον δὲ κακίας ἦλθεν, ὥστε
ἅμα μὲν διὰ τὴν πρὸς ἐκείνους πίστιν ὑμᾶς
κατεδουλώσατο, διὰ δὲ τὴν πρὸς ὑμᾶς τοὺς
68 φίλους ἀπώλεσε. τιμώμενος δὲ καὶ τῶν μεγίστων
ἀξιούμενος, αὐτὸς ἐπαγγειλάμενος σώσειν τὴν
πόλιν αὐτὸς ἀπώλεσε, φάσκων πρᾶγμα ηὑρηκέναι
μέγα καὶ πολλοῦ ἄξιον. ὑπέσχετο δὲ εἰρήνην
ποιήσειν μήτε ὅμηρα δοὺς μήτε τὰ τείχη καθελὼν
μήτε τὰς ναῦς παραδούς· ταῦτα δὲ εἰπεῖν μὲν
οὐδενὶ ἠθέλησεν, ἐκέλευσε δὲ αὐτῷ πιστεύειν.
69 ὑμεῖς δέ, ὦ ἄνδρες ᾿Αθηναῖοι, πραττούσης μὲν
τῆς ἐν ᾿Αρείῳ πάγῳ βουλῆς σωτήρια, ἀντιλεγόν-
των δὲ πολλῶν Θηραμένει, εἰδότες δὲ ὅτι οἱ μὲν
ἄλλοι ἄνθρωποι τῶν πολεμίων ἕνεκα τἀπόρρητα
ποιοῦνται, ἐκεῖνος δ' ἐν τοῖς αὑτοῦ πολίταις οὐκ
ἠθέλησεν εἰπεῖν ταῦτα ἃ πρὸς τοὺς πολεμίους
ἔμελλεν ἐρεῖν, ὅμως ἐπετρέψατε αὐτῷ πατρίδα
70 καὶ παῖδας καὶ γυναῖκας καὶ ὑμᾶς αὐτούς. ὁ
δὲ ὧν μὲν ὑπέσχετο οὐδὲν ἔπραξεν, οὕτως δὲ
ἐνετεθύμητο ὡς χρὴ μικρὰν καὶ ἀσθενῆ γενέσθαι
τὴν πόλιν, ὥστε περὶ ὧν οὐδεὶς πώποτε οὔτε τῶν
πολεμίων ἐμνήσθη οὔτε τῶν πολιτῶν ἤλπισε,
ταῦθ' ὑμᾶς ἔπεισε πρᾶξαι, οὐχ ὑπὸ Λακεδαιμονίων ἀναγκαζόμενος, ἀλλ' αὐτὸς ἐκείνοις ἐπαγγελλόμενος, τοῦ τε Πειραιῶς τὰ τείχη περιελεῖν
καὶ τὴν ὑπάρχουσαν πολιτείαν καταλῦσαι, εὖ
εἰδὼς ὅτι, εἰ μὴ πασῶν τῶν ἐλπίδων ἀποστερή-
σεσθε, ταχεῖαν παρ' αὐτοῦ τὴν τιμωρίαν
71 κομιεῖσθε. καὶ τὸ τελευταῖον, ὦ ἄνδρες δικα-

σταί, οὐ πρότερον εἴασε τὴν ἐκκλησίαν γενέσθαι, ἕως ὁ λεγόμενος ὑπ' ἐκείνου[11] καιρὸς ἐπιμελῶς ὑπ' αὐτοῦ ἐτηρήθη, καὶ μετεπέμψατο μὲν τὰς μετὰ Λυσάνδρου ναῦς ἐκ Σάμου, ἐπεδήμησε δὲ τὸ τῶν πολεμίων στρατόπεδον. τότε δὲ τούτων 72
ὑπαρχόντων, καὶ παρόντων Λυσάνδρου καὶ Φιλοχάρους καὶ Μιλτιάδου, περὶ τῆς πολιτείας τὴν ἐκκλησίαν ἐποίουν, ἵνα μήτε ῥήτωρ αὐτοῖς μηδεὶς ἐναντιοῖτο μηδὲ ἀπειλοῖ, ὑμεῖς τε μὴ τὰ τῇ πόλει συμφέροντα ἕλοισθε, ἀλλὰ τἀκείνοις δοκοῦντα ψηφίσαισθε. ἀναστὰς δὲ Θηραμένης 73
ἐκέλευσεν ὑμᾶς τριάκοντα ἀνδράσιν ἐπιτρέψαι τὴν πόλιν, καὶ τῇ πολιτείᾳ χρῆσθαι ἣν Δρακοντίδης ἀπέφαινεν. ὑμεῖς δ' ὅμως καὶ οὕτω διακείμενοι ἐθορυβεῖτε ὡς οὐ ποιήσοντες ταῦτα· ἐγιγνώσκετε γὰρ ὅτι περὶ δουλείας καὶ ἐλευθερίας ἐν ἐκείνῃ τῇ ἡμέρᾳ ἐξεκλησιάζετε. Θηραμένης 74
δέ, ὦ ἄνδρες δικασταί, (καὶ τούτων ὑμᾶς αὐτοὺς μάρτυρας παρέξομαι) εἶπεν ὅτι οὐδὲν αὐτῷ μέλοι τοῦ ὑμετέρου θορύβου, ἐπειδὴ πολλοὺς μὲν Ἀθηναίων εἰδείη τοὺς τὰ ὅμοια πράττοντας αὐτῷ, δοκοῦντα δὲ Λυσάνδρῳ καὶ Λακεδαιμονίοις λέγοι. μετ' ἐκεῖνον δὲ Λύσανδρος ἀναστὰς ἄλλα τε πολλὰ εἶπε καὶ ὅτι παρασπόνδους ὑμᾶς ἔχοι, καὶ ὅτι οὐ περὶ πολιτείας ὑμῖν ἔσται ἀλλὰ περὶ σωτηρίας, εἰ μὴ ποιήσεθ' ἃ Θηραμένης κελεύει. τῶν δ' ἐν τῇ ἐκκλησίᾳ ὅσοι ἄνδρες ἀγαθοὶ 75
ἦσαν, γνόντες τὴν παρασκευὴν καὶ τὴν ἀνάγκην, οἱ μὲν αὐτοῦ μένοντες ἡσυχίαν ἦγον, οἱ δὲ

[11] *West.* ὡμολογημένος. *Scheibe* ἐκείνων.

ᾤχοντο ἀπιόντες, τοῦτο γοῦν σφίσιν αὐτοῖς
συνειδότες, ὅτι οὐδὲν κακὸν τῇ πόλει ἐψηφίσαντο·
ὀλίγοι δέ τινες καὶ πονηροὶ καὶ κακῶς βουλευό-
76 μενοι τὰ προσταχθέντα ἐχειροτόνησαν. παρήγγελτο γὰρ αὐτοῖς δέκα μὲν οὓς Θηραμένης
ἀπέδειξε χειροτονῆσαι, δέκα δὲ οὓς οἱ καθεστη-
κότες ἔφοροι κελεύοιεν, δέκα δ' ἐκ τῶν παρόντων·
οὕτω γὰρ τὴν ὑμετέραν ἀσθένειαν ἑώρων καὶ
τὴν αὑτῶν δύναμιν ἠπίσταντο, ὥστε πρότερον
ᾔδεσαν τὰ μέλλοντα ἐν τῇ ἐκκλησίᾳ πραχθήσε-
77 σθαι. ταῦτα δὲ οὐκ ἐμοὶ δεῖ πιστεῦσαι, ἀλλὰ
ἐκείνῳ· πάντα γὰρ τὰ ὑπ' ἐμοῦ εἰρημένα ἐν τῇ
βουλῇ ἀπολογούμενος ἔλεγεν, ὀνειδίζων μὲν τοῖς
φεύγουσιν, ὅτι δι' αὐτὸν κατέλθοιεν, οὐδὲν φρον-
τιζόντων Λακεδαιμονίων, ὀνειδίζων δὲ τοῖς τῆς
πολιτείας μετέχουσιν ὅτι πάντων τῶν πεπραγμένων τοῖς εἰρημένοις τρόποις ὑπ' ἐμοῦ αὐτὸς
αἴτιος γεγενημένος τοιούτων τυγχάνοι, πολλὰς
πίστεις αὐτὸς ἔργῳ δεδωκὼς καὶ παρ' ἐκείνων
78 ὅρκους εἰληφώς. καὶ τοσούτων καὶ ἑτέρων κακῶν καὶ αἰσχρῶν καὶ πάλαι καὶ νεωστὶ καὶ
μικρῶν καὶ μεγάλων αἰτίῳ γεγενημένῳ τολμήσουσιν αὐτοὺς φίλους ὄντας ἀποφαίνειν, οὐχ
ὑπὲρ ὑμῶν ἀποθανόντος Θηραμένους ἀλλ' ὑπὲρ
τῆς αὑτοῦ πονηρίας, καὶ δικαίως μὲν ἐν ὀλιγαρχίᾳ
δίκην δόντος (ἤδη γὰρ αὐτὴν κατέλυσε), δικαίως
δ' ἂν ἐν δημοκρατίᾳ· δὶς γὰρ ὑμᾶς κατεδουλώσατο, τῶν μὲν παρόντων καταφρονῶν, τῶν δὲ
ἀπόντων ἐπιθυμῶν, καὶ τῷ καλλίστῳ ὀνόματι
χρώμενος δεινοτάτων ἔργων διδάσκαλος καταστάς.

§ 7. *So much for Theramenes. It is now your imperative duty to show no pity, but to punish his adherents, especially Eratosthenes; and yet Eratosthenes is in much better plight than the loyal citizens were whom he slew. They perished without fair trial, he enjoys the advantages of legal proceedings and an opportunity of self-defence. Besides, he can die but once,—an inadequate retaliation for the numerous murders and robberies in which he has taken part. He also, be sure, has a party at his back into which you must by his condemnation strike awe.*

Περὶ μὲν τοίνυν Θηραμένους ἱκανά μοί 79
ἐστι τὰ κατηγορημένα· ἥκει δ' ὑμῖν ἐκεῖνος ὁ
καιρός, ἐν ᾧ δεῖ συγγνώμην καὶ ἔλεον μὴ εἶναι
ἐν ταῖς ὑμετέραις γνώμαις, ἀλλὰ παρὰ Ἐρατοσθένους καὶ τῶν τουτουὶ συναρχόντων δίκην
λαβεῖν, μηδὲ μαχομένους μὲν κρείττους εἶναι
τῶν πολεμίων, ψηφιζομένους δὲ ἥττους τῶν
ἐχθρῶν. μηδ' ὧν φασι μέλλειν πράξειν πλείω 80
χάριν αὐτοῖς ἴστε, ἢ ὧν ἐποίησαν ὀργίζεσθε·
μηδ' ἀποῦσι μὲν τοῖς τριάκοντα ἐπιβουλεύετε,
παρόντας δ' ἀφῆτε· μηδὲ τῆς τύχης, ἣ τούτους
παρέδωκε τῇ πόλει, κάκιον ὑμῖν αὐτοῖς βοηθή-
σητε. κατηγορεῖτε δὲ καὶ [12] τῶν τούτου φίλων, 81
οἷς τὰς ἀπολογίας ἀνοίσει καὶ μεθ' ὧν αὐτῷ
ταῦτα πέπρακται. ὁ μέντοι ἀγὼν οὐκ ἐξ ἴσου
τῇ πόλει καὶ Ἐρατοσθένει· οὗτος μὲν γὰρ κατή-
γορος καὶ δικαστὴς αὐτὸς ἦν τῶν γινομένων,[13]
ἡμεῖς δὲ νυνὶ εἰς κατηγορίαν καὶ ἀπολογίαν

[12] κατηγορεῖτε δὲ καί. Sic *Madv.* Advers. Crit., p. 453. *Scheibe* κατηγόρηται δὴ Ἐρατοσθένους καί. MSS. κατηγορεῖτε δὲ Ἐρ. κτλ.

[13] γινομένων. *Reiskius* et *Scheibe* κρινομένων, quod cum ἀκρίτους, § 82, male jungitur. Num idem κρινόμενοι et ἄκριτοι sunt?

82 καθεσταμεν. καὶ οὗτοι μὲν τοὺς οὐδὲν ἀδικοῦντας ἀκρίτους ἀπέκτειναν, ὑμεῖς δὲ τοὺς ἀπολέ-
σαντας τὴν πόλιν κατὰ τὸν νόμον ἀξιοῦτε κρίνειν,
παρ᾽ ὧν οὐδ᾽ ἂν παρανόμως βουλόμενοι δίκην
λαμβάνειν ἀξίαν τῶν ἀδικημάτων ὧν τὴν πόλιν
ἠδικήκασι λάβοιτε. τί γὰρ ἂν παθόντες δίκην
83 τὴν ἀξίαν εἴησαν τῶν ἔργων δεδωκότες; πότερον
εἰ αὐτοὺς ἀποκτείνοιτε καὶ τοὺς παῖδας αὐτῶν,
ἱκανὴν ἂν τοῦ φόνου δίκην λάβοιμεν, ὧν οὗτοι
πατέρας καὶ υἱεῖς καὶ ἀδελφοὺς ἀκρίτους ἀπέκτειναν; ἀλλὰ γὰρ εἰ τὰ χρήματα τὰ φανερὰ
δημεύσαιτε, καλῶς ἂν ἔχοι ἢ τῇ πόλει, ἧς οὗτοι
πολλὰ εἰλήφασιν, ἢ τοῖς ἰδιώταις, ὧν οἰκίας
84 ἐξεπόρθησαν; ἐπειδὴ τοίνυν πάντα ποιοῦντες
δίκην παρ᾽ αὐτῶν* οὐκ ἂν δύναισθε λαβεῖν, πῶς
οὐκ αἰσχρὸν ὑμῖν καὶ ἡντινοῦν ἀπολιπεῖν, ἥντινά
τις βούλοιτο παρὰ τούτων λαμβάνειν; πᾶν δ᾽
ἄν μοι δοκεῖ τολμῆσαι, ὅστις νυνὶ οὐχ ἑτέρων
ὄντων τῶν δικαστῶν ἀλλ᾽ αὐτῶν τῶν κακῶς
πεπονθότων, ἥκει ἀπολογησόμενος πρὸς αὐτοὺς
τοὺς μάρτυρας τῆς τούτου πονηρίας· τοσοῦτον
ἢ ὑμῶν καταπεφρόνηκεν ἢ ἑτέροις πεπίστευκεν.
85 ὧν ἀμφοτέρων ἄξιον ἐπιμεληθῆναι, ἐνθυμουμένους
ὅτι οὔτ᾽ ἂν ἐκεῖνα ἐδύναντο ποιεῖν μὴ ἑτέρων
συμπραττόντων οὔτ᾽ ἂν νῦν ἐπεχείρησαν ἐλθεῖν
μὴ ὑπὸ τῶν αὐτῶν οἰόμενοι σωθήσεσθαι, οἳ οὐ
τούτοις ἥκουσι βοηθήσοντες, ἀλλὰ ἡγούμενοι
πολλὴν ἄδειαν σφίσιν ἔσεσθαι τῶν πεπραγμένων
καὶ τοῦ λοιποῦ ποιεῖν ὅ τι ἂν βούλωνται, εἰ τοὺς
μεγίστων κακῶν αἰτίους λαβόντες ἀφήσετε.

* *Weidn.* αὐτῶν ἀξίαν.

§ 8. *To those respectable men who plead for the defendants, I can only say I could wish that they had shown equal zeal to save the city from the tyrants. And to the witnesses in their favour I would say, that they show more courage in taking part against you all than they did when, for fear of Eratosthenes, they shrank from attending the funerals of the proscribed.*

They say that Eratosthenes was the least criminal of the Thirty. But your verdict should rest on this principle, that you will declare openly now whether you approve of what has been done, or are determined to show your anger at it, and exact due punishment.

Ἀλλὰ καὶ τῶν συνερούντων αὐτοῖς ἄξιον 86
θαυμάζειν, πότερον ὡς καλοὶ κἀγαθοὶ αἰτήσονται,
τὴν αὐτῶν ἀρετὴν πλείονος ἀξίαν ἀποφαίνοντες
τῆς τούτων πονηρίας· ἐβουλόμην μέντ᾽ ἂν αὐτοὺς
οὕτω προθύμους εἶναι σώζειν τὴν πόλιν, ὥσπερ
οὗτοι ἀπολλύναι· ἢ ὡς δεινοὶ λέγειν ἀπολογή-
σονται καὶ τὰ τούτων ἔργα πολλοῦ ἄξια ἀπο-
φανοῦσιν. ἀλλ᾽ οὐχ ὑπὲρ ὑμῶν οὐδεὶς αὐτῶν
οὐδὲ τὰ δίκαια πώποτε ἐπεχείρησεν εἰπεῖν.
ἀλλὰ τοὺς μάρτυρας ἄξιον ἰδεῖν, οἳ τούτοις 87
μαρτυροῦντες αὐτῶν κατηγοροῦσι, σφόδρα ἐπι-
λήσμονας καὶ εὐήθεις νομίζοντες ὑμᾶς εἶναι, εἰ
διὰ μὲν τὸ ὑμέτερον πλῆθος[14] ἀδεῶς ἡγοῦνται
τοὺς τριάκοντα σώσειν, διὰ δὲ Ἐρατοσθένην
καὶ τοὺς συνάρχοντας αὐτοῦ δεινὸν ἦν καὶ τῶν
τεθνεώτων ἐπ᾽ ἐκφορὰν ἐλθεῖν. καίτοι οὗτοι μὲν 88
σωθέντες πάλιν ἂν δύναιντο τὴν πόλιν ἀπολέσαι·
ἐκεῖνοι δέ, οὓς οὗτοι ἀπώλεσαν, τελευτήσαντες

[14] τὸ ὑμέτερον πλῆθος *Dobr.* et *Scheib.* Alii et MSS. τοῦ ὑμετέρου πλήθους.

τὸν βίον πέρας ἔχουσι τῆς παρὰ τῶν ἐχθρῶν
τιμωρίας. οὐκ οὖν δεινὸν εἰ τῶν μὲν ἀδίκως
τεθνεώτων οἱ φίλοι συναπώλλυντο, αὐτοῖς δὲ
τοῖς τὴν πόλιν ἀπολέσασιν δήπου ἐπ' ἐκφορὰν
πολλοὶ ἥξουσιν, ὁπότε βοηθεῖν τοσοῦτοι παρα-
89 σκευάζονται; καὶ μὲν δὴ πολλῷ[15] ῥᾷον ἡγοῦμαι
εἶναι ὑπὲρ ὧν ὑμεῖς ἐπάσχετε ἀντειπεῖν, ἢ ὑπὲρ
ὧν οὗτοι πεποιήκασιν ἀπολογήσασθαι. καίτοι
λέγουσιν ὡς Ἐρατοσθένει ἐλάχιστα τῶν τριάκοντα
κακὰ εἴργασται, καὶ διὰ τοῦτο αὐτὸν ἀξιοῦσι
σωθῆναι· ὅτι δὲ τῶν ἄλλων Ἑλλήνων πλεῖστα
εἰς ὑμᾶς ἐξημάρτηκεν, οὐκ οἴονται χρῆναι αὐτὸν
90 ἀπολέσθαι. ὑμεῖς δὲ δείξετε ἥν τινα γνώμην
ἔχετε περὶ τῶν πραγμάτων. εἰ μὲν γὰρ τούτου
καταψηφιεῖσθε, δῆλοι ἔσεσθε ὡς ὀργιζόμενοι τοῖς
πεπραγμένοις· εἰ δὲ ἀποψηφιεῖσθε, ὀφθήσεσθε
τῶν αὐτῶν ἔργων ἐπιθυμηταὶ τούτοις ὄντες, καὶ
οὐχ ἕξετε λέγειν ὅτι τὰ ὑπὸ τῶν τριάκοντα
91 προσταχθέντα ἐποιεῖτε· νυνὶ μὲν γὰρ οὐδεὶς
ὑμᾶς ἀναγκάζει παρὰ τὴν ὑμετέραν γνώμην ἀποψηφίζεσθαι. ὥστε συμβουλεύω μὴ τούτων ἀπο-
ψηφισαμένους ὑμῶν αὐτῶν καταψηφίσασθαι.
μηδ' οἴεσθε κρύβδην εἶναι τὴν ψῆφον· φανερὰν
γὰρ τῇ πόλει τὴν ὑμετέραν γνώμην ποιήσετε.

§ 9. *Finally, I appeal to you all, whether you were of the City party or the Peiræus party.*

92 Βούλομαι δὲ ὀλίγα ἑκατέρους ἀναμνήσας
καταβαίνειν, τούς τε ἐξ ἄστεος καὶ τοὺς ἐκ

[15] πολλῷ *Scheibe.* Al. πολύ. MSS. nonnull. πολλοί.

Πειραιῶς, ἵνα τὰς ὑμῖν διὰ τούτων γεγενημένας συμφορὰς παραδείγματα ἔχοντες τὴν ψῆφον φέρητε.

(1.) *If the first, remember that these men caused you to join in an unnatural and unprofitable war against your friends and relatives.*

Καὶ πρῶτον μὲν ὅσοι ἐξ ἄστεός ἐστε, σκέψασθε
ὅτι ὑπὸ τούτων οὕτω σφόδρα ἤρχεσθε, ὥστε
ἀδελφοῖς καὶ υἱέσι καὶ πολίταις ἠναγκάζεσθε
πολεμεῖν τοιοῦτον πόλεμον, ἐν ᾧ ἡττηθέντες μὲν
τοῖς νικήσασι τὸ ἴσον ἔχετε, νικήσαντες δ' ἂν
τούτοις ἐδουλεύετε. καὶ τοὺς ἰδίους οἴκους οὗτοι 93
μὲν ἂν ἐκ τῶν πραγμάτων μεγάλους ἐκτήσαντο,
ὑμεῖς δὲ διὰ τὸν πρὸς ἀλλήλους πόλεμον ἐλάτ-
τους ἔχετε· συνωφελεῖσθαι μὲν γὰρ ὑμᾶς οὐκ
ἠξίουν, συνδιαβάλλεσθαι δ' ἠνάγκαζον, εἰς τοσοῦτον ὑπεροψίας ἐλθόντες ὥστε οὐ τῶν ἀγαθῶν
κοινούμενοι πιστοὺς ὑμᾶς ἐκτῶντο, ἀλλὰ τῶν
ὀνειδῶν μεταδιδόντες εὔνους ᾤοντο εἶναι. ἀνθ' 94
ὧν ὑμεῖς νῦν ἐν τῷ θαρραλέῳ ὄντες, καθ' ὅσον
δύνασθε, καὶ ὑπὲρ ὑμῶν αὐτῶν καὶ ὑπὲρ τῶν ἐκ
Πειραιῶς τιμωρήσασθε, ἐνθυμηθέντες μὲν ὅτι
ὑπὸ τούτων πονηροτάτων ὄντων ἤρχεσθε, ἐνθυμηθέντες δὲ ὅτι μετ' ἀνδρῶν νῦν ἀρίστων πολι-
τεύεσθε καὶ τοῖς πολεμίοις μάχεσθε καὶ περὶ
τῆς πόλεως βουλεύεσθε, ἀναμνησθέντες δὲ τῶν
ἐπικούρων, οὓς οὗτοι φύλακας τῆς σφετέρας
ἀρχῆς καὶ τῆς ὑμετέρας δουλείας εἰς τὴν ἀκρόπολιν κατέστησαν. καὶ πρὸς ὑμᾶς μὲν ἔτι 95
πολλῶν ὄντων εἰπεῖν τοσαῦτα λέγω.

(2.) *If the latter, remember that by these men you were deprived of your arms: banished from the city: demanded back from the towns in which you had taken refuge: saw your friends dragged to slaughter from market-place and temple, forced to put an end to their own lives, and left unburied; while those of you who escaped death wandered miserably from place to place, leaving wives and children in foreign lands, or in your own country grown more hostile than they.*

Ὅσοι δ' ἐκ Πειραιῶς ἐστε, πρῶτον μὲν τῶν
ὅπλων ἀναμνήσθητε, ὅτι πολλὰς μάχας ἐν τῇ
ἀλλοτρίᾳ μαχεσάμενοι οὐχ ὑπὸ τῶν πολεμίων
ἀλλ' ὑπὸ τούτων εἰρήνης οὔσης ἀφῃρέθητε τὰ
ὅπλα, ἔπειθ' ὅτι ἐξεκηρύχθητε μὲν ἐκ τῆς πόλεως,
ἣν ὑμῖν οἱ πατέρες παρέδοσαν, φεύγοντας δὲ
96 ὑμᾶς ἐκ τῶν πόλεων ἐξῃτοῦντο. ἀνθ' ὧν ὀργίσ-
θητε μὲν ὥσπερ ὅτ' ἐφεύγετε, ἀναμνήσθητε δὲ
καὶ τῶν ἄλλων κακῶν ἃ πεπόνθατε ὑπ' αὐτῶν,
οἳ τοὺς μὲν ἐκ τῆς ἀγορᾶς τοὺς δ' ἐκ τῶν ἱερῶν
συναρπάζοντες βιαίως ἀπέκτειναν, τοὺς δὲ ἀπὸ
τέκνων καὶ γονέων καὶ γυναικῶν ἀφέλκοντες
φονέας αὑτῶν ἠνάγκασαν γενέσθαι καὶ οὐδὲ ταφῆς
τῆς νομιζομένης εἴασαν τυχεῖν, ἡγούμενοι τὴν
αὑτῶν ἀρχὴν βεβαιοτέραν εἶναι τῆς παρὰ τῶν
97 θεῶν τιμωρίας. ὅσοι δὲ τὸν θάνατον διέφυγον,
πολλαχοῦ κινδυνεύσαντες καὶ εἰς πολλὰς πόλεις
πλανηθέντες καὶ πανταχόθεν ἐκκηρυττόμενοι,
ἐνδεεῖς ὄντες τῶν ἐπιτηδείων, οἱ μὲν ἐν πολεμίᾳ
τῇ πατρίδι τοὺς παῖδας καταλιπόντες, οἱ δ' ἐν
ξένῃ γῇ, πολλῶν ἐναντιουμένων ἤλθετε εἰς τὸν
Πειραιᾶ. πολλῶν δὲ καὶ μεγάλων κινδύνων

ὑπαρξάντων ἄνδρες ἀγαθοὶ γενόμενοι τοὺς μὲν
ἠλευθερώσατε, τοὺς δ' εἰς τὴν πατρίδα κατη-
γάγετε. εἰ δὲ ἐδυστυχήσατε καὶ τούτων ἡμάρ- 98
τετε, αὐτοὶ μὲν ἂν δείσαντες ἐφεύγετε μὴ πάθητε
τοιαῦτα οἷα καὶ πρότερον, καὶ οὔτ' ἂν ἱερὰ οὔτε
βωμοὶ ὑμᾶς ἀδικουμένους διὰ τοὺς τούτων τρό-
πους ὠφέλησαν, ἃ καὶ τοῖς ἀδικοῦσι σωτήρια
γίνεται· οἱ δὲ παῖδες ὑμῶν, ὅσοι μὲν ἐνθάδε
ἦσαν, ὑπὸ τούτων ἂν ὑβρίζοντο, οἱ δ' ἐπὶ ξένης
μικρῶν ἂν ἕνεκα συμβολαίων ἐδούλευον ἐρημίᾳ
τῶν ἐπικουρησόντων.

§ 10. *The crimes of these men extend to innumerable particulars, and require not one only, but many accusers to expose them in detail. I have done my best. In the name of everything dear and sacred to you, condemn them.*

Ἀλλὰ γὰρ οὐ τὰ μέλλοντα ἔσεσθαι βού- 99
λομαι λέγειν, τὰ πραχθέντα ὑπὸ τούτων οὐ
δυνάμενος εἰπεῖν· οὐδὲ γὰρ ἑνὸς κατηγόρου οὐδὲ
δυοῖν ἔργον ἐστίν, ἀλλὰ πολλῶν. ὅμως δὲ τῆς
ἐμῆς προθυμίας οὐδὲν ἐλλέλειπται, ὑπέρ τε τῶν
ἱερῶν, ἃ οὗτοι τὰ μὲν ἀπέδοντο τὰ δ' εἰσιόντες
ἐμίαινον, ὑπέρ τε τῆς πόλεως, ἣν μικρὰν ἐποίουν,
ὑπέρ τε τῶν νεωρίων, ἃ καθεῖλον, καὶ ὑπὲρ τῶν
τεθνεώτων, οἷς ὑμεῖς, ἐπειδὴ ζῶσιν ἐπαμῦναι οὐκ
ἠδύνασθε, ἀποθανοῦσι βοηθήσατε. οἶμαι δ' 100
αὐτοὺς ἡμῶν τε ἀκροᾶσθαι καὶ ὑμᾶς εἴσεσθαι
τὴν ψῆφον φέροντας, ἡγουμένους, ὅσοι μὲν ἂν
τούτων ἀποψηφίσησθε, αὐτῶν θάνατον κατα-
ψηφιεῖσθαι, ὅσοι δ' ἂν παρὰ τούτων δίκην

λάβωσιν, ὑπὲρ αὐτῶν τὰς τιμωρίας πεποιημένους. παύσομαι κατηγορῶν. ἀκηκόατε, ἑωράκατε, πεπόνθατε, ἔχετε. δικάζετε.

ORATION VII. [14.]

For the Prosecution: against Alcibiades for Desertion. Before a Military Court presided over by the Strategi.

§ 1. *No preface is needed; the defendant's whole life shows hopeless depravity. I have inherited as well as personal reasons for endeavouring to secure his punishment, and I shall speak on the points passed over by Archestratides.*

Ἡγοῦμαι μέν, ὦ ἄνδρες δικασταί, οὐδεμίαν
ὑμᾶς ποθεῖν ἀκοῦσαι πρόφασιν παρὰ τῶν βουλομένων Ἀλκιβιάδου κατηγορεῖν· τοιοῦτον γὰρ
πολίτην ἑαυτὸν ἐξ ἀρχῆς παρέσχεν, ὥστε καὶ εἰ
μή τις ἰδίᾳ ἀδικούμενος ὑπ' αὐτοῦ τυγχάνει,
οὐδὲν ἧττον προσήκει ἐκ τῶν ἄλλων ἐπιτηδευμάτων ἐχθρὸν αὐτὸν ἡγεῖσθαι. οὐ γὰρ μικρὰ τὰ 2
ἁμαρτήματα οὐδὲ συγγνώμης ἄξια, οὐδ' ἐλπίδα

29 *Francken* conj. οὐχ ὁμόψηφοι τοῖς ἐχθροῖς ἔσεσθε . . .

παρέχοντα ὡς ἔσται τοῦ λοιποῦ βελτίων, ἀλλ'
οὕτω πεπραγμένα καὶ εἰς τοσοῦτο κακίας ἀφιγ-
μένα, ὥστ' ἐπ' ἐνίοις[1] ὧν οὗτος φιλοτιμεῖται τοὺς
ἐχθροὺς αἰσχύνεσθαι. ἐγὼ μέντοι, ὦ ἄνδρες
δικασταί, καὶ πρότερον πρὸς τοὺς πατέρας ἡμῖν
διαφορᾶς ὑπαρχούσης, καὶ πάλαι τοῦτον ἐχθρὸν
ἡγούμενος, καὶ νῦν ὑπ' αὐτοῦ πεπονθὼς κακῶς,
πειράσομαι περὶ πάντων τῶν πεπραγμένων μεθ'
3 ὑμῶν αὐτὸν τιμωρήσασθαι. περὶ μὲν οὖν τῶν
ἄλλων Ἀρχεστρατίδης ἱκανῶς κατηγόρησε· καὶ
γὰρ τοὺς νόμους ἐπέδειξε καὶ μάρτυρας πάντων
παρέσχετο· ὅσα δ' οὗτος παραλέλοιπεν, ἐγὼ
καθ' ἕκαστον ὑμᾶς διδάξω.

§ 2. *You have an important constitutional point to settle. The accused pleads that the law as to desertion* (λειποταξία) *only refers to desertion in actual battle: and that there having been no battle, he does not come under its provisions. I, on the contrary, contend that it applies to every non-appearance in the ranks on active service* (στρατιᾷ), *whether there be actual fighting or not.*

4 Εἰκὸς τοίνυν ἐστίν, ὦ ἄνδρες δικασταί, ἐξ οὗ τὴν εἰρήνην ἐποιησάμεθα, πρῶτον περὶ τούτων νυνὶ δικάζοντας μὴ μόνον δικαστὰς ἀλλὰ καὶ νομοθέτας αὐτοὺς γενέσθαι,[2] εὖ εἰδότας ὅτι, ὅπως ἂν ὑμεῖς νυνὶ περὶ αὐτῶν γνῶτε, οὕτω καὶ τὸν ἄλλον χρόνον ἡ πόλις αὐτοῖς χρήσεται. δοκεῖ δέ μοι καὶ πολίτου χρηστοῦ καὶ δικαστοῦ δικαίου ἔργον εἶναι ταύτῃ τοὺς νόμους διαλαμβάνειν,

[1] ἐπ' ἐνίοις *Reiskius*: MSS. ἐπινικίοις. al. ἐπ' ἐκείνοις.
[2] *Francken* αὐτοὺς ἡγεῖσθαι.

ὅπῃ εἰς τὸν λοιπὸν χρόνον μέλλει συνοίσειν τῇ
πόλει. τολμῶσι γάρ τινες λέγειν ὡς οὐδεὶς 5
ἔνοχός ἐστι λιποταξίου οὐδὲ δειλίας· μάχην
γὰρ οὐδεμίαν γεγονέναι, τὸν δὲ νόμον κελεύειν,
ἐάν τις λίπῃ τὴν τάξιν εἰς τοὔπισω δειλίας ἕνεκα, μαχομένων
τῶν ἄλλων, περὶ τούτου τοὺς στρατιώτας δικάζειν.
ὁ δὲ νόμος οὐ περὶ τούτων κελεύει μόνον, ἀλλὰ
καὶ ὁπόσοι ἂν μὴ παρῶσιν ἐν τῇ πεζῇ στρατιᾷ.
ἀνάγνωθί μοι τὸν νόμον.

Law as to "Desertion" put in.

§ 3. *The law, you see, defines two classes of offenders: (1) those who fall out in the presence of the enemy; (2) those who do not put in an appearance in their proper rank.*

The question is, who is bound to appear? Those of course who are (1) of proper age, (2) put in the list by the Strategi.

If he pleads that he served in the cavalry, and so did not cheat the State, I shall in return show that thereby he exposed himself to the provisions of another law, which forbids any one serving in the cavalry who has not passed his scrutiny (ἀδοκίμαστος). *His motives were (1) sheer cowardice; (2) a contempt for the State, which he expected to fall, and so not be able to punish him.*

Ἀκούετε, ὦ ἄνδρες δικασταί, ὅτι περὶ ἀμφο- 6
τέρων κεῖται, καὶ ὅσοι ἂν μάχης οὔσης εἰς τοὔπισω
ἀναχωρήσωσι, καὶ ὅσοι ἂν ἐν τῇ πεζῇ στρατιᾷ
μὴ παρῶσι. σκέψασθε δὲ τίνες εἰσὶν οὓς δεῖ
παρεῖναι. οὐχ οἵτινες ἂν τὴν ἡλικίαν ταύτην
ἔχωσιν; οὐχ οὓς ἂν οἱ στρατηγοὶ καταλέξωσιν;

7 ἡγοῦμαι δ' ὦ ἄνδρες δικασταί, ὅλῳ τῷ νόμῳ
μόνον αὐτὸν τῶν πολιτῶν ἔνοχον εἶναι. ἀστρατείας μὲν γὰρ δικαίως ἂν αὐτὸν ἁλῶναι, ὅτι
καταλεγεὶς ὁπλίτης οὐκ ἐξῆλθε μεθ' ὑμῶν στρατοπεδευομένων, οὐδὲ παρέσχε μετὰ τῶν ἄλλων
ἑαυτὸν τάξαι,—δειλίας δέ, ὅτι δέον[2] αὐτὸν μετὰ
8 τῶν ὁπλιτῶν κινδυνεύειν ἱππεύειν εἵλετο. καίτοι
φασὶν αὐτὸν ταύτην τὴν ἀπολογίαν ποιήσεσθαι,
ὡς ἐπειδήπερ ἵππευεν, οὐδὲν ἠδίκει τὴν πόλιν.
ἐγὼ δ' ἡγοῦμαι διὰ τοῦθ' ὑμᾶς δικαίως ἂν αὐτῷ
ὀργίζεσθαι, ὅτι τοῦ νόμου κελεύοντος, ἐάν τις
ἀδοκίμαστος ἱππεύῃ, ἄτιμον εἶναι, ἐτόλμησεν
ἀδοκίμαστος ἱππεύειν. καί μοι ἀνάγνωθι τὸν
νόμον.

LAW PUT IN AS TO THE SERVING OF *ἀδοκίμαστοι* IN THE CAVALRY.

9 Οὗτος τοίνυν εἰς τοῦτ' ἦλθε πονηρίας, καὶ
οὕτως ὑμῶν κατεφρόνησε καὶ τοὺς πολεμίους
ἔδεισε καὶ ἱππεύειν ἐπεθύμησε καὶ τῶν νόμων
οὐκ ἐφρόντισεν, ὥστε οὐδὲν αὐτῷ τούτων τῶν
κινδύνων ἐμέλησεν, ἀλλ' ἐβουλήθη καὶ ἄτιμος
εἶναι καὶ τὰ χρήματ' αὐτοῦ δημευθῆναι καὶ
πάσαις ταῖς κειμέναις ζημίαις ἔνοχος γενέσθαι
μᾶλλον ἢ μετὰ τῶν πολιτῶν εἶναι καὶ ὁπλίτης
10 γενέσθαι. καὶ ἕτεροι μὲν οὐδεπώποτε ὁπλιτεύ-

[2] δέον dedi ego; quod ante ab aliis propositum jam reperio. *Scheibe*, alii, δεῖν. *Francken* pro δέον (δεῖν) αὐτὸν conj. δείσας. Totum locum ἀστρατείας . . . εἵλετο sæpissime ab edd. vexatum mutatumque auctoritati Scheibii permisi, nisi quod στρατοπεδευομένων [al. os] . . δέον scripsi.

σαντες, ἱππεύσαντες δὲ τὸν ἄλλον χρόνον καὶ πολλὰ κακὰ τοὺς πολεμίους πεποιηκότες, οὐκ ἐτόλμησαν ἐπὶ τοὺς ἵππους ἀναβῆναι, δεδιότες ὑμᾶς καὶ τὸν νόμον· οὕτω γὰρ ἦσαν παρεσκευασμένοι, οὐχ ὡς ἀπολουμένης τῆς πόλεως, ἀλλ' ὡς σωθησομένης καὶ μεγάλης ἐσομένης καὶ τιμωρησομένης τοὺς ἀδικοῦντας· Ἀλκιβιάδης δ' ἐτόλμησεν ἀναβῆναι, οὔτε εὔνους ὢν τῷ πλήθει οὔτε πρότερον ἱππεύσας οὔτε νῦν ἐπιστάμενος οὔτε ὑφ' ὑμῶν δοκιμασθείς, ὡς οὐκ ἐξεσόμενον τῇ πόλει δίκην παρὰ τῶν ἀδικούντων λαμβάνειν.

§ 4. *Such insubordination, if suffered to pass, makes law useless. And it is no more cowardly for a man to shirk the first rank on the approach of an enemy than to appear among the cavalry when he is assigned to the infantry. You should punish him to deter others from the same conduct, all the more because he is a conspicuous person. Thus the law will be feared: without which fear numberless men put on the lists of service would gladly yield to the temptation of shirking, the motives to which are many and strong.*

Ἐνθυμηθῆναι δὲ χρὴ ὅτι, εἰ ἐξέσται ὅ τι ἂν 11
τις βούληται ποιεῖν, οὐδὲν ὄφελος νόμους κεῖσθαι
ἢ ὑμᾶς συλλέγεσθαι ἢ στρατηγοὺς αἱρεῖσθαι.
θαυμάζω δέ, ὦ ἄνδρες δικασταί, εἴ τις ἀξιοῖ, ἐὰν
μέν τις προσιόντων τῶν πολεμίων τῆς πρώτης
τάξεως τεταγμένος τῆς δευτέρας γένηται, τούτου
μὲν δειλίαν καταψηφίζεσθαι, ἐὰν δέ τις ἐν τοῖς
ὁπλίταις τεταγμένος ἐν τοῖς ἱππεῦσιν ἀναφανῇ,
τούτῳ συγγνώμην ἔχειν. καὶ μὲν δή, ὦ ἄνδρες 12

δικασταί, ἡγοῦμαι δικάζειν ὑμᾶς οὐ μόνον τῶν
ἐξαμαρτανόντων ἕνεκα, ἀλλ' ἵνα καὶ τοὺς ἄλλους
τῶν ἀκοσμούντων σωφρονεστέρους ποιῆτε. ἐὰν
μὲν τοίνυν τοὺς ἀγνῶτας κολάζητε, οὐδεὶς ἔσται
τῶν ἄλλων βελτίων· οὐδεὶς γὰρ εἴσεται τὸν ὑφ'
ὑμῶν καταψηφισθέντα· ἐὰν δὲ τοὺς ἐπιφανεστά-
τους τῶν ἐξαμαρτανόντων τιμωρῆσθε, πάντες
πεύσονται, ὥστε τούτῳ παραδείγματι χρώμενοι
13 βελτίους ἔσονται οἱ πολῖται. ἐὰν τοίνυν τούτου
καταψηφίσησθε,[3] οὐ μόνον οἱ ἐν τῇ πόλει εἴσονται, ἀλλὰ καὶ οἱ σύμμαχοι αἰσθήσονται καὶ οἱ
πολέμιοι πεύσονται, καὶ ἡγήσονται πολὺ πλείονος
ἀξίαν εἶναι τὴν πόλιν, ἐὰν ὁρῶσιν ἐπὶ τοῖς τοιού-
τοις τῶν ἁμαρτημάτων μάλισθ' ὑμᾶς ὀργιζομένους
καὶ μηδεμιᾶς συγγνώμης τοὺς ἀκοσμοῦντας ἐν
14 τῷ πολέμῳ τυγχάνοντας. ἐνθυμεῖσθε δ', ὦ
ἄνδρες δικασταί, ὅτι τῶν στρατιωτῶν οἱ μὲν
κάμνοντες ἐτύγχανον, οἱ δὲ ἐνδεεῖς ὄντες τῶν
ἐπιτηδείων, καὶ ἡδέως ἂν οἱ μὲν ἐν ταῖς πόλεσι
καταμείναντες ἐθεραπεύοντο, οἱ δὲ οἴκαδ' ἀπελ-
θόντες τῶν οἰκείων ἐπεμέλοντο, οἱ δὲ ψιλοὶ
ἐστρατεύοντο, οἱ δ' ἐν τοῖς ἱππεῦσιν ἐκινδύνευον·
15 ἀλλ' ὅμως οὐκ ἐτολμᾶτε ἀπολιπεῖν τὰς τάξεις
οὐδὲ τἀρεστὰ ὑμῖν αὐτοῖς αἱρεῖσθαι, ἀλλὰ πολὺ
μᾶλλον ἐφοβεῖσθε τοὺς τῆς πόλεως νόμους ἢ τὸν
πρὸς τοὺς πολεμίους κίνδυνον. ὧν χρὴ μεμνημένους ὑμᾶς νυνὶ τὴν ψῆφον φέρειν, καὶ πᾶσι
φανερὸν ποιεῖν ὅτι Ἀθηναίων οἱ μὴ βουλόμενοι
τοῖς πολεμίοις μάχεσθαι ὑφ' ὑμῶν κακῶς πείσονται.

[3] καταψηφίσησθε. MSS. καταψηφιεῖσθε.

§ 5. *If an appeal is made in the defendant's behalf on the ground of his father's greatness, I answer that it would have been a good thing for the city if the famous Alcibiades had been executed for his first act of insubordination; and as he was afterwards condemned to death, it is a curious claim, that his son should ask to be acquitted for his sake. If men are to be excused for their father's services, who will get satisfaction for us for the losses we sustain by their ill conduct? No; the only possible defence for Alcibiades is to prove either that he did serve as an hoplite, or had passed his scrutiny before serving in the cavalry.*

Ἡγοῦμαι δ', ὦ ἄνδρες δικασταί, περὶ μὲν τοῦ 16
νόμου καὶ αὐτοῦ τοῦ πράγματος οὐχ ἕξειν αὐτοὺς
ὅ τι λέξουσιν· ἀναβαίνοντες δ' ὑμᾶς ἐξαιτήσονται
καὶ ἀντιβολήσουσιν, οὐκ ἀξιοῦντες τοῦ Ἀλκιβιάδου υἱέος τοσαύτην δειλίαν καταγνῶναι, ὡς
ἐκεῖνον πολλῶν ἀγαθῶν ἀλλ' οὐχὶ πολλῶν κακῶν
αἴτιον γεγενημένον, ὃν εἰ τηλικοῦτον ὄντα ἀπε-
κτείνατε, ὅτε πρῶτον εἰς ὑμᾶς ἐλάβετε ἐξαμαρτάνοντα, οὐκ ἂν ἐγένοντο συμφοραὶ τοσαῦται τῇ 17
πόλει. δεινὸν δέ μοι δοκεῖ, ὦ ἄνδρες δικασταί,
εἶναι, εἰ αὐτοῦ μὲν ἐκείνου θάνατον κατέγνωτε,
τοῦ δὲ υἱοῦ ἀδικοῦντος δι' ἐκεῖνον ἀποψηφιεῖσθε,
ὃς αὐτὸς μὲν οὐκ ἐτόλμα μεθ' ὑμῶν μάχεσθαι,
ὁ δὲ πατὴρ αὐτοῦ μετὰ τῶν πολεμίων ἠξίου
στρατεύεσθαι. καὶ ὅτε μὲν παῖς ὢν οὔπω δῆλος
ἦν ὁποῖός τις ἔσται, διὰ τὰ τοῦ πατρὸς ἁμαρτήματα ὀλίγου τοῖς ἕνδεκα παρεδόθη· ἐπειδὴ δὲ
πρὸς τοῖς ἐκείνῳ πεπραγμένοις ἐπίστασθε καὶ
τὴν τούτου πονηρίαν, διὰ τὸν πατέρα ἐλεεῖν
αὐτὸν ἀξιώσετε; οὐκ οὖν δεινόν, ὦ ἄνδρες δικα- 18

σταί, τούτους μὲν οὕτως εὐτυχεῖς εἶναι, ὥστ',
ἐπειδὰν ἐξαμαρτάνοντες ληφθῶσι, διὰ τὸ αὑτῶν
γένος σώζεσθαι, ἡμᾶς δέ, εἰ ἐδυστυχήσαμεν διὰ
τοὺς οὕτως ἀτακτοῦντας, μηδὲν ἂν δύνασθαι
παρὰ τῶν πολεμίων ἐξαιτήσασθαι διὰ[4] τὰς τῶν
19 προγόνων ἀρετάς; καίτοι πολλαὶ καὶ μεγάλαι
καὶ ὑπὲρ ἁπάντων τῶν Ἑλλήνων γεγόνασι, καὶ
οὐδὲν ὅμοιαι τοῖς ὑπὸ τούτων περὶ τὴν πόλιν
πεπραγμένοις, ὦ ἄνδρες δικασταί. εἰ δ' ἐκεῖνοι
δοκοῦσι βελτίους εἶναι σώζοντες τοὺς φίλους,
δῆλον ὅτι καὶ ὑμεῖς ἀμείνους δόξετε εἶναι τιμωρού-
20 μενοι τοὺς ἐχθρούς. ἀξιῶ δ', ὦ ἄνδρες δικασταί,
ἐὰν μέν τινες τῶν συγγενῶν αὐτὸν ἐξαιτῶνται,
ὀργίζεσθαι ὅτι τούτου μὲν οὐκ ἐπεχείρησαν· δεη-
θῆναι, ἢ δεηθέντες οὐκ ἐδύναντο εὑρέσθαι, ποιεῖν
τὰ ὑπὸ τῆς πόλεως προσταττόμενα, ὑμᾶς δὲ
πείθειν πειρῶνται ὡς οὐ χρὴ παρὰ τῶν ἀδικούν-
21 των δίκην λαμβάνειν· ἐὰν δέ τινες τῶν ἀρχόντων
βοηθῶσιν αὐτῷ ἐπίδειξιν μὲν τῆς ἑαυτῶν δυνά-
μεως ποιούμενοι, φιλοτιμούμενοι δὲ ὅτι καὶ τοὺς
φανερῶς ἡμαρτηκότας σώζειν δύνανται, ὑμᾶς δὲ
χρὴ ὑπολαμβάνειν πρῶτον μὲν ὅτι, εἰ πάντες
Ἀλκιβιάδῃ ὅμοιοι ἐγένοντο, οὐδὲν ἂν ἔδει τοῦ
στρατηγεῖν (οὐδὲ γὰρ ἂν εἶχον ὅτου ἡγοῖντο),
ἔπειθ' ὅτι πολὺ μᾶλλον αὐτοὺς προσήκει τῶν
λιπόντων τὴν τάξιν κατηγορεῖν ἢ ὑπὲρ τῶν τοιούτων ἀπολογεῖσθαι. τίς γάρ ἐστιν ἐλπὶς τοὺς

[4] διά. *Scheibe*, alii, μηδ' ἄν. Codex Laur. μηδὲ διά, quorum *Cobetus* διὰ verum esse posse, μηδὲ alienum putat. ἐξαιτήσασθαι τὰς ἀρετὰς fortasse intelligi potest, sed non bene verbis διὰ τὸ αὑτῶν γένος respondet.

ἄλλους ἐθελήσειν ποιεῖν τὰ ὑπὸ τῶν στρατηγῶν
προσταττόμενα, ὅταν αὐτοὶ οὗτοι τοὺς ἀκοσμοῦντας σώζειν πειρῶνται; ἐγὼ τοίνυν ἀξιῶ, 22
ἂν μὲν ἀποδείξωσιν οἱ λέγοντες καὶ αἰτούμενοι
ὑπὲρ Ἀλκιβιάδου ὡς ἐστρατεύσατο ἐν τοῖς ὁπλίταις ἢ ὡς ἱππεύει δεδοκιμασμένος, ἀποψηφίσα-
σθαι· ἐὰν δὲ μηδὲν ἔχοντες δίκαιον κελεύωσιν
αὐτοῖς χαρίζεσθαι, μεμνῆσθαι χρὴ ὅτι διδάσκου-
σιν ὑμᾶς ἐπιορκεῖν καὶ τοῖς νόμοις μὴ πείθεσθαι,
καὶ ὅτι λίαν προθύμως τοῖς ἀδικοῦσι βοηθοῦντες
πολλοὺς τῶν αὐτῶν ἔργων ἐπιθυμεῖν ποιήσουσι.

§ 6. *But even if it were admitted that the good personal character of a man was a reason for absolving him of some actual misconduct, Alcibiades could not claim this indulgence; for he spent a youth and early manhood defiled by debauchery, treachery, and piracy,—and that too though he was the son of a father whose treasons he ought to have tried to compensate by his own regularity and strict morality.*

Θαυμάζω δὲ μάλιστα, ὦ ἄνδρες δικασταί, εἴ 23
τις ὑμῶν τὸν Ἀλκιβιάδην ἀξιώσει διὰ μὲν τοὺς
βοηθοῦντας σώζεσθαι, διὰ δὲ τὴν αὑτοῦ πονηρίαν
μὴ ἀπολέσθαι. ἧς ἄξιον ὑμᾶς ἀκοῦσαι, ἵν'
ἐπίστησθε ὅτι οὐκ ἂν εἰκότως αὐτοῦ ἀποψηφίζοι-
σθε, ὡς ταῦτα μὲν ἡμαρτηκότος, τὰ δ' ἄλλα
πολίτου χρηστοῦ γεγενημένου· ἐκ γὰρ τῶν ἄλλων
τῶν τούτῳ πεπραγμένων δικαίως ἂν αὐτοῦ θάνατον καταψηφίζοισθε. προσήκει δ' ὑμῖν περὶ 24
αὐτῶν εἰδέναι· ἐπειδὴ γὰρ καὶ τῶν ἀπολογουμένων ἀποδέχεσθε λεγόντων τὰς σφετέρας αὐτῶν

ἀρετὰς καὶ τὰς τῶν προγόνων εὐεργεσίας, εἰκὸς
ὑμᾶς καὶ τῶν κατηγόρων ἀκροᾶσθαι, ἐὰν ἀπο-
φαίνωσι τοὺς φεύγοντας πολλὰ εἰς ὑμᾶς ἡμαρτηκότας καὶ τοὺς προγόνους αὐτῶν πολλῶν κακῶν
25 αἰτίους γεγενημένους. οὗτος γὰρ παῖς μὲν ὢν
παρ' Ἀρχεδήμῳ τῷ γλάμωνι, οὐκ ὀλίγα τῶν
ὑμετέρων ὑφῃρημένῳ, πολλῶν ὁρώντων ἔπινε μὲν
ὑπὸ τῷ αὐτῷ ἱματίῳ[5] κατακείμενος ἐκώμαζε δὲ
μεθ' ἡμέραν, ἄνηβος ἑταίραν ἔχων, μιμούμενος τοὺς
ἑαυτοῦ προγόνους, καὶ ἡγούμενος οὐκ ἂν δύνασθαι
πρεσβύτερος ὢν λαμπρὸς γενέσθαι, εἰ μὴ νέος
26 ὢν πονηρότατος δόξει εἶναι. μετεπέμφθη δ' ὑπὸ
Ἀλκιβιάδου, ἐπειδὴ φανερῶς ἐξημάρτανε. καίτοι
ποῖόν τινα χρὴ αὐτὸν ὑφ' ὑμῶν νομίζεσθαι εἶναι,
ὅστις κἀκείνῳ τοιαῦτ' ἐπιτηδεύων διεβέβλητο, ὃς
τοὺς ἄλλους ταῦτ' ἐδίδασκε; μετὰ Θεοτίμου δὲ
ἐπιβουλεύσας τῷ πατρὶ Ὠρεὸν[6] προὔδωκεν. ὁ
δὲ παραλαβὼν τὸ χωρίον πρότερον μὲν ὕβριζεν
αὐτὸν ὡραῖον ὄντα, τελευτῶν δὲ δήσας ἀργύριον

[5] *ἔπινε . . ἑταίραν ἔχων.* Textum *Cobeti* jam [3ª edit.] edidi. *Scheibius* [a *Bergkio*] *ἔπινε μὲν ὑπὸ ἀετώματι . . ἐκώμαζε δὲ.* Codex X sic locum exhibet, *ἔτι μὲν ὑπὸ τῷ αὐτόματι κατακείμενος ἐκώμαζε μεθ' ἡμέραν κ.τ.λ.* Nihili est *αὐτόματι.* *Augerus* latere credidit *τῷ αὐτῷ στρώματι.* Sed ex duobus fragm. Aristotelis [fr. 565 (*Bekker*) *Ἀριστοτέλης ἐν Τυρρηνῶν νομίμοις· οἱ δὲ Τυρρηνοὶ δειπνοῦσι μετὰ τῶν γυναικῶν ἀνακείμενος ὑπὸ τῷ αὐτῷ ἱματίῳ.* (2) Exc. Pol. 17, *Τυρρηνῶν πάντες ὑπὸ τῷ αὐτῷ ἱματίῳ κατακεῖνται κἂν παρῶσί τινες*] recte judicasse *Cobetum* apparet. Sic *πίνειν . . κωμάζειν* opponuntur in Demosth. (?) 1356, *κἀπὶ δεῖπνα ἔχοι' αὐτὴν πανταχοῖ ἐπορεύετο, ὅποι πίνοι, ἐκώμαζέ τε ἀεὶ μετ' αὐτῆς.* Cp. Soph. Trach. 540, Ovid, Am. 1, 4, 47.

[6] *Ὠρεὸν.* *Markl.* *Ὀρνεὰς.* *Cod. Pal.* *ὀρνεοὺς.* Cod. Laur. *ὡρεούς* quod *Cobetus* edidit. Nec Oreus nec Orneæ ullo modo ad hunc locum pertinent. Alcibiades in Thracia esse videtur. *Ridgeway* noster conj. *ὠρεῖον.* Vid. C. I. G. 2554, v. 195, *ὠρεῖα* = *castella.* Cp. Hesych. *ὤρεια· φυλακτήρια.*

εἰσεπράττετο. ὁ δὲ πατὴρ αὐτὸν οὕτως ἐμίσει 27
σφόδρα, ὥστ' οὐδ' ἂν ἀποθανόντος ἔφασκε τὰ
ὀστᾶ κομίσασθαι. τελευτήσαντος δ' ἐκείνου
ἐραστὴς γενόμενος Ἀρχεβιάδης αὐτὸν ἐλύσατο.
οὐ πολλῷ δὲ χρόνῳ ὕστερον κατακυβεύσας τὰ
ὄντα, ἐκ Λευκῆς ἀκτῆς ὁρμώμενος τοὺς φίλους
κατεπόντιζεν. ὅσα μὲν οὖν, ὦ ἄνδρες δικασταί, 28
ἢ εἰς τοὺς πολίτας ἢ εἰς τοὺς οἰκείους ἢ περὶ
τοὺς αὑτοῦ ξένους ἢ περὶ τοὺς ἄλλους ἡμάρτηκε,
μακρὸν ἂν εἴη λέγειν· Ἱππόνικος δὲ πολλοὺς
παρακαλέσας ἐξέπεμψε τὴν αὑτοῦ γυναῖκα,
φάσκων τοῦτον ὡς οὐκ ἀδελφὸν[7] ἀλλ' ὡς ἄνδρα
ἐκείνης εἰς τὴν οἰκίαν εἰσιέναι τὴν αὑτοῦ. καὶ 29
τοιαῦθ' ἡμαρτηκότι καὶ οὕτω δεινὰ καὶ πολλὰ
καὶ μεγάλα πεποιηκότι οὔτε τῶν πεπραγμένων
αὐτῷ μεταμέλει οὔτε τῶν μελλόντων ἔσεσθαι,
ἀλλ' ὃν[8] ἔδει κοσμιώτατον εἶναι τῶν πολιτῶν,
ἀπολογίαν ποιούμενον τὸν ἑαυτοῦ βίον τῶν
τοῦ πατρὸς ἁμαρτημάτων, οὗτος ἑτέρους ὑβρίζειν
πειρᾶται, ὥσπερ δυνάμενος ἂν πολλοστὸν μέρος
τῶν ὀνειδῶν τῶν ἑαυτῷ προσόντων τοῖς ἄλλοις
μεταδοῦναι, καὶ ταῦθ' υἱὸς ὢν Ἀλκιβιάδου, ὃς 30
ἔπεισε μὲν Δεκέλειαν Λακεδαιμονίους ἐπιτειχίσαι,
ἐπὶ δὲ τὰς νήσους ἀποστήσων ἔπλευσε, διδάσκαλος δὲ τῶν τῆς πόλεως κακῶν ἐγένετο, πλεο-
νάκις δὲ μετὰ τῶν ἐχθρῶν ἐπὶ τὴν πατρίδα
ἐστρατεύσατο ἢ μετὰ τῶν πολιτῶν ἐπ' ἐκείνους.

[7] *ἀδελφὸν.* MSS. *ἀδελφὸν αὐτῆς*, quod manente *ἐκείνης* nihili est : nec in *αὐτοῦ* bene vertendum est si *εἰς τὴν οἰκίαν τὴν αὐτοῦ* respicias.

[8] *ἀλλ' ὃν Scheibe.* Al. *ὃν μᾶλλον.*

ἀνθ' ὧν καὶ ὑμῖν καὶ τοῖς μέλλουσιν ἔσεσθαι
τιμωρεῖσθαι προσήκει ὅντινα λαμβάνετε τούτων.
31 καίτοι σφόδρα εἴθισται λέγειν ὡς· οὐκ εἰκός ἐστι
τὸν μὲν πατέρα αὐτοῦ κατελθόντα δωρεὰς παρὰ
τοῦ δήμου λαβεῖν, τοῦτον δ' ἀδίκως διὰ τὴν
φυγὴν τὴν ἐκείνου διαβεβλῆσθαι. ἐμοὶ δὲ δοκεῖ
δεινὸν εἶναι, εἰ τὰς μὲν δωρεὰς αὐτοῦ ἀφείλεσθε
ὡς οὐ δικαίως δεδωκότες, τούτου δὲ ἀδικοῦντος
ἀποψηφιεῖσθε ὡς τοῦ πατρὸς χρηστοῦ περὶ
τὴν πόλιν γεγενημένου.

§ 7. *His appealing to the achievements of his father is a great piece of audacity; for he dares to compare his operations against the city to yours when trying to recover it. And as to Alcibiades' great power, of which he spoke, it consisted in his unscrupulousness. Who could not inflict damage on his country if he chose to betray all her vulnerable points to the enemy? This is what Alcibiades did, nor did he ever venture to stand an audit as to the money he took from the public under pretence of his influence with the king of Persia.*

32 Καὶ μὲν δή, ὦ ἄνδρες δικασταί, ἄλλων τε
πολλῶν ἄξιον εἵνεκα αὐτοῦ καταψηφίσασθαι, καὶ
ὅτι ταῖς ὑμετέραις ἀρεταῖς χρῆται παραδείγματι
περὶ τῆς ἑαυτοῦ πονηρίας. τολμᾷ γὰρ λέγειν
ὡς Ἀλκιβιάδης οὐδὲν δεινὸν εἴργασται ἐπὶ τὴν
33 πατρίδα στρατεύσας· καὶ γὰρ ὑμᾶς φεύγοντας
Φυλὴν καταλαβεῖν καὶ δένδρα τεμεῖν καὶ πρὸς
τὰ τείχη προσβαλεῖν, καὶ ταῦτα ποιήσαντας οὐκ
ὄνειδος τοῖς παισὶ καταλιπεῖν, ἀλλὰ τιμὴν παρὰ
πᾶσιν ἀνθρώποις κτήσασθαι, ὡς τῶν αὐτῶν ὄντας

ἀξίους ὅσοι φυγόντες μετὰ τῶν πολεμίων ἐπὶ τὴν
χώραν ἐστράτευσαν, καὶ ὅσοι κατῄεσαν Λακεδαιμονίων ἐχόντων τὴν πόλιν. καὶ μὲν δὴ πᾶσιν 34
ἡγοῦμαι δῆλον εἶναι ὅτι οὗτοι μὲν ἐζήτουν κατιέναι
ὡς τὴν μὲν τῆς θαλάττης ἀρχὴν Λακεδαιμονίοις
παραδώσοντες, αὐτοὶ δ' ὑμῶν ἄρξοντες· τὸ δ'
ὑμέτερον πλῆθος κατελθὸν τοὺς μὲν πολεμίους
ἐξήλασε, τῶν δὲ πολιτῶν καὶ τοὺς βουλομένους
δουλεύειν ἠλευθέρωσεν· ὥστ' οὐχ ὁμοίων τῶν ἔργων
ἀμφοτέροις γεγενημένων τοὺς λόγους ποιεῖται.
'Αλλ' ὅμως τοσούτων συμφορῶν καὶ οὕτως αὐτῷ 35
μεγάλων ὑπαρχουσῶν ἐπὶ τῇ τοῦ πατρὸς πονηρίᾳ
φιλοτιμεῖται, καὶ λέγει ὡς οὕτως ἐκεῖνος μέγα
ἐδύνατο, ὥστε τῇ πόλει πάντων κακῶν αἴτιος
γεγένηται. καίτοι τίς οὕτως ἄπειρος τῆς ἑαυτοῦ
πατρίδος, ὃς οὐκ ἂν βουλόμενος εἶναι πονηρὸς
εἰσηγήσαιτο μὲν τοῖς πολεμίοις ἃ χρὴ καταλαβεῖν τῶν χωρίων, δηλώσειε δ' ἂν ἃ κακῶς φυλάτ-
τεται τῶν φρουρίων, διδάξειε δ' ἂν ἃ πονηρῶς
ἔχει τῶν πραγμάτων, μηνύσειε δ' ἂν τοὺς βουλομένους ἀφίστασθαι τῶν συμμάχων; οὐ γὰρ 36
δήπου, ὅτε μὲν ἔφευγε, διὰ τὴν δύναμιν κακῶς
οἷός τ' ἦν ποιεῖν τὴν πόλιν, ἐπειδὴ δὲ ὑμᾶς
ἐξαπατήσας κατῆλθε καὶ πολλῶν ἦρξε τριήρων,
οὔτε τοὺς πολεμίους ἐδύνατο ἐκ τῆς χώρας
ἐκβαλεῖν, οὔτε Χίους οὓς ἀπέστησε πάλιν φίλους
ποιῆσαι, οὔτε ἄλλο οὐδὲν ἀγαθὸν ὑμᾶς ἐργάσασθαι. ὥστ' οὐ χαλεπὸν γνῶναι ὅτι 'Αλκιβιάδης 37
δυνάμει μὲν οὐδὲν τῶν ἄλλων διέφερε, πονηρίᾳ
δὲ τῶν πολιτῶν πρῶτος ἦν. ἃ μὲν γὰρ ᾔδει τῶν

ὑμετέρων κακῶς ἔχοντα, μηνυτὴς αὐτῶν τοῖς
Λακεδαιμονίοις ἐγένετο· ἐπειδὴ δ' ἔδει αὐτὸν
στρατηγεῖν, οὐδὲν κακὸν ποιεῖν ἐκείνους ἐδύνατο,
ἀλλ' ὑποσχόμενος δι' ἑαυτὸν παρέξειν βασιλέα
χρήματα, πλέον ἢ διακόσια τάλαντα τῆς πόλεως
38 ὑφείλετο. καὶ οὕτω πολλὰ ἐνόμιζεν εἰς ὑμᾶς
ἡμαρτηκέναι, ὥστε λέγειν δυνάμενος καὶ φίλων
ὄντων καὶ χρήματα κεκτημένος οὐδέποτ' ἐλθὼν
εὐθύνας ἐτόλμησε δοῦναι, ἀλλὰ φυγὴν αὑτοῦ
καταγνοὺς καὶ Θρᾴκης καὶ πάσης πόλεως ἐβούλετο πολίτης γενέσθαι μᾶλλον ἢ τῆς πατρίδος
εἶναι τῆς ἑαυτοῦ. καὶ τὸ τελευταῖον, ὦ ἄνδρες
δικασταί, ὑπερβολὴν ποιησάμενος τῆς προτέρας
πονηρίας ἐτόλμησε τὰς ναῦς Λυσάνδρῳ μετὰ
39 Ἀδειμάντου προδοῦναι. ὥστε εἴ τις ὑμῶν ἢ
τοὺς τεθνεῶτας ἐν τῇ ναυμαχίᾳ ἐλεεῖ, ἢ ὑπὲρ
τῶν δουλευσάντων τοῖς πολεμίοις αἰσχύνεται, ἢ
τῶν τειχῶν καθῃρημένων ἀγανακτεῖ, ἢ Λακεδαιμονίους μισεῖ, ἢ τοῖς τριάκοντα ὀργίζεται, τούτων
ἁπάντων χρὴ τὸν τούτου πατέρα αἴτιον ἡγεῖσθαι,
καὶ ἐνθυμηθῆναι ὅτι Ἀλκιβιάδην μὲν τὸν πρόπαππον αὐτοῦ καὶ τὸν πατρὸς πρὸς μητρὸς
πάππον Μεγακλέα οἱ ὑμέτεροι πρόγονοι δὶς
ἀμφοτέρους ἐξωστράκισαν, τοῦ δὲ πατρὸς αὐτοῦ
οἱ πρεσβύτεροι ὑμῶν θάνατον κατέγνωσαν, ὥστε
40 νῦν χρὴ ἡγησαμένους πατρικὸν ἐχθρὸν τοῦτον
εἶναι τῇ πόλει καταψηφίσασθαι, καὶ μήτε ἔλεον
μήτε συγγνώμην μήτε χάριν μηδεμίαν περὶ
πλείονος ποιήσασθαι τῶν νόμων τῶν κειμένων
καὶ τῶν ὅρκων οὓς ὠμόσατε.

§ 8. *You can have no motive for sparing such men as the defendant or his father, stained as they are with the most hideous crimes and debaucheries. Neither is there any hope—as in some cases—of his improving if mercy is shown him; nor is he of such manly or intrepid character as to be an object of fear if you make him an enemy.*

Condemn him therefore for the sake of example, and to be rid of him from the State; seeing that he is clearly guilty under this indictment, though I have not been able to state a tithe of his misdeeds or those of his father.

Σκέψασθαι δὲ χρή, ὦ ἄνδρες δικασταί, διὰ τί 41
ἄν τις τοιούτων ἀνδρῶν φείσαιτο; πότερον ὡς
πρὸς μὲν τὴν πόλιν δεδυστυχήκασιν, ἄλλως δὲ
κόσμιοί εἰσι καὶ σωφρόνως βεβιώκασιν; οὐχ οἱ
μὲν πολλοὶ αὐτῶν ἡταιρήκασιν, οἱ δὲ ἀδελφαῖς
συγγεγόνασι, τοῖς δ' ἐκ θυγατέρων παῖδες γεγό-
νασιν, οἱ δὲ μυστήρια πεποιήκασι καὶ τοὺς 42
Ἑρμᾶς περικεκόφασι καὶ περὶ πάντας τοὺς θεοὺς
ἠσεβήκασι καὶ εἰς ἅπασαν τὴν πόλιν ἡμαρτή-
κασιν, ἀδίκως καὶ παρανόμως καὶ πρὸς τοὺς
ἄλλους διακείμενοι καὶ πρὸς σφᾶς αὐτοὺς πολιτευόμενοι, οὐδεμιᾶς τόλμης ἀπεχόμενοι, οὐδὲ
ἔργου δεινοῦ ἄπειροι γεγενημένοι; ἀλλὰ καὶ
πεπόνθασι καὶ πεποιήκασιν ἅπαντα. οὕτω γὰρ
διάκεινται, ὥστ' ἐπὶ μὲν τοῖς καλοῖς αἰσχύνεσθαι,
ἐπὶ δὲ τοῖς κακοῖς φιλοτιμεῖσθαι. Καὶ μὲν δή, 43
ὦ ἄνδρες δικασταί, ἤδη τινῶν ἀπεψηφίσασθε
ἀδικεῖν μὲν νομίσαντες, οἰόμενοι δ' εἰς τὸ λοιπὸν
χρησίμους ὑμῖν ἔσεσθαι. τίς οὖν ἐλπὶς ὑπὸ
τούτου τι ἀγαθὸν πείσεσθαι τὴν πόλιν, ὃν ὑμεῖς,
ὅτι μὲν οὐδενὸς ἄξιός ἐστιν, ἐπειδὰν ἀπολογῆται,

εἴσεσθε, ὅτι δὲ πονηρός ἐστιν, ἐκ τῶν ἄλλων
44 ἐπιτηδευμάτων ᾔσθησθε; Ἀλλὰ μὲν δὴ οὐδ' ἂν
ἐξελθὼν ἐκ τῆς πόλεως οὐδὲν δύναιτο κακὸν ὑμᾶς
ἐργάσασθαι, δειλὸς ὢν καὶ πένης καὶ πράττειν
ἀδύνατος καὶ τοῖς οἰκείοις διάφορος καὶ ὑπὸ τῶν
ἄλλων μισούμενος. ὥστ' οὐδὲ τούτων ἕνεκα
45 αὐτὸν ἄξιον φυλάττεσθαι, ἀλλὰ πολὺ μᾶλλον
παράδειγμα ποιῆσαι καὶ τοῖς ἄλλοις καὶ τοῖς
τούτου φίλοις, οἳ τὰ μὲν προσταττόμενα ποιεῖν
οὐκ ἐθέλουσι, τοιούτων δ' ἔργων ἐπιθυμοῦσι, καὶ
περὶ τῶν σφετέρων αὐτῶν κακῶς βουλευσάμενοι
περὶ τῶν ὑμετέρων δημηγοροῦσιν.

46 Ἐγὼ μὲν οὖν ὡς ἐδυνάμην ἄριστα κατηγόρηκα,
ἐπίσταμαι δ' ὅτι οἱ μὲν ἄλλοι τῶν ἀκροωμένων
θαυμάζουσιν, ὅπως ποθ' οὕτως ἀκριβῶς ἐδυνήθην
ἐξευρεῖν τὰ τούτων ἁμαρτήματα, οὗτος δέ μου
καταγελᾷ, ὅτι οὐδὲ πολλοστὸν μέρος εἴρηκα τῶν
47 τούτοις ὑπαρχόντων κακῶν. ὑμεῖς οὖν καὶ τὰ
εἰρημένα καὶ τὰ παραλελειμμένα ἀναλογισάμενοι
πολὺ μᾶλλον αὐτοῦ καταψηφίσασθε, ἐνθυμηθέντες ὅτι ἔνοχος μέν ἐστι τῇ γραφῇ, μεγάλη δ'
εὐτυχία τὸ τοιούτων πολιτῶν ἀπαλλαγῆναι πόλει.
Ἀνάγνωθι δ' αὐτοῖς τοὺς νόμους καὶ τοὺς ὅρκους
καὶ τὴν γραφήν· καὶ τούτων μεμνημένοι ψηφι-
οῦνται τὰ δίκαια.

Recitation of Laws on which the Speaker relies; the Oath of the Jurors; and Text of the Indictment.

ORATION X. [19.]

FOR THE DEFENDANT, CHARGED WITH THE CONCEALMENT BY HIS OWN OR FATHER'S ACT OF SOME OF THE CONFISCATED PROPERTY OF ARISTOPHANES.

§ 1. *The gravity of the issues of this trial, my own inexperience, and the disadvantages necessarily attaching to a defendant, make me of course anxious. Many a man has perished on a charge, the falsity of which has been discovered too late. Pause, then, and hear what I have to say.*

Πολλήν μοι ἀπορίαν παρέχει ὁ ἀγὼν οὑτοσί,
ὦ ἄνδρες δικασταί, ὅταν ἐνθυμηθῶ ὅτι, ἂν ἐγὼ
μὲν μὴ νῦν εὖ εἴπω, οὐ μόνον ἐγὼ ἀλλὰ καὶ ὁ
πατὴρ δόξει ἄδικος εἶναι καὶ τῶν ὄντων ἁπάντων
στερήσομαι. ἀνάγκη οὖν, εἰ καὶ μὴ δεινὸς πρὸς
ταῦτα πέφυκα, βοηθεῖν τῷ πατρὶ καὶ ἐμαυτῷ
2 οὕτως ὅπως ἂν δύνωμαι. τὴν μὲν οὖν παρασκευὴν καὶ προθυμίαν τῶν ἐχθρῶν ὁρᾶτε, καὶ
οὐδὲν δεῖ περὶ τούτων λέγειν· τὴν δ' ἐμὴν ἀπειρίαν πάντες ἴσασιν, ὅσοι ἐμὲ γιγνώσκουσιν.
αἰτήσομαι οὖν ὑμᾶς δίκαια καὶ ῥᾴδια χαρίσασθαι,
ἄνευ ὀργῆς καὶ ἡμῶν ἀκοῦσαι, ὥσπερ τῶν κατη-
3 γόρων. ἀνάγκη γὰρ τὸν ἀπολογούμενον, κἂν ἐξ
ἴσου ἀκροᾶσθε, ἔλαττον ἔχειν. οἱ μὲν γὰρ ἐκ
πολλοῦ χρόνου ἐπιβουλεύοντες, αὐτοὶ ἄνευ κινδύνων ὄντες, τὴν κατηγορίαν ἐποιήσαντο, ἡμεῖς
δὲ ἀγωνιζόμεθα μετὰ δέους καὶ διαβολῆς καὶ

κινδύνου μεγίστου. εἰκὸς οὖν ὑμᾶς εὔνοιαν
πλείω ἔχειν τοῖς ἀπολογουμένοις. οἶμαι γὰρ 4
πάντας ὑμᾶς εἰδέναι ὅτι πολλοὶ ἤδη πολλὰ καὶ
δεινὰ κατηγορήσαντες παραχρῆμα ἐξηλέγχθησαν
ψευδόμενοι οὕτω φανερῶς, ὥστε ὑπὲρ πάντων
τῶν πεπραγμένων μισηθέντες ἀπελθεῖν· οἱ δ' αὖ
μαρτυρήσαντες τὰ ψευδῆ καὶ ἀδίκως ἀπολέσαντες
ἀνθρώπους ἑάλωσαν, ἡνίκα οὐδὲν ἦν πλέον τοῖς
πεπονθόσιν. ὅτ' οὖν τοιαῦτα πολλὰ γεγένηται, 5
ὡς ἐγὼ ἀκούω, εἰκὸς ὑμᾶς, ὦ ἄνδρες δικασταί,
μήπω τοὺς τῶν κατηγόρων λόγους ἡγεῖσθαι
πιστούς, πρὶν ἂν καὶ ἡμεῖς εἴπωμεν. ἀκούω γὰρ
ἔγωγε, καὶ ὑμῶν δὲ τοὺς πολλοὺς οἶμαι εἰδέναι,
ὅτι πάντων δεινότατόν ἐστι διαβολή. μάλιστα 6
δὲ τοῦτο ἔχοι ἄν τις ἰδεῖν, ὅταν πολλοὶ ἐπὶ τῇ
αὐτῇ αἰτίᾳ εἰς ἀγῶνα καταστῶσιν. ὡς γὰρ ἐπὶ
τὸ πολὺ οἱ τελευταῖοι κρινόμενοι σῴζονται·
πεπαυμένοι γὰρ τῆς ὀργῆς αὐτῶν ἀκροᾶσθε, καὶ
τοὺς ἐλέγχους ἤδη θέλοντες ἀποδέχεσθε.

§ 2. *What a hard case is mine! Nikophemus and his son Aristophanes (my brother-in-law) were put to death without trial; were refused burial; their property was confiscated; and the children of Aristophanes, thus deprived of means, are dependent on* me. *And yet* I *am now also in danger of losing what my father—that liberal patriot—left me, on the ground of being in possession of part of his property; at a time too when the treasury is so poor that any one engaged in a suit affecting the revenue is at a special disadvantage.*

Ἐνθυμεῖσθε οὖν ὅτι Νικόφημος καὶ Ἀριστο- 7

φάνης ἄκριτοι ἀπέθανον, πρὶν παραγενέσθαι τινὰ
αὐτοῖς ἐλεγχομένοις ὡς ἠδίκουν. οὐδεὶς γὰρ οὐδ᾽
εἶδεν ἐκείνους μετὰ τὴν σύλληψιν· οὐδὲ γὰρ
θάψαι τὰ σώματ᾽ αὐτῶν ἀπέδωκαν, ἀλλ᾽ οὕτω
δεινὴ ἡ συμφορὰ γεγένηται ὥστε πρὸς τοῖς ἄλλοις
8 καὶ τούτου ἐστέρηνται. ἀλλὰ ταῦτα μὲν ἐάσω·
οὐδὲν γὰρ ἂν περαίνοιμι· πολὺ δὲ ἀθλιώτεροι
δοκοῦσί μοι οἱ παῖδες οἱ Ἀριστοφάνους. οὐδένα
γὰρ οὔτ᾽ ἰδίᾳ οὔτε δημοσίᾳ ἠδικηκότες οὐ μόνον
τὰ πατρῷα ἀπολωλέκασι παρὰ τοὺς νόμους τοὺς
ὑμετέρους, ἀλλὰ καὶ ἣ ὑπόλοιπος ἐλπὶς ἦν, ὑπὸ
τοῦ πάππου ἐκτραφῆναι, ἐν οὕτω δεινῷ καθέ-
9 στηκεν. ἔτι δ᾽ ἡμεῖς ἐστερημένοι μὲν κηδεστῶν,
ἐστερημένοι δὲ τῆς προικός, παιδάρια δὲ τρία
ἠναγκασμένοι τρέφειν, προσέτι συκοφαντούμεθα,
καὶ κινδυνεύομεν περὶ ὧν οἱ πρόγονοι ἡμῖν κατέ-
λιπον κτησάμενοι ἐκ τοῦ δικαίου. καίτοι, ὦ
ἄνδρες δικασταί, ὁ ἐμὸς πατὴρ ἐν ἅπαντι τῷ βίῳ
πλείω εἰς τὴν πόλιν ἀνάλωσεν ἢ εἰς αὑτὸν καὶ
τοὺς οἰκείους, τετραπλάσια[1] δὲ ἢ νῦν ἔστιν ἡμῖν,
ὡς ἐγὼ λογιζομένῳ αὐτῷ πολλάκις παρεγενόμην.
10 μὴ οὖν προκαταγινώσκετε ἀδικίαν τοῦ εἰς αὑτὸν
μὲν μικρὰ δαπανῶντος, ὑμῖν δὲ πολλὰ καθ᾽
ἕκαστον τὸν ἐνιαυτόν,* ἀλλ᾽ ὅσοι καὶ τὰ πατρῷα
καὶ ἄν τί ποθεν λάβωσιν,[2] εἰς τὰς αἰσχίστας
11 ἡδονὰς εἰθισμένοι εἰσὶν ἀναλίσκειν. χαλεπὸν
μὲν οὖν, ὦ ἄνδρες δικασταί, ἀπολογεῖσθαι πρὸς

[1] τετραπλάσια (*i.e.* δ´ πλάσια) "nunc e Spengelii emendatione scripsi. Coll., § 59 et 61." *Scheibe.* Vulgo διπλάσια.

[2] λάβωσιν, Codex X μὴ δῶσιν. Alii aliter correxerunt. *Francken* μεταδῷ τις.

* *W.* add. ἐπιδιδόντος.

δόξαν ἣν ἔνιοι ἔχουσι περὶ τῆς Νικοφήμου οὐσίας, καὶ διὰ σπάνιν ἀργυρίου ἣ νῦν ἐστιν ἐν τῇ πόλει, καὶ τοῦ ἀγῶνος πρὸς τὸ δημόσιον ὄντος· ὅμως δὲ καὶ τούτων ὑπαρχόντων ῥᾳδίως γνώσεσθε ὅτι οὐκ ἀληθῆ ἐστι τὰ κατηγορημένα. δέομαι δ' ὑμῶν πάσῃ τέχνῃ καὶ μηχανῇ μετ' εὐνοίας ἀκροασαμένους ἡμῶν διὰ τέλους, ὅ τι ἂν ὑμῖν ἄριστον καὶ εὐορκότατον νομίζητε εἶναι, τοῦτο ψηφίσασθαι.

§ 3. *Now, was my father likely to have fraudulently withheld this money? Remember he did not seek the alliance with Aristophanes for his daughter, but gave her on the request of Conon. Moreover, his whole conduct,—his marriage with my portionless mother, his selection of poor men as husbands for his daughters, of a portionless wife for me, his son,—proves that he was not likely to be grasping.*

Πρῶτον μὲν οὖν, ᾧ τρόπῳ κηδεσταὶ ἡμῖν ἐγέ- 12
νοντο. διδάξω ὑμᾶς. στρατηγῶν γὰρ Κόνων
περὶ Πελοπόννησον, τριηραρχήσαντι τῷ ἐμῷ
πατρὶ πάλαι φίλος γεγενημένος, ἐδεήθη δοῦναι
τὴν ἀδελφὴν αἰτοῦντι τῷ υἱεῖ τῷ Νικοφήμου. ὁ 13
δὲ ὁρῶν αὐτοὺς ὑπ' ἐκείνου τε πεπιστευμένους
γεγονότας τε ἐπιεικεῖς τῇ τε πόλει ἔν γε τῷ τότε
χρόνῳ ἀρέσκοντας, ἐπείσθη δοῦναι, οὐκ εἰδὼς τὴν
ἐσομένην διαβολήν, ἀλλ' ὅτε καὶ ὑμῶν ὁστισοῦν
ἂν ἐκείνοις ἠξίωσε κηδεστὴς γενέσθαι, ἐπεὶ ὅτι
γε οὐ χρημάτων ἕνεκα, ῥᾴδιον γνῶναι ἐκ τοῦ
βίου παντὸς καὶ τῶν ἔργων τῶν τοῦ πατρός.
ἐκεῖνος γὰρ ὅτ' ἦν ἐν ἡλικίᾳ, παρὸν μετὰ πολλῶν 14

χρημάτων γῆμαι ἄλλην, τὴν ἐμὴν μητέρα ἔλαβεν
οὐδὲν ἐπιφερομένην, ὅτι δὲ Ξενοφῶντος ἦν θυγάτηρ τοῦ Εὐριπίδου υἱέος, ὃς οὐ μόνον ἰδίᾳ
χρηστὸς ἐδόκει εἶναι, ἀλλὰ καὶ στρατηγεῖν αὐτὸν
15 ἠξιώσατε, ὡς ἐγὼ ἀκούω. τὰς τοίνυν ἐμὰς
ἀδελφὰς θελόντων τινῶν λαβεῖν ἀπροίκους πάνυ
πλουσίων οὐκ ἔδωκεν,[3] ὅτι ἐδόκουν κάκιον γεγονέναι, ἀλλὰ τὴν μὲν Φιλομήλῳ τῷ Παιανιεῖ, ὃν
οἱ πολλοὶ βελτίονα ἡγοῦνται εἶναι ἢ πλουσιώτερον, τὴν δὲ πένητι γεγενημένῳ οὐ διὰ κακίαν,
ἀδελφιδῷ δὲ Φαίδρῳ τῷ Μυρρινουσίῳ, ἐπιδοὺς
τετταράκοντα μνᾶς, καὶ Ἀριστοφάνει τὸ ἴσον.
16 πρὸς δὲ τούτοις ἐμοὶ πολλὴν ἐξὸν πάνυ προῖκα
λαβεῖν ἐλάττω συνεβούλευσεν, ὥστε εὖ εἰδέναι
ὅτι κηδεσταῖς χρησοίμην κοσμίοις καὶ σώφροσι.
καὶ νῦν ἔχω γυναῖκα τὴν Κριτοδήμου θυγατέρα
τοῦ Ἀλωπεκῆθεν, ὃς ὑπὸ Λακεδαιμονίων ἀπέθανεν, ὅτε ἡ ναυμαχία ἐγένετο ἐν Ἑλλησπόντῳ.
17 καίτοι, ὦ ἄνδρες δικασταί, ὅστις αὐτός τε ἄνευ
χρημάτων ἔγημε ταῖν τε θυγατέροιν πολὺ ἀργύριον ἐπέδωκε τῷ τε υἱεῖ ὀλίγην προῖκα ἔλαβε,
πῶς οὐκ εἰκὸς περὶ τούτου πιστεύειν ὡς οὐχ
ἕνεκα χρημάτων τούτοις κηδεστὴς ἐγένετο;

§ 4. *Again, was Aristophanes likely to leave much property? He spent freely in his desire for political distinction. It was he that undertook the mission to Dionysius in hopes of detaching him from Sparta, and uniting him with Evagoras. Again, he contributed largely to the subvention asked for from Cyprus: in this*

[3] οὐκ ἔδωκεν, *Reiske et Scheibe.* Vulgo οὐ δέδωκεν.

matter he spared neither his own nor his brother's fortune, and borrowed of my father besides. To show you how he had impoverished himself I will tell you this. Demus asked me to raise money on a gold cup he had, and bring it to Cyprus: I asked Aristophanes, accordingly, to lend sixteen minæ. He replied that not only had he not got so much, but that he had had to borrow from friends. On another occasion, when entertaining the ambassadors of Evagoras, he had to borrow the necessary plate. Finally, the inventory will show how little moveable property he left.

Ἀλλὰ μὴν ὅ γε Ἀριστοφάνης ἤδη ἔχων τὴν 18
γυναῖκα ὅτι πολλοῖς ἂν[4] μᾶλλον ἐχρῆτο ἢ τῷ
ἐμῷ πατρί, ῥᾴδιον γνῶναι. ἥ τε γὰρ ἡλικία
πολὺ διάφορος, ἥ τε φύσις ἔτι πλέον· ἐκείνῳ
μὲν γὰρ ἦν τὰ ἑαυτοῦ πράττειν, Ἀριστοφάνης
δὲ οὐ μόνον τῶν ἰδίων ἀλλὰ καὶ τῶν κοινῶν
ἐβούλετο ἐπιμελεῖσθαι, καὶ εἴ τι ἦν αὐτῷ ἀργύριον,
ἀνήλωσεν ἐπιθυμῶν τιμᾶσθαι. γνώσεσθε δὲ ὅτι 19
ἀληθῆ λέγω ἐξ αὐτῶν ὧν ἐκεῖνος ἔπραττε. πρῶτον μὲν γὰρ βουλομένου Κόνωνος πέμπειν τινὰ
εἰς Σικελίαν, ᾤχετο ὑποστὰς μετὰ Εὐνόμου,
Διονυσίου* φίλου ὄντος καὶ ξένου, τὸ πλῆθος τὸ
ὑμέτερον πλεῖστα ἀγαθὰ πεποιηκότος, ὡς ἐγὼ
ἀκήκοα τῶν ἐν Πειραιεῖ παραγενομένων.[5] ἦσαν 20
δ' ἐλπίδες τοῦ πλοῦ πεῖσαι Διονύσιον κηδεστὴν
μὲν γενέσθαι Εὐαγόρᾳ, πολέμιον δὲ Λακεδαιμονίοις, φίλον δὲ καὶ σύμμαχον τῇ πόλει τῇ
ὑμετέρᾳ. καὶ ταῦτ' ἔπραττον πολλῶν κινδύνων
ὑπαρχόντων πρὸς τὴν θάλασσαν καὶ τοὺς πο-

[4] πολλοῖς ἂν MSS. πολλοῖς δὴ *Scheibe.*

[5] *Scheibe* τῶν παραγενομένων.

* Διονυσίου *Sauppius*: legebatur καὶ Λυσίου.

λεμίους, καὶ ἔπεισαν Διονύσιον μὴ πέμψαι
τριήρεις ἃς τότε παρεσκευάσατο Λακεδαιμονίοις.
21 μετὰ δὲ ταῦτα ἐπειδὴ οἱ πρέσβεις ἧκον ἐκ
Κύπρου ἐπὶ τὴν βοήθειαν, οὐδὲν ἐνέλιπε προθυμίας σπεύδων. ὑμεῖς δὲ τριήρεις αὐτοῖς ἔδοτε
καὶ τἆλλα ἐψηφίσασθε, ἀργυρίου δ' εἰς τὸν
ἀπόστολον ἠπόρουν. ὀλίγα μὲν γὰρ ἦλθον
ἔχοντες χρήματα, πολλῶν δὲ προσεδεήθησαν·
οὐ γὰρ μόνον εἰς τὰς ναῦς, ἀλλὰ καὶ πελταστὰς
22 ἐμισθώσαντο καὶ ὅπλα ἐπρίαντο. Ἀριστοφάνης
δ' οὖν τῶν χρημάτων τὰ μὲν πλεῖστα αὐτὸς
παρέσχεν· ἐπειδὴ δὲ οὐχ ἱκανὰ ἦν, τοὺς φίλους
ἔπειθε δεόμενος καὶ ἐγγυώμενος, καὶ τοῦ ἀδελφοῦ
τοῦ ὁμοπατρίου ἀποκειμένας παρ' αὐτῷ τεσσαρά-
κοντα μνᾶς ἔχων[6] κατεχρήσατο. τῇ δὲ προ-
τεραίᾳ ᾗ ἀνήγετο, εἰσελθὼν ὡς τὸν πατέρα τὸν
ἐμὸν ἐκέλευσε χρῆσαι ὅ τι εἴη ἀργύριον. προσ-
δεῖν γὰρ ἔφη πρὸς τὸν μισθὸν τοῖς πελτασταῖς.
ἦσαν δ' ἡμῖν ἔνδον ἑπτὰ μναῖ· ὁ δὲ καὶ ταύτας
23 λαβὼν κατεχρήσατο. τίνα γὰρ οἴεσθε, ὦ ἄνδρες
δικασταί, φιλότιμον μὲν ὄντα, ἐπιστολῶν δ'
αὐτῷ ἡκουσῶν παρὰ τοῦ πατρὸς μηδὲν ἀπορήσειν
ἐκ Κύπρου, ᾑρημένον δὲ πρεσβευτὴν καὶ μέλλοντα
πλεῖν ὡς Εὐαγόραν, ὑπολιπέσθαι ἄν τι τῶν
ὄντων, ἀλλ' οὐκ εἰ ἦν δυνατὸς πάντα παρασχόντα
χαρίσασθαι ἐκείνῳ τε καὶ κομίσασθαι μὴ ἐλάττω;
ὡς τοίνυν ταῦτ' ἐστὶν ἀληθῆ, κάλει μοι Εὔνομον.

[6] *ἔχων Cobetus.* Alii *εἰπὼν* [MS. X], *λαβών*, *πείθων*, *ἀπορῶν*. *ἀπιὼν* nunc probat *Scheibe.* *αὐτῷ* ego scripsi : sed vide vii. 64.

Witnesses as to the Proceedings of Aristophanes in the Matter of his Mission to Evagoras.

Τῶν μὲν μαρτύρων ἀκούετε, οὐ μόνον ὅτι 24
ἔχρησαν*ἐκείνου δεηθέντος, ἀλλὰ καὶ ὅτι ἀπειλή-
φασιν· ἐκομίσθη γὰρ αὐτοῖς ἐπὶ τῆς τριήρους.
ῥᾴδιον μὲν οὖν ἐκ τῶν εἰρημένων γνῶναι ὅτι
τοιούτων καιρῶν συμπεσόντων οὐδενὸς ἂν ἐφείσατο
τῶν ἑαυτοῦ· ὃ δὲ μέγιστον τεκμήριον· Δῆμος 25
γὰρ ὁ Πυριλάμπους, τριηραρχῶν εἰς Κύπρον,
ἐδεήθη μου προσελθεῖν αὐτῷ, λέγων ὅτι ἔλαβε
σύμβολον παρὰ βασιλέως τοῦ μεγάλου φιάλην
χρυσῆν,[7] καὶ λαβεῖν ἑκκαίδεκα μνᾶς ἐπ' αὐτῇ,
ἃς ἔχοι ἀναλίσκειν εἰς τὰ τῆς τριηραρχίας·
ἐπειδὴ δὲ εἰς Κύπρον ἀφίκοιτο, λύσεσθαι ἀποδοὺς
εἴκοσι μνᾶς· πολλῶν γὰρ ἀγαθῶν καὶ ἄλλων καὶ
χρημάτων εὐπορήσειν διὰ τὸ σύμβολον ἐν πάσῃ
τῇ ἠπείρῳ. Ἀριστοφάνης τοίνυν ἀκούων μὲν 26
ταῦτα Δήμου, δεομένου δ' ἐμοῦ, μέλλων δ' ἄξειν
τὸ χρυσίον, τέτταρας δὲ μνᾶς τόκον λήψεσθαι,
οὐκ ἔφη εἶναι, ἀλλ' ὤμνυ καὶ προσδεδανεῖσθαι
τοῖς ξένοις ἄλλοθεν, ἐπειδὴ ἥδιστ' ἂν ἀνθρώπων
ἄγειν τε εὐθὺς ἐκεῖνο τὸ σύμβολον καὶ χαρίσασθαι ἡμῖν ἃ ἐδεόμεθα. ὡς δὲ ταῦτ' ἐστὶν ἀληθῆ, 27
μάρτυρας ὑμῖν παρέξομαι.

* Al. ἔχρησαν τὸ ἀργύριον.

7 Omisi ὡς Ἀριστοφάνην, quae verba seclusit *Scheibe*.

Witness as to Aristophanes refusing to lend on the Security of the Gold Cup.

Ὅτι μὲν τοίνυν οὐ κατέλιπεν Ἀριστοφάνης ἀργύριον οὐδὲ χρυσίον, ῥᾴδιον γνῶναι ἐκ τῶν εἰρημένων καὶ μεμαρτυρημένων· χαλκώματα δὲ σύμμικτα οὐ πολλὰ ἐκέκτητο. ἀλλὰ καὶ ὅθ' εἱστία τοὺς παρ' Εὐαγόρου πρεσβεύοντας, αἰτησάμενος ἐχρήσατο. ἃ δὲ κατέλιπεν, ἀναγνώσεται ὑμῖν.

Schedule of the personal Property of Aristophanes.

§ 5. *The list is small. But remember that before the battle of Cnidus* [B.C. 394] *he had nothing but a small estate at Rhamnus. That was about five years before his death, and in that interval he twice supplied a chorus, served as trierarch three years running, gave many contributions to the State, bought a town house and more than 300 plethra of land. He was not therefore likely to leave much personal property behind.*

28 Ἴσως ἐνίοις ὑμῶν, ὦ ἄνδρες δικασταί, δοκεῖ
ὀλίγα εἶναι· ἀλλ' ἐκεῖνο ἐνθυμεῖσθε, ὅτι πρὶν
τὴν ναυμαχίαν νικῆσαι ἡμᾶς, οὐκ ἦν ἀλλ' ἢ
χωρίδιον μικρὸν Ῥαμνοῦντι. ἐγένετο δ' ἡ ναυ-
29 μαχία ἐπ' Εὐβούλου ἄρχοντος. ἐν οὖν τέτταρσιν
ἢ πέντε ἔτεσι, πρότερον μὴ ὑπαρχούσης οὐσίας,
χαλεπόν, ὦ ἄνδρες δικασταί, τραγῳδοῖς τε δὶς
χορηγῆσαι, ὑπὲρ αὑτοῦ τε καὶ τοῦ πατρός, καὶ
τρία ἔτη συνεχῶς τριηραρχῆσαι, εἰσφοράς τε
πολλὰς εἰσενηνοχέναι, οἰκίαν τε πεντήκοντα μνῶν
πρίασθαι, γῆς τε πλέον ἢ τριακόσια πλέθρα

κτήσασθαι· ἔτι δὲ πρὸς τούτοις οἴεσθε χρῆναι
ἔπιπλα πολλὰ καταλελοιπέναι; ἀλλ' οὐδ' οἱ 30
πάλαι πλούσιοι δοκοῦντες εἶναι ἄξια λόγου
ἔχοιεν ἂν ἐξενεγκεῖν· ἐνίοτε γὰρ οὐκ ἔστιν, οὐδ'
ἐάν τις πάνυ ἐπιθυμῇ, πρίασθαι τοιαῦτα ἃ κτησα-
μένῳ εἰς τὸν λοιπὸν χρόνον ἡδονὴν ἂν παρέχοι.

§ 6. *Another proof that the State has his personal property in full. We took care that his goods should not be exposed to plunder by the doors of his house being wrenched off, as often happens, and no one left in charge. I will swear too most solemnly, not only that I have none of his goods, but that he died owing us my sister's portion, and seven minae besides. It is hard to suffer this loss, to be saddled with the widow and children, and yet to be punished as though I had embezzled his goods.*

Ἀλλὰ τόδε σκοπεῖτε. τῶν ἄλλων ὅσων ἐδη- 31
μεύσατε τὰ χρήματα, οὐχ ὅπως σκεύη ἀπέδοσθε,
ἀλλὰ καὶ αἱ θύραι ἀπὸ τῶν οἰκημάτων ἀφηρ-
πάσθησαν· ἡμεῖς δὲ ἤδη δεδημευμένων καὶ ἐξελη-
λυθυίας τῆς ἐμῆς ἀδελφῆς φύλακα κατεστήσαμεν
ἐν τῇ οἰκίᾳ, ἵνα μήτε θυρώματα μήτε ἀγγεῖα μήτε
ἄλλο μηδὲν ἀπόλοιτο. ἔπιπλα δὲ ἀπεφαίνετο[8]
πλεῖον ἢ χιλίων δραχμῶν, ὅσα οὐδενός πώποτ'
ἐλάβετε. πρὸς δὲ τούτοις καὶ πρότερον πρὸς 32
τοὺς συνδίκους καὶ νῦν ἐθέλομεν πίστιν δοῦναι,
ἥτις ἐστὶ μεγίστη τοῖς ἀνθρώποις, μὴ ἔχειν τῶν
Ἀριστοφάνους χρημάτων, ὀφείλεσθαι δὲ τὴν
προῖκα τῆς ἀδελφῆς καὶ ἑπτὰ μνᾶς, ἃς ᾤχετο
λαβὼν παρὰ τοῦ πατρὸς τοῦ ἐμοῦ. πῶς ἂν οὖν 33

[8] ἀπεφαίνετο *Cobetus.* *Scheibe et vulgo* ἀπεφαίνοντο.

εἶεν ἄνθρωποι ἀθλιώτεροι, ἢ εἰ τὰ σφέτερ' αὐτῶν ἀπολωλεκότες δοκοῖεν τἀκείνων ἔχειν; ὃ δὲ πάντων δεινότατον, τὴν ἀδελφὴν ὑποδέξασθαι παιδία ἔχουσαν πολλά, καὶ ταῦτα τρέφειν, μηδ' αὐτοὺς ἔχοντας μηδέν, ἐὰν ὑμεῖς τὰ ὄντ' ἀφέλησθε.

§ 7. *Take what might be an analogous case,—that of Conon. He was much richer than Nikophemus. Suppose now the property of his son Timotheos to be confiscated. Would his relations be prosecuted because the property turned out to be, as it did, less than was expected? Now, considering the money sunk by Aristophanes, as I have described, it is rather a wonder that his personal property was as much as a third of that of Conon, without counting what his father Nikophemus had at Cyprus.*

34 Φέρε πρός θεῶν Ὀλυμπίων· οὕτω γὰρ σκοπεῖτε, ὦ δικασταί. εἴ τις ὑμῶν ἔτυχε δοὺς
Τιμοθέῳ τῷ Κόνωνος τὴν θυγατέρα ἢ τὴν ἀδελ-
φήν, καὶ ἐκείνου ἀποδημήσαντος καὶ ἐν διαβολῇ
γενομένου ἐδημεύθη ἡ οὐσία, καὶ μὴ ἐγένετο
τῇ πόλει πραθέντων ἁπάντων τέτταρα τάλαντα
ἀργυρίου, διὰ τοῦτο ἠξιοῦτε ἂν τοὺς ἀναγκαίους
τοὺς ἐκείνου καὶ τοὺς προσήκοντας ἀπολέσαι, ὅτι
οὐδὲ πολλοστὸν μέρος τῆς δόξης τῆς παρ' ὑμῖν
35 ἐφάνη τὰ χρήματα; ἀλλὰ μὴν τούτων πάντες
ἐπίστασθε Κόνωνα μὲν ἄρχοντα, Νικόφημον δὲ
ποιοῦντα ὅ τι ἐκεῖνος προστάττοι. τῶν οὖν
ὠφελειῶν Κόνωνα εἰκὸς πολλοστὸν μέρος ἄλλῳ
τινὶ μεταδιδόναι, ὥστ' εἰ οἴονται πολλὰ γενέσθαι
Νικοφήμῳ, ὁμολογήσειαν ἂν τὰ Κόνωνος εἶναι
36 πλείονα ἢ δεκαπλάσια. ἔτι δὲ φαίνονται οὐδὲν

πώποτε διενεχθέντες, ὥστ' εἰκὸς καὶ περὶ τῶν
χρημάτων ταὐτὰ γνῶναι, ἱκανὰ μὲν[9] ἐνθάδε τῷ
υἱεῖ ἑκάτερον καταλιπεῖν, τὰ δὲ ἄλλα παρ' αὑτοῖς
ἔχειν· ἦν γὰρ Κόνωνι μὲν υἱὸς ἐν Κύπρῳ καὶ
γυνή, Νικοφήμῳ δὲ γυνὴ καὶ θυγάτηρ, ἡγοῦντο
δὲ καὶ τὰ ἐκεῖ ὁμοίως σφίσιν εἶναι σᾶ[10] ὥσπερ καὶ
τὰ ἐνθάδε. πρὸς δὲ τούτοις ἐνθυμεῖσθε ὅτι καὶ 37
εἴ τις μὴ κτησάμενος ἀλλὰ παρὰ τοῦ πατρὸς
παραλαβὼν τοῖς παισὶ διένειμεν, οὐκ ἐλάχιστα
ἂν αὑτῷ ὑπέλιπε· βούλονται γὰρ πάντες ὑπὸ
τῶν παίδων θεραπεύεσθαι ἔχοντες χρήματα μᾶλλον ἢ ἐκείνων δεῖσθαι ἀποροῦντες. νῦν τοίνυν 38
εἰ δημεύσαιτε τὰ Τιμοθέου,—ὃ μὴ γένοιτο, εἰ μή
τι μέλλει μέγα ἀγαθὸν* ἔσεσθαι τῇ πόλει,—
ἐλάττονα δὲ ἐξ αὐτῶν λάβοιτ' ἢ ἐκ τῶν Ἀριστοφάνους γεγένηται, τούτου ἕνεκα ἂν ἀξιοῖτε τοὺς
ἀναγκαίους τοὺς ἐκείνου τὰ σφέτερ' αὐτῶν ἀπολέσαι; ἀλλ' οὐκ εἰκός, ὦ ἄνδρες δικασταί· ὁ 39
γὰρ Κόνωνος θάνατος καὶ αἱ διαθῆκαι, ἃς διέθετο
ἐν Κύπρῳ, σαφῶς ἐδήλωσαν ὅτι πολλοστὸν
μέρος ἦν τὰ χρήματα ὧν ὑμεῖς προσεδοκᾶτε· τῇ
μὲν γὰρ Ἀθηνᾷ καθιέρωσεν εἰς ἀναθήματα καὶ
τῷ Ἀπόλλωνι εἰς Δελφοὺς πεντακισχιλίους
στατῆρας· τῷ δὲ ἀδελφιδῷ τῷ ἑαυτοῦ, ὃς ἐφύ- 40
λαττεν αὐτῷ καὶ ἐταμίευε πάντα τὰ ἐν Κύπρῳ,
ἔδωκεν ὡς μυρίας δραχμάς, τῷ δὲ ἀδελφῷ τρία
τάλαντα· τὰ δὲ λοιπὰ τῷ υἱεῖ κατέλιπε, τάλαντα
ἑπτακαίδεκα. τούτων δὲ κεφάλαιον γίγνεται

[9] *Cobetus* vult τὰ μέν.
[10] σᾶ, 'quod Atticum est pro σῶα.'—*Cobetus.* Vulg. ἴσα.
* *Rauch.* μέγα κακόν. *W.* μέγ' ἄλλο κακόν.

περὶ τετταράκοντα τάλαντα. καὶ οὐδενὶ οἷόν τε
εἰπεῖν ὅτι διηρπάσθη ἢ ὡς οὐ δικαίως ἀπεφάνθη·
41 αὐτὸς γὰρ ἐν τῇ νόσῳ ὢν εὖ φρονῶν διέθετο.
καί μοι κάλει τούτων μάρτυρας.

Witnesses as to Conon's Will and the amount of his Personalty.

42 Ἀλλὰ μὴν ὁστισοῦν, ὦ ἄνδρες δικασταί, πρὶν
ἀμφότερα δῆλα γενέσθαι, πολλοστὸν μέρος τὰ
Νικοφήμου τῶν Κόνωνος χρημάτων ᾠήθη ἂν
εἶναι. Ἀριστοφάνης τοίνυν γῆν μὲν καὶ οἰκίαν
ἐκτήσατο πλέον ἢ πέντε ταλάντων, κατεχορήγησε
δὲ ὑπὲρ αὑτοῦ καὶ τοῦ πατρὸς πεντακισχιλίας
δραχμάς, τριηραρχῶν δὲ ἀνήλωσεν ὀγδοήκοντα
43 μνᾶς. εἰσενήνεκται δὲ ὑπὲρ ἀμφοτέρων οὐκ
ἔλαττον μνῶν τετταράκοντα. εἰς δὲ τὸν ἐπὶ
Σικελίας πλοῦν ἀνήλωσεν ἑκατὸν μνᾶς. εἰς δὲ
τὸν ἀπόστολον τῶν τριήρων, ὅτε οἱ Κύπριοι
ἦλθον καὶ ἔδοτε αὐτοῖς τὰς δέκα ναῦς, καὶ τῶν
πελταστῶν τὴν μίσθωσιν καὶ τῶν ὅπλων τὴν
ὠνὴν παρέσχε τρισμυρίας δραχμάς. καὶ τούτων
κεφάλαιον πάντων γίγνεται μικροῦ λείποντος
44 πεντεκαίδεκα τάλαντα. ὥστε οὐκ ἂν εἰκότως
ἡμᾶς αἰτιάσαισθε, ἐπεὶ τῶν Κόνωνος, τῶν ὁμολο-
γουμένων δικαίως ἀποφανθῆναι ὑπ' αὐτοῦ ἐκείνου,
πολλαπλασίων δοκούντων εἶναι πλέον ἢ τρίτον
μέρος φαίνεται τὰ Ἀριστοφάνους. καὶ οὐ προσ-
λογιζόμεθα ὅσα αὐτὸς ἐν Κύπρῳ ἔσχε Νικόφημος,
οὔσης αὐτῷ ἐκεῖ γυναικὸς καὶ θυγατρός.

§ 8. *Aristophanes is not the first person whose property at his death turned out less than was expected. I can quote many others: Ischomachus, Stephanus, Cleophon, Diotimus, and Alcibiades. With such facts before you, be merciful to me. It is no disgrace to own that you were mistaken.*

Ἐγὼ μὲν οὐκ ἀξιῶ, ὦ ἄνδρες δικασταί, οὕτω 45
πολλὰ καὶ μεγάλα τεκμήρια παρασχομένους ἡμᾶς
ἀπολέσθαι ἀδίκως. ἀκήκοα γὰρ ἔγωγε καὶ τοῦ
πατρὸς καὶ ἄλλων πρεσβυτέρων, ὅτι οὐ νῦν
μόνον ἀλλὰ καὶ ἐν τῷ ἔμπροσθεν χρόνῳ πολλῶν
ἐψεύσθητε τῆς οὐσίας, καὶ ζῶντες μὲν πλουτεῖν
ἐδόκουν, ἀποθανόντες δὲ πολὺ παρὰ τὴν δόξαν
τὴν ὑμετέραν ἐφάνησαν. αὐτίκα Ἰσχομάχῳ, ἕως 46
ἔζη, πάντες ᾤοντο εἶναι πλεῖν ἢ ἑβδομήκοντα
τάλαντα, ὡς ἐγὼ ἀκούω· ἐνειμάσθην δὲ τὼ υἱέε
οὐδὲ δέκα τάλαντα ἑκάτερος ἀποθανόντος. Στε-
φάνῳ δὲ τῷ Θάλλου ἐλέγετο εἶναι πλεῖν ἢ
πεντήκοντα τάλαντα, ἀποθανόντος δ' ἡ οὐσία
ἐφάνη περὶ ἕνδεκα τάλαντα. ὁ τοίνυν Νικίου 47
οἶκος προσεδοκᾶτο εἶναι οὐκ ἔλαττον ἢ ἑκατὸν
ταλάντων, καὶ τούτων τὰ πολλὰ ἔνδον·[11] Νική-
ρατος δὲ ὅτ' ἀπέθνησκεν, ἀργύριον μὲν ἢ χρυσίον
οὐδ' αὐτὸς ἔφη καταλείπειν οὐδέν, ἀλλὰ τὴν
οὐσίαν ἣν κατέλιπε τῷ υἱεῖ, οὐ πλείονος ἀξία
ἐστὶν ἢ τεττάρων καὶ δέκα ταλάντων. Καλλίας 48
τοίνυν ὁ Ἱππονίκου, ὅτε νεωστὶ ἐτεθνήκει ὁ
πατήρ, πλεῖστα τῶν Ἑλλήνων ἐδόκει κεκτῆσθαι,
καὶ ὥς φησι, διακοσίων ταλάντων ἐτιμήσατο

[11] Post ἔνδον sequebatur ἦν. *Scheibe* seclusit. *Taylorus*, alii, εἶναι voluerunt. Defendit ἦν *Reiskius*.

αὐτοῦ ὁ πάππος. τὸ τούτου τοίνυν[12] τίμημα οὐδὲ
δυοῖν ταλάντοιν ἐστί. Κλεοφῶντα δὲ πάντες
ἴστε, ὅτι πολλὰ ἔτη διεχείρισε τὰ τῆς πόλεως
πάντα καὶ προσεδοκᾶτο πάνυ πολλὰ ἐκ τῆς
ἀρχῆς ἔχειν· ἀποθανόντος δ' αὐτοῦ οὐδαμοῦ δῆλα
τὰ χρήματα, ἀλλὰ καὶ οἱ προσήκοντες καὶ οἱ
κηδεσταί, παρ' οἷς κατέλιπεν, ὁμολογουμένως
49 πένητές εἰσι. φαινόμεθα δὴ καὶ τῶν ἀρχαιοπλούτων πολὺ ἐψευσμένοι καὶ τῶν νεωστὶ ἐν δόξῃ
γεγενημένων. αἴτιον δέ μοι δοκεῖ εἶναι, ὅτι
ῥᾳδίως τινὲς τολμῶσι λέγειν ὡς ὁ δεῖνα ἔχει
τάλαντα πολλὰ ἐκ τῆς ἀρχῆς. καὶ ὅσα μὲν
περὶ τεθνεώτων λέγουσιν, οὐ πάνυ θαυμάζω (οὐ
γὰρ ὑπό γε ἐκείνων ἐξελεγχθεῖεν ἄν), ἀλλ' ὅσα
50 ζώντων ἐπιχειροῦσι καταψεύδεσθαι. αὐτοὶ γὰρ
ἔναγχος ἠκούετε ἐν τῇ ἐκκλησίᾳ, ὡς Διότιμος
ἔχοι τάλαντα τετταράκοντα πλείω ἢ ὅσα αὐτὸς
ὡμολόγει παρὰ τῶν ναυκλήρων καὶ ἐμπόρων·
καὶ ταῦτα, ἐπειδὴ ἦλθεν, ἐκείνου ἀπογράφοντος
καὶ χαλεπῶς φέροντος ὅτι ἀπὼν διεβάλλετο, οὐδεὶς ἐξήλεγξε, δεομένης μὲν τῆς πόλεως χρημάτων,
51 ἐθέλοντος δὲ ἐκείνου λογίσασθαι. ἐνθυμεῖσθε
τοίνυν οἷον ἂν ἐγένετο, εἰ Ἀθηναίων ἁπάντων
ἀκηκοότων ὅτι τετταράκοντα τάλαντα ἔχοι Διότιμος, εἶτα ἔπαθέ τι πρὶν καταπλεῦσαι δεῦρο.
εἶτα οἱ προσήκοντες ἂν αὐτοῦ ἐν κινδύνῳ ἦσαν
τῷ μεγίστῳ, εἰ ἔδει αὐτοὺς πρὸς τοσαύτην δια-
βολὴν ἀπολογεῖσθαι, μὴ εἰδότας μηδὲν τῶν

[12] *Scheibe, ὁ πάππος τότε, τούτου τὸ νῦν κ.τ.λ.* Si mutandum sit malim *ποτέ*, quando enim est *τότε* ?

πεπραγμένων. αἴτιοι οὖν εἰσι καὶ ὑμῖν πολλῶν ἤδη ψευσθῆναι καὶ δὴ ἀδίκως γέ τινας ἀπολέσθαι οἱ ῥᾳδίως τολμῶντες ψεύδεσθαι καὶ συκοφαντεῖν ἀνθρώπους ἐπιθυμοῦντες. ἔπειτ' οἴομαι ὑμᾶς 52 εἰδέναι ὅτι Ἀλκιβιάδης τέτταρα ἢ πέντε ἔτη ἐφεξῆς ἐστρατήγει ἐπικρατῶν καὶ νενικηκὼς Λακεδαιμονίους, καὶ διπλάσια ἐκείνῳ ἠξίουν αἱ πόλεις διδόναι ἢ ἄλλῳ τινὶ τῶν στρατηγῶν, ὥστ' ᾤοντο εἶναί τινες αὐτῷ πλέον ἢ ἑκατὸν τάλαντα. ὁ δ' ἀποθανὼν ἐδήλωσεν ὅτι οὐκ ἀληθῆ ταῦτα ἦν· ἐλάττω γὰρ οὐσίαν κατέλιπε τοῖς παισὶν ἢ αὐτὸς παρὰ τῶν ἐπιτροπευσάντων παρέλαβεν.

Ὅτι μὲν οὖν καὶ ἐν τῷ ἔμπροσθεν χρόνῳ 53 τοιαῦτα ἐγίγνετο, ῥᾴδιον γνῶναι· φασὶ δὲ καὶ τοὺς ἀρίστους καὶ σοφωτάτους μάλιστα ἐθέλειν μεταγιγνώσκειν. εἰ οὖν δοκοῦμεν εἰκότα λέγειν καὶ ἱκανὰ τεκμήρια παρέχεσθαι, ὦ ἄνδρες δικασταί, πάσῃ τέχνῃ καὶ μηχανῇ ἐλεήσατε, ὡς ἡμεῖς τῆς μὲν διαβολῆς οὕτω μεγάλης οὔσης ἀεὶ προσεδοκῶμεν κρατήσειν μετὰ τοῦ ἀληθοῦς· ὑμῶν δὲ μηδενὶ τρόπῳ ἐθελησάντων πεισθῆναι οὐδ' ἐλπὶς οὐδεμία σωτηρίας ἐδόκει ἡμῖν εἶναι. ἀλλὰ πρὸς 54 θεῶν Ὀλυμπίων, ὦ ἄνδρες δικασταί, βούλεσθε ἡμᾶς δικαίως σῶσαι μᾶλλον ἢ ἀδίκως ἀπολέσαι, καὶ πιστεύετε τούτοις ἀληθῆ λέγειν, οἳ ἂν καὶ σιωπῶντες ἐν ἅπαντι τῷ βίῳ παρέχωσι σώφρονας σφᾶς αὐτοὺς καὶ δικαίους.

§ 9. *My character and that of my father should be my warrant. I am thirty, and never was in a law court before. My father, from pure patriotism, not from the hope of recouping himself by office, spent no less than 9 talents 2000 drachmæ on the public service; and was ever liberal to his fellow-citizens in helping to portion their daughters and perform their funerals.*

55 Περὶ μὲν οὖν αὐτῆς τῆς γραφῆς, καὶ ᾧ τρόπῳ
κηδεσταὶ ἡμῖν ἐγένοντο, καὶ ὅτι οὐκ ἐξήρκει τὰ
ἐκείνου εἰς τὸν ἔκπλουν, ἀλλὰ καὶ ὡς ἄλλοθεν
προσεδανείσατο ἀκηκόατε καὶ μεμαρτύρηται ὑμῖν·
περὶ δ' ἐμαυτοῦ βραχέα βούλομαι ὑμῖν εἰπεῖν.
ἐγω γὰρ ἔτη γεγονὼς ἤδη τριάκοντα οὔτε τῷ
πατρὶ οὐδὲν πώποτε ἀντεῖπον, οὔτε τῶν πολιτῶν
οὐδείς μοι ἐνεκάλεσεν, ἐγγύς τε οἰκῶν τῆς ἀγορᾶς
οὐδὲ πρὸς δικαστηρίῳ οὐδὲ πρὸς βουλευτηρίῳ
ὤφθην οὐδεπώποτε, πρὶν ταύτην τὴν συμφορὰν
56 γενέσθαι. περὶ μὲν οὖν ἐμαυτοῦ τοσαῦτα λέγω,
περὶ δὲ τοῦ πατρός, ἐπειδὴ ὥσπερ ἀδικοῦντος αἱ
κατηγορίαι γεγένηνται, συγγνώμην ἔχετε, ἐὰν
λέγω ἃ ἀνήλωσεν εἰς τὴν πόλιν καὶ εἰς τοὺς
φίλους· οὐ γὰρ φιλοτιμίας ἕνεκεν ἀλλὰ τεκμήριον
ποιούμενος ὅτι οὐ τοῦ αὐτοῦ ἐστιν ἀνδρὸς ἄνευ
ἀνάγκης τε πολλὰ ἀναλίσκειν καὶ μετὰ κινδύνου
τοῦ μεγίστου ἐπιθυμῆσαι ἔχειν τι τῶν κοινῶν.
57 εἰσὶ δέ τινες οἱ προαναλίσκοντες οὐ μόνον τούτου
ἕνεκεν, ἀλλ' ἵνα ἄρχειν ὑφ' ὑμῶν ἀξιωθέντες
διπλάσια κομίσωνται. ὁ τοίνυν ἐμὸς πατὴρ
ἄρχειν μὲν οὐδεπώποτε ἐπεθύμησε, τὰς δὲ χορηγίας ἁπάσας κεχορήγηκε, τετριηράρχηκε δὲ ἑπτά-
κις, εἰσφορὰς δὲ πολλὰς καὶ μεγάλας εἰσενήνοχεν.
ἵνα δὲ εἰδῆτε καὶ ὑμεῖς, καὶ καθ' ἑκάστην ἀναγνώσεται.

A List of Services performed by Defendant's Father.

'Ακούετε, ὦ ἄνδρες δικασταί, τὸ πλῆθος. πεν- 58
τήκοντα γὰρ ἔτη ἐστὶν ὅσα ὁ πατὴρ καὶ τοῖς
χρήμασι καὶ τῷ σώματι τῇ πόλει ἐλειτούργει.
ἐν οὖν τοσούτῳ χρόνῳ δοκοῦντά τι ἐξ ἀρχῆς
ἔχειν οὐδεμίαν εἰκὸς δαπάνην[13] πεφευγέναι.
ὅμως δὲ καὶ μάρτυρας ὑμῖν παρέξομαι.

Witnesses as to the liberal manner in which Defendant's Father performed his 'Liturgies.'

Τούτων συμπάντων κεφάλαιόν ἐστιν ἐννέα 59
τάλαντα καὶ δισχίλιαι δραχμαί. ἔτι τοίνυν καὶ
ἰδίᾳ τισὶ τῶν πολιτῶν ἀποροῦσι συνεξέδωκε
θυγατέρας καὶ ἀδελφάς, τοὺς δ' ἐλύσατο ἐκ τῶν
πολεμίων, τοῖς δ' εἰς ταφὴν παρεῖχεν ἀργύριον.
καὶ ταῦτ' ἐποίει ἡγούμενος εἶναι ἀνδρὸς ἀγαθοῦ
ὠφελεῖν τοὺς φίλους, καὶ εἰ μηδεὶς μέλλοι εἴσεσθαι·
νῦν δὲ πρέπον ἐστὶ καὶ ὑμᾶς ἀκοῦσαί μου.* καί
μοι κάλει τὸν καὶ τόν.

Further Witnesses to the Liberality of Defendant's Father.

§ 10. *Now, a man could not keep up a hypocritical pretence of liberality through a long life of seventy years.*

[13] *Reiskius* voluit δίκην, sed de impensis sui patris non de litibus agit orator. * *W.* μαρτύρων.

Facts speak for themselves. He once had a large property. If you now confiscate it, you will find barely two talents; and on this small remnant I am at this moment serving a trierarchy, and intend to follow in my father's path of disinterested patriotism.

60 Τῶν μὲν οὖν μαρτύρων ἀκηκόατε· ἐνθυμεῖσθε
δὲ ὅτι ὀλίγον μὲν χρόνον δύναιτ' ἄν τις πλάσασθαι
τὸν τρόπον τὸν αὑτοῦ, ἐν ἑβδομήκοντα δὲ ἔτεσιν
οὐδ' ἂν εἷς λάθοι πονηρὸς ὤν. τῷ τοίνυν πατρὶ
τῷ ἐμῷ ἄλλα μὲν ἄν τις ἔχοι ἐπικαλέσαι ἴσως,
εἰς χρήματα δὲ οὐδεὶς οὐδὲ τῶν ἐχθρῶν ἐτόλμησε
61 πώποτε. οὔκουν ἄξιον τοῖς τῶν κατηγόρων
λόγοις πιστεῦσαι μᾶλλον ἢ τοῖς ἔργοις, ἃ ἐπράχθη
ἐν ἅπαντι τῷ βίῳ, καὶ τῷ χρόνῳ, ὃν ὑμεῖς σαφέ-
στατον ἔλεγχον τοῦ ἀληθοῦς νομίσατε. εἰ γὰρ
μὴ ἦν τοιοῦτος, οὐκ ἂν ἐκ πολλῶν ὀλίγα κατέλιπεν, ἐπεὶ εἰ νῦν γε ἐξαπατηθείητε ὑπὸ τούτων
καὶ δημεύσαιθ' ἡμῶν τὴν οὐσίαν, οὐδὲ δύο τάλαντα
λάβοιτ' ἄν. ὥστε οὐ μόνον πρὸς δόξαν ἀλλὰ
καὶ εἰς χρημάτων λόγον λυσιτελεῖ μᾶλλον ὑμῖν
ἀποψηφίσασθαι· πολὺ γὰρ πλείω ὠφελήσεσθε,
62 ἂν ἡμεῖς ἔχωμεν. σκοπεῖτε δὲ ἐκ τοῦ παρεληλυθότος χρόνου, ὅσα φαίνεται ἀνηλωμένα εἰς τὴν
πόλιν· καὶ νῦν ἀπὸ τῶν ὑπολοίπων τριηραρχῶ
μὲν ἐγώ, τριηραρχῶν δὲ ὁ πατὴρ ἀπέθανεν,
πειράσομαι δ', ὥσπερ ἐκεῖνον ἑώρων, ὀλίγα κατὰ
μικρὸν παρασκευάσασθαι εἰς τὰς κοινὰς ὠφελείας.
ὥστε τῷ γ' ἔργῳ τῆς πόλεως[14] ταῦτ' ἐστί, καὶ
οὔτ' ἐγὼ ἀφῃρημένος ἀδικεῖσθαι οἰήσομαι, ὑμῖν δὲ

[14] τῆς πόλεως, vulgo πάλαι. Alii aliter correxerunt, πάλαι ὑμέτερα, πάλαι τῆς πόλεως, πάλαι ταῦτ' ἐστι κοινά. Francken vult ἔσται. *W.* πάλιν τῆς πόλεως ταῦτ' ἔσται.

πλείους οὕτως αἱ ὠφέλειαι ἢ εἰ δημεύσαιτε. πρὸς 63
δὲ τούτοις ἄξιον ἐνθυμηθῆναι οἵαν φύσιν εἶχεν ὁ
πατήρ. ὅσα γὰρ ἔξω τῶν ἀναγκαίων ἐπεθύμησεν
ἀναλίσκειν, πάντα φανήσεται τοιαῦτα ὅθεν καὶ
τῇ πόλει τιμὴ ἔμελλεν ἔσεσθαι. αὐτίκα ὅτε
ἵππευεν, οὐ μόνον ἵππους ἐκτήσατο λαμπροὺς
ἀλλὰ καὶ ἀθλητάς, οἷς ἐνίκησεν Ἰσθμοῖ καὶ
Νεμέᾳ, ὥστε τὴν πόλιν κηρυχθῆναι καὶ αὐτὸν
στεφανωθῆναι. δέομαι οὖν ὑμῶν, ὦ ἄνδρες 64
δικασταί, καὶ τούτων καὶ τῶν ἄλλων μεμνημένους
ἁπάντων τῶν εἰρημένων βοηθεῖν ἡμῖν καὶ μὴ
περιιδεῖν ὑπὸ τῶν ἐχθρῶν ἀναιρεθέντας. καὶ
ταῦτα ποιοῦντες τά τε δίκαια ψηφιεῖσθε καὶ
ὑμῖν αὐτοῖς τὰ συμφέροντα.

ORATION XI. [22.]

For the Prosecution. Against the Corn Dealers for 'Engrossing.'

§ 1. *Though the prosecution of 'engrossers' in corn is legal, yet there is a certain prejudice against the promoter. I must first show that I do not act from spite. Originally the Boulè wished to deliver these men without trial to the Eleven for execution. I then spoke against that course, and advised that the ordinary form of trial should be used. I incurred odium for that, and I now wish to show that I was acting not from favour to the dealers but for the sake of legality.*

Πολλοί μοι προσεληλύθασιν, ὦ ἄνδρες δικα-

σταί, θαυμάζοντες ὅτι ἐγὼ τῶν σιτοπωλῶν ἐν τῇ
βουλῇ κατηγόρουν, καὶ λέγοντες ὅτι ὑμεῖς, εἰ ὡς
μάλιστα αὐτοὺς ἀδικεῖν ἡγεῖσθε, οὐδὲν ἧττον καὶ
τοὺς περὶ τούτων ποιουμένους λόγους συκοφαντεῖν
νομίζετε. ὅθεν οὖν ἠνάγκασμαι κατηγορεῖν αὐτῶν,
περὶ τούτων πρῶτον εἰπεῖν βούλομαι.
2 Ἐπειδὴ γὰρ οἱ πρυτάνεις ἀπέδοσαν εἰς τὴν
βουλὴν περὶ αὐτῶν, οὕτως ὠργίσθησαν αὐτοῖς,
ὥστε ἔλεγόν τινες τῶν ῥητόρων ὡς ἀκρίτους
αὐτοὺς χρὴ τοῖς ἕνδεκα παραδοῦναι θανάτῳ
ζημιῶσαι. ἡγούμενος δὲ ἐγὼ δεινὸν εἶναι τοιαῦτα
ἐθίζεσθαι ποιεῖν τὴν βουλήν, ἀναστὰς εἶπον ὅτι
μοι δοκοίη κρίνειν τοὺς σιτοπώλας κατὰ τὸν
νόμον, νομίζων, εἰ μέν εἰσιν ἄξια θανάτου εἰργασμένοι, ὑμᾶς οὐδὲν ἧττον ἡμῶν γνώσεσθαι τὰ
δίκαια, εἰ δὲ μηδὲν ἀδικοῦσιν, οὐ δεῖν αὐτοὺς
3 ἀκρίτους* ἀπολωλέναι. πεισθείσης δὲ τῆς βουλῆς
ταῦτα, διαβάλλειν ἐπεχείρουν με λέγοντες ὡς
ἐγὼ σωτηρίας ἕνεκα τῆς τῶν σιτοπωλῶν τοὺς
λόγους τούτους ἐποιούμην. πρὸς μὲν οὖν τὴν
βουλήν, ὅτ' ἦν αὐτοῖς ἡ κρίσις, ἔργῳ ἀπελογη-
σάμην· τῶν γὰρ ἄλλων ἡσυχίαν ἀγόντων ἀναστὰς
αὐτῶν κατηγόρουν, καὶ πᾶσι φανερὸν ἐποίησα
ὅτι οὐχ ὑπὲρ τούτων ἔλεγον, ἀλλὰ τοῖς νόμοις
4 τοῖς κειμένοις ἐβοήθουν. ἠρξάμην μὲν οὖν τούτων ἕνεκα, δεδιὼς τὰς αἰτίας· αἰσχρὸν δ' ἡγοῦμαι
πρότερον παύσασθαι, πρὶν ἂν ὑμεῖς περὶ αὐτῶν
ὅ τι ἂν βούλησθε ψηφίσησθε.

§ 2. *First, I will show by an examination of the*

* *Röhl* ἀδίκως.

dealers that they have broken the law in buying up above the legal quantity of corn. They plead that they were acting under the orders of the corn-inspectors. That is no defence to the charge, unless the law contains a clause giving the inspectors such dispensing power. But I will prove that the plea is false. The only advice they got from an inspector was to cease bidding against each other, and to be content with the legal profit.

Καὶ πρῶτον μὲν ἀνάβηθι καὶ εἰπὲ σὺ ἐμοί, 5
μέτοικος εἶ; Ναί. Μετοικεῖς δὲ πότερον ὡς
πεισόμενος τοῖς νόμοις τοῖς τῆς πόλεως, ἢ ὡς
ποιήσων ὅ τι ἂν βούλῃ; Ὡς πεισόμενος. Ἄλλο
τι οὖν ἢ ἀξιοῖς ἀποθανεῖν, εἴ τι πεποίηκας παρὰ
τοὺς νόμους, ἐφ' οἷς θάνατος ἡ ζημία; Ἔγωγε.
Ἀπόκριναι δή μοι, εἰ ὁμολογεῖς πλείω σῖτον
συμπρίασθαι πεντήκοντα φορμῶν, ὧν ὁ νόμος
ἐξεῖναι κελεύει. Ἐγὼ τῶν ἀρχόντων κελευόντων
συνεπριάμην.

Ἂν μὲν τοίνυν ἀποδείξῃ, ὦ ἄνδρες δικασταί, 6
ὡς ἔστι νόμος ὃς κελεύει τοὺς σιτοπώλας συνωνεῖσθαι τὸν σῖτον, ἂν οἱ ἄρχοντες κελεύωσιν,
ἀποψηφίσασθε· εἰ δὲ μή, δίκαιον ὑμᾶς καταψηφίσασθαι. ἡμεῖς γὰρ ὑμῖν παρεσχόμεθα τὸν
νόμον, ὃς ἀπαγορεύει μηδένα τῶν ἐν τῇ πόλει
πλείω σῖτον πεντήκοντα φορμῶν συνωνεῖσθαι.

Χρῆν μὲν τοίνυν, ὦ ἄνδρες δικασταί, ἱκανὴν 7
εἶναι ταύτην τὴν κατηγορίαν, ἐπειδὴ οὗτος μὲν
ὁμολογεῖ συμπρίασθαι ὁ δὲ νόμος ἀπαγορεύων
φαίνεται, ὑμεῖς δὲ κατὰ τοὺς νόμους ὀμωμόκατε
ψηφιεῖσθαι· ὅμως δ' ἵνα πεισθῆτε ὅτι καὶ κατὰ
τῶν ἀρχόντων ψεύδονται, ἀνάγκη καὶ μακρότεροι

8 εἰπεῖν περὶ αὐτῶν. ἐπειδὴ γὰρ οὗτοι τὴν αἰτίαν
εἰς ἐκείνους ἀνέφερον, παρακαλέσαντες τοὺς ἄρχοντας ἠρωτῶμεν. καὶ οἱ μὲν τέσσαρες οὐδὲν
ἔφασαν εἰδέναι τοῦ πράγματος, Ἄνυτος δ' ἔλεγεν
ὡς τοῦ προτέρου χειμῶνος, ἐπειδὴ τίμιος ἦν ὁ
σῖτος, τούτων ὑπερβαλλόντων ἀλλήλους καὶ πρὸς
σφᾶς αὐτοὺς μαχομένων συμβουλεύσειεν αὐτοῖς
παύσασθαι φιλονεικοῦσιν, ἡγούμενος συμφέρειν
ὑμῖν τοῖς παρὰ τούτων ὠνουμένοις ὡς ἀξιώτατον
τούτους πρίασθαι· δεῖν γὰρ αὐτοὺς ὀβολῷ μόνον
9 πωλεῖν τιμιώτερον. ὡς τοίνυν οὐ συμπριαμένους
καταθέσθαι ἐκέλευεν αὐτούς, ἀλλὰ μὴ ἀλλήλοις
ἀντωνεῖσθαι συνεβούλευεν, αὐτὸν ὑμῖν Ἄνυτον
μάρτυρα παρέξομαι, καὶ ὡς οὗτος μὲν ἐπὶ τῆς
προτέρας βουλῆς τούτους εἶπε τοὺς λόγους, οὗτοι
δ' ἐπὶ τῆσδε[1] συνωνούμενοι φαίνονται.

Deposition of Anytus that he did not advise the Corn Dealers to accumulate Corn.

10 Ὅτι μὲν τοίνυν οὐχ ὑπὸ τῶν ἀρχόντων κελευσθέντες συνεπρίαντο τὸν σῖτον, ἀκηκόατε· ἡγοῦμαι δ', ἂν ὡς μάλιστα περὶ τούτων ἀληθῆ λέγωσιν, οὐχ ὑπὲρ αὐτῶν αὐτοὺς ἀπολογήσεσθαι, ἀλλὰ τούτων κατηγορήσειν· περὶ γὰρ ὧν εἰσι νόμοι διαρρήδην γεγραμμένοι, πῶς οὐ χρὴ διδόναι δίκην καὶ τοὺς μὴ πειθομένους καὶ τοὺς κελεύοντας τούτοις τἀναντία πράττειν;

[1] ἐπὶ τῆσδε. MSS. ἐπίτηδες. W. ἔτι τῆτες.

§ 3. *They will plead that they acted for your benefit in amassing corn that they might sell it cheap. This is false, for they often varied the selling price as much as a drachma in a day.*

Ἀλλὰ γάρ, ὦ ἄνδρες δικασταί, οἴομαι αὐτοὺς 11
ἐπὶ μὲν τοῦτον τὸν λόγον οὐκ ἐλεύσεσθαι·* ἴσως
δ' ἐροῦσιν, ὥσπερ καὶ ἐν τῇ βουλῇ, ὡς ἐπ' εὐνοίᾳ
τῆς πόλεως συνεωνοῦντο τὸν σῖτον, ἵν' ὡς ἀξιώτατον ἡμῖν πωλοῖεν. μέγιστον δ' ὑμῖν ἐρῶ καὶ
περιφανέστατον τεκμήριον ὅτι ψεύδονται. ἐχρῆν 12
γὰρ αὐτούς, εἴπερ ὑμῶν ἕνεκα ἔπραττον ταῦτα,
φαίνεσθαι τῆς αὐτῆς τιμῆς πολλὰς ἡμέρας πω-
λοῦντας, ἕως ὁ συνεωνημένος αὐτοὺς ἐπέλιπε·
νυνὶ δ' ἐνίοτε τῆς αὐτῆς ἡμέρας ἐπώλουν δραχμῇ
τιμιώτερον, ὥσπερ κατὰ μέδιμνον συνωνούμενοι.
καὶ τούτων ὑμῖν μάρτυρας παρέξομαι.

Evidence to show that the Corn Dealers have varied the Price of their stored Corn.

§ 4. *Is it likely that men, who, when State contributions are wanted, plead poverty, should, entirely for your profit, risk death by an infraction of a law? Indeed public disasters benefit them by making corn dearer. And the city is reduced by them in time of peace almost to a state of siege as regards provisions. This is why corn inspectors are appointed.*

Δεινὸν δέ μοι δοκεῖ εἶναι, εἰ ὅταν μὲν εἰσφορὰν 13
εἰσενεγκεῖν δέῃ, ἣν πάντες εἴσεσθαι μέλλουσιν,
οὐκ ἐθέλουσιν, ἀλλὰ πενίαν προφασίζονται, ἐφ'
οἷς δὲ θάνατός ἐστιν ἡ ζημία καὶ λαθεῖν αὐτοῖς

* *Cob.* τρέψεσθαι. *W.* ἐπὶ τούτῳ . . ἐλεήσεσθαι.

συνέφερε, ταῦτα ἐπ' εὐνοίᾳ φασὶ τῇ ὑμετέρᾳ
παρανομῆσαι. καίτοι πάντες ἐπίστασθε ὅτι
τούτοις ἥκιστα προσήκει τοιούτους ποιεῖσθαι
λόγους. τἀναντία γὰρ αὐτοῖς καὶ τοῖς ἄλλοις
συμφέρει· τότε γὰρ πλεῖστα κερδαίνουσιν, ὅταν
κακοῦ τινος ἀπαγγελθέντος τῇ πόλει τίμιον τὸν
14 σῖτον πωλῶσιν. οὕτω δ' ἄσμενοι τὰς συμφορὰς
τὰς ὑμετέρας ὁρῶσιν, ὥστε τὰς μὲν πρότεροι τῶν
ἄλλων πυνθάνονται, τὰς δ' αὐτοὶ λογοποιοῦσιν,
ἢ τὰς ναῦς διεφθάρθαι τὰς ἐν τῷ Πόντῳ, ἢ
ὑπὸ Λακεδαιμονίων ἐκπλεούσας συνειλῆφθαι, ἢ
τὰ ἐμπόρια κεκλεῖσθαι, ἢ τὰς σπονδὰς μέλλειν
ἀπορρηθήσεσθαι, καὶ εἰς τοῦτ' ἔχθρας ἐληλύθασιν,
15 ὥστ' ἐν τούτοις τοῖς καιροῖς ἐπιβουλεύουσιν ἡμῖν,
ἐν οἷσπερ οἱ πολέμιοι. ὅταν γὰρ μάλιστα σίτου
τυγχάνητε δεόμενοι, ἀναρπάζουσιν οὗτοι καὶ οὐκ
ἐθέλουσι πωλεῖν, ἵνα μὴ περὶ τῆς τιμῆς διαφερώ-
μεθα, ἀλλ' ἀγαπῶμεν ἂν ὁποσουτινοσοῦν πριά-
μενοι παρ' αὐτῶν ἀπέλθωμεν· ὥστ' ἐνίοτε εἰρήνης
16 οὔσης ὑπὸ τούτων πολιορκούμεθα. οὕτω δὲ
πάλαι περὶ τῆς τούτων πανουργίας καὶ κακονοίας
ἡ πόλις ἔγνωκεν, ὥστ' ἐπὶ μὲν τοῖς ἄλλοῖς ὠνίοις
ἅπασι τοὺς ἀγορανόμους φύλακας κατεστήσατε,
ἐπὶ δὲ ταύτῃ μόνῃ τῇ τέχνῃ χωρὶς σιτοφύλακας
ἀποκληροῦτε·[2] καὶ πολλάκις ἤδη παρ' ἐκείνων
πολιτῶν ὄντων δίκην τὴν μεγίστην ἐλάβετε, ὅτι
οὐχ οἷοί τ' ἦσαν τῆς τούτων πονηρίας ἐπικρατῆσαι.
καίτοι τί χρὴ αὐτοὺς τοὺς ἀδικοῦντας ὑφ' ὑμῶν
πάσχειν, ὁπότε καὶ τοὺς οὐ δυναμένους φυλάττειν
ἀποκτείνετε;

[2] *Scheibe, Markland,* ἀπεκληροῦτε sed 'agitur de consuetudine.' *Francken.*

§ 5. *If there were a conflict of testimony, you might acquit them; but now you have their own confession. Condemn them as a warning to others. Remember that the practice is so profitable as to tempt many to risk the penalties. More worthy of your pity are the people they helped to starve, the merchants against whom they combined, and the inspectors who have before now suffered death for not being able to prevent their practices.*

Ἐνθυμεῖσθαι δὲ χρὴ ὅτι ἀδύνατον ὑμῖν ἐστὶν 17
ἀποψηφίσασθαι. εἰ γὰρ ἀπογνώσεσθε ὁμολογούντων αὐτῶν ἐπὶ τοὺς ἐμπόρους συνίστασθαι,
δόξεθ' ὑμεῖς ἐπιβουλεύειν τοῖς εἰσπλέουσιν. εἰ
μὲν γὰρ ἄλλην τινὰ ἀπολογίαν ἐποιοῦντο, οὐδεὶς
ἂν εἶχε τοῖς ἀποψηφισαμένοις ἐπιτιμᾶν· ἐφ'
ὑμῖν γὰρ ὁποτέροις βούλεσθε πιστεύειν· νῦν δὲ
πῶς οὐ δεινὰ ἂν δόξαιτε ποιεῖν, εἰ τοὺς ὁμολο-
γοῦντας παρανομεῖν ἀζημίους ἀφήσετε; ἀνα- 18
μνήσθητε δέ, ὦ ἄνδρες δικασταί, ὅτι πολλῶν ἤδη
ἐχόντων ταύτην τὴν αἰτίαν[3] καὶ μάρτυρας παρε-
χομένων θάνατον κατέγνωτε, πιστοτέρους ἡγησά-
μενοι τοὺς τῶν κατηγόρων λόγους. καίτοι πῶς
ἂν οὐ θαυμαστὸν εἴη, εἰ περὶ τῶν αὐτῶν ἁμαρτημάτων δικάζοντες μᾶλλον ἐπεθυμεῖτε παρὰ τῶν
ἀρνουμένων δίκην λαμβάνειν; Καὶ μὲν δή, ὦ 19
ἄνδρες δικασταί, πᾶσιν ἡγοῦμαι φανερὸν εἶναι
ὅτι οἱ περὶ τῶν τοιούτων ἀγῶνες κοινότατοι
τυγχάνουσιν ὄντες τοῖς ἐν τῇ πόλει, ὥστε πεύσονται ἥντινα γνώμην περὶ αὐτῶν ἔχετε, ἡγούμενοι,
ἂν μὲν θάνατον τούτων καταγνῶτε, κοσμιωτέρους

[3] λαμβάνειν ejeci cum *Cobeto*, *Sauppio*, aliis. *Dobr.* vult καὶ ἀρνουμένων καί. *Kayser* λανθάνειν δὲ πειρωμένων. *West.* τοῦ μὴ δίκην λαμβάνειν. *Weidn.* ἀλλ' ἀρνουμένων.

ἔσεσθαι τοὺς λοιπούς· ἂν δ' ἀζημίους ἀφῆτε,
πολλὴν ἄδειαν αὐτοῖς ἐψηφισμένοι ἔσεσθε ποιεῖν
20 ὅ τι ἂν βούλωνται. χρὴ δέ, ὦ ἄνδρες δικασταί,
μὴ μόνον τῶν παρεληλυθότων ἕνεκα αὐτοὺς
κολάζειν, ἀλλὰ καὶ παραδείγματος ἕνεκα τῶν
μελλόντων ἔσεσθαι· οὕτω γὰρ ἔσονται μόγις
ἀνεκτοί. ἐνθυμεῖσθε δὲ ὅτι ἐκ ταύτης τῆς τέχνης
πλεῖστοι περὶ τοῦ σώματός εἰσιν ἠγωνισμένοι·
καὶ οὕτω μεγάλα ἐξ αὐτῆς ὠφελοῦνται, ὥστε
μᾶλλον αἱροῦνται καθ' ἑκάστην ἡμέραν περὶ τῆς
ψυχῆς κινδυνεύειν ἢ παύσασθαι παρ' ὑμῶν
21 ἀδίκως κερδαίνοντες. καὶ μὲν δὴ οὐδ' ἂν ἀντιβο-
λῶσιν ὑμᾶς καὶ ἱκετεύωσι, δικαίως ἂν αὐτοὺς
ἐλεήσαιτε, ἀλλὰ πολὺ μᾶλλον τῶν τε πολιτῶν
οἳ διὰ τὴν τούτων πονηρίαν ἀπέθνησκον, καὶ τοὺς
ἐμπόρους ἐφ' οὓς οὗτοι συνέστησαν· οἷς ὑμεῖς
χαριεῖσθε καὶ προθυμοτέρους ποιήσετε, δίκην
παρὰ τούτων [4] λαμβάνοντες. εἰ δὲ μή, τίν' αὐτοὺς
οἴεσθε γνώμην ἕξειν, ἐπειδὰν πύθωνται ὅτι τῶν
καπήλων, οἳ τοῖς εἰσπλέουσιν ὡμολόγησαν ἐπιβουλεύειν, ἀπεψηφίσασθε;
22 Οὐκ οἶδ' ὅ τι δεῖ πλείω λέγειν· περὶ μὲν γὰρ
τῶν ἄλλων τῶν ἀδικούντων, ὅτου δικάζονται, δεῖ
παρὰ τῶν κατηγόρων πυθέσθαι, τὴν δὲ τούτων
πονηρίαν ἅπαντες ἐπίστασθε. ἂν οὖν τούτων
καταψηφίσησθε, τά τε δίκαια ποιήσετε καὶ ἀξιώ-
τερον τὸν σῖτον ὠνήσεσθε· εἰ δὲ μή, τιμιώτερον.

[4] τούτων *Tayl. Dobr. Francken* pro αὐτῶν.

Hermann refers to C. F. Hermann's 'Manual of the Political Antiquities of Greece.' English translation. 1836.

Cobet to 'Variæ Lectiones' of C. G. Cobet. 1873.

Boeckh. refers to 'Public Economy of Athens,' translated by G. C. Lewis. 1842.

The grammatical references are as follow :—

Goodwin, with section (§), refers to Professor Goodwin's 'Elementary Greek Grammar.' Macmillan and Co. 1880.

Goodwin, M. and T., to the same writer's Greek 'Moods and Tenses.' 1872 and 1889.

Madvig to Browne's translation of Madvig's 'Syntax of the Greek Language.' 2d Ed. 1873.

Clyde to Dr. J. Clyde's 'Greek Syntax.' 1870.

Donaldson to J. W. Donaldson's 'Complete Greek Grammar.' 1862.

Veitch to W. Veitch's 'Greek Verbs.' 1871.

Rutherford to 'The New Phrynichus.' 1881.

For Philological information reference is made to Curtius' 'Principles of Greek Etymology,' Wilkins and England's Translation, 1875 ; the references being by the numbers in the margin.

NOTES.

ORATION IV. [10.]

* [The last case arose from a charge of slandering a magistrate; we now have a case of the slander of a private person in a speech delivered apparently in the Ecclesia.

Theomnestus had been impeached (εἰσαγγελία, § 7) by Lysitheos for *speaking in the assembly* after throwing away his shield. He was acquitted (§ 22); and then prosecuted for perjury one of the witnesses against him, Dionysios, and obtained his disfranchisement (§ 22); and also brought a suit against a certain Theon for slander (§ 12).

The present speaker had been one of the witnesses against Theomnestus, who in his reply had asserted that the witness had killed his own father. Thereupon the speaker prosecuted Theomnestus for slander, and the case (δίκη κακολογίας), having first been heard before an arbitrator (§ 6), was tried before an ordinary court under the presidency of the Thesmothetæ.

The speech, in itself spirited and interesting, is curious from the line of defence set up by Theomnestus. He seems to have admitted the fact, but to have pleaded that his words were not actionable, because he had used the expression ἀποκτονέναι, whereas the word forbidden (ἀπόρρητον) in the law was ἀνδροφόνος. The speech therefore is in a great degree taken up with this special plea, showing its absurdity by quotations from old laws, still in force, though containing obsolete words.

* For the law of slander, see Orat. iii. l. 58. The penalty for the offence was a fine of 500 drachmæ [§ 12].

The date of the speech is shown by § 4. He says that it is the twentieth year since the restoration of the Democracy, which took place in 404-3 B.C. The date therefore is B.C. 384-3.

Readers of Aristophanes will know how common the imputation of this act of cowardice, 'throwing away the shield,' was, and how

Cleonymus is again and again attacked for it. *Vide* Vesp. 19, 82-3; Av. 289, 1481. The motive of course of throwing away the heavy shield was to fly more quickly. Cf. Thucyd. vii. 45, 2, after the unsuccessful attack on Epipolæ, ὅπλα μέντοι ἔτι πλείω ἢ κατὰ τοὺς νεκροὺς ἐλήφθη, which he explains by stating that in retreating down the high ground they threw away their shields, and some escaped and others were killed. Cf. Horace's description of his retreat at Philippi, *relicta non bene parmula.*]

3. **δικάζοντας** 'sitting on the jury.'

4-5. **εἰσήγγελλε . . δημηγορεῖν** 'was impeaching Theomnestus for speaking in the assembly after having thrown away his shield.' A man guilty of cowardice in the field was tried before the Strategi; but in this case Lysitheus seems to have accused him of 'speaking in the assembly' after having been guilty of such a crime, the penalty of which was ἀτιμία. But though the impeachment was raised on this issue, the whole case would depend on the proof of his having 'thrown away his shield,' without proof of which the other charge necessarily fell to the ground. The εἰσαγγελία seems to have been to the Ecclesia, not the Boulè. The infinitive after εἰσαγγέλλειν is not common.

5. **οὐκ ἐξὸν** 'when it was not lawful for him to do so:' because if he had shown cowardice he was ἄτιμος. οἷς ἔξεστι is the phrase describing men without any disability in respect to any civil function.

9. **φαῦλον** 'common-place and insignificant.'

ἡγούμην 'I should have considered:' for ἄν omitted, see
* ii. l. 216. Weidn. read φαῦλον γὰρ ἄν.

12. **φιλόδικον** 'pettifogging' or 'litigious.' δικάζεσθαι 'to go to law with;' δικάζειν 'to act as judge.' The offence, as in Lat., is in the genitive, **κακηγορίας** 'for slander.'

13. **νυνὶ δὲ** 'but in the circumstances,' *i.e.* considering what a dreadful thing he has said of me.

14. **οὕτω πολλοῦ . . πόλει** 'a man who had performed such notable services to you and the State.' W. reads ἡμῖν.

17. **ἐξαίρετόν ἐστι** 'the special privilege is allowed,' a metaphor from the division of booty.

19-21. **ἐμοὶ . . τουτί.** This serves to date the speech; he says, 'this is the twentieth year since the restoration,' *i.e.* since the re-establishment of the Democracy after the rule of the Thirty Tyrants; that is, the year B.C. 384-3. He himself is now thirty-three, and therefore was thirteen in the year of anarchy.

23. **οὔτε τί ἐστιν . . ἠπιστάμην** 'could neither have any understanding of what constitutes an oligarchy.'

24. **ἐκείνῳ** *i.e.* my father. For **ἂν** W. gives *αὖ*.

25. **καὶ μὲν δὴ** 'Moreover, I could have had no good reason to plot his death as far as money went.' **καὶ μὲν δὴ** introduces a new point in his argument, as often in Lysias, cp. l. 191. He proceeds to show that he was a loser and not a gainer by his father's death, owing to his elder brother's rapacity.

30. **προσῆκέ μοι** 'it was for my interest.' W. *προσήκειν*.

32. **σχεδὸν ἐπίστασθε** 'you know well enough:' so we use 'pretty well' almost ironically for 'quite well.'

35. **πρὸς ὑμᾶς** 'before you.'

36. **πρὸς τὸν διαιτητήν** 'before the arbitrator.' (Müll. *τῷ διαιτητῇ*.) The case had been tried before one of the forty official arbitrators [four annually elected by lot from each tribe]. Against their decisions there was always an appeal; and before the time of Demosthenes all civil suits were heard first before one of them, that, if possible, an appeal to a higher court might be saved. It seems uncertain when this ceased to be the invariable practice; it had evidently been followed in this case.

37. **τῶν ἀπορρήτων** 'one of the forbidden words,' *i.e.* one of the words for which a man might be prosecuted for libel if he applied it to another.

39. **οὐκ ἀπαγορεύειν** 'does not forbid.' 'The infinitive in *indirect discourse* regularly has *οὐ*, not *μή*, to retain the negative of the *direct discourse*; but some exceptions occur.'—Goodwin, § 283, 3. Cf. Madv. § 205.

οὐκ ἐᾶν 'prohibits;' the negative, as in *οὔ φημι* 'nego,' is inseparable from this verb in this sense.

41-42. **ὀνομάτων** 'words.' Not the letters, but the spirit.

τῆς . . διανοίας 'their meaning.'

διαφέρεσθαι 'curare,' 'to care about,' 'take into account.'

Dem. Phil. i. p. 112: *φάσκειν δ' εἰρήνην ἄγειν ὥσπερ ἐκεῖνος οὐ διαφέρομαι = οὐ μοι διαφέρει.*

46. **περὶ ἑνὸς**, sc. *ὀνόματος*. 'When he mentioned one term (for the act) his meaning embraced all.' He clearly showed his intention as to any other term that might be used.

48. **δήπου** 'I presume,' introducing what seems to the speaker an absurd case. Note: the negative stands first in such sentences in Greek, for it is the emphatic word, but in English we must put it more closely with the verb. 'For I presume you would not have held a man guilty who called you a father-beater, and yet have looked on him as innocent if he had said that you "struck" your father.' Or, 'I presume you would no more have held a man innocent of slander who said that you "struck" your parent, than if he had said that you were a "parent-beater."'

If **οὐ** is taken with the first clause, **δέ** must be translated 'and yet.'

53. **περὶ τοῦτο γὰρ** *i.e.* on the subject of throwing away a shield; of which Theomnestus had been accused, and acquitted: hence *καὶ ποιεῖν καὶ λέγειν.*

56. **φάσκῃ** 'assert.' There seems often an idea of insincerity or malice attached to this word.

ὑπόδικον 'liable to be prosecuted.'

57. **οὐκ** 'nonne.' **ἀλλ' ἐξήρκει . . ἀποβεβληκέναι** 'but in the case of some one saying that you had thrown away your shield, would you have been satisfied with saying, "Oh, it's nothing to me, for 'throwing' and 'flinging' are two different things"?'

60-4. **ἀποδέξαιο.** 'Nor could you admit the charge, if you were one of the eleven, and a person arrested another complaining that his "cloak or shirt had been stripped off;" but on this same principle you would have to let the prisoner off, because he was not specifically called a *λωποδύτης*.'

The Eleven [ten magistrates elected one from each tribe, with a clerk] had twofold functions:

I. Administrative—

(*a*) They had the care of the prison, were responsible for the safe custody of the prisoners, and for their recapture if they escaped.

(*b*) Consequently they had to see that executions were carried out by the public executioner (*δημόκοινος*).

(*c*) They were present at the examination by torture of slaves.

(*d*) They had cognisance of the lists of confiscated property before they were brought into court; and after the court decided were charged with the execution of the decree.

II. Judicial—

(*a*) Criminal cases generally to which the death penalty was attached.

(*b*) Cases of State debtors refusing to pay.

(*c*) Cases of summary arrest (*ἀπαγωγή*).

It is in this last capacity that they are referred to here. They could not, however, inflict the penalty in the cases in which they acted as magistrates, unless the accused confessed; if he did not do so, they had only the power of bringing the case into the regular court (*εἰσαγωγὴ εἰς τὸ δικαστήριον*).

ἀπάγοι 'summarily arrest.' See Wayte, or Dem. Andr. 601. Three ways of proceeding in criminal charges will be useful to observe as covering a large number of cases :—

(1) To summarily arrest a man and bring him before the Eleven [*ἀπαγωγή*]; in this case he must have been taken in the
* act [*ἐπ' αὐτοφώρῳ*, vi. § 85]. This is distinct from an *ἀπαγωγή* following *ἔνδειξις*.

(2) To bring some magistrate to the spot to witness the
* crime [*ἐφήγησις*, ii. § 22].

(3) By calling, if possible, bystanders to witness, and then laying an information [*ἔνδειξις*] before the magistrate [ii. § 20]. This would be followed by an *ἀπαγωγή*, as in vi. § 85.

λωποδύτης 'a stripper of clothes' [**λῶπος δύω** (the feminine **λώπη** is used in Homer for clothes)]. It is used as a general name for a 'robber from the person in the street.'

61. **θοιμάτιον** sc. *τὸ ἱμάτιον* the outer garment, consisting of a square piece of cloth, called also *χλαῖνα*.

χιτωνίσκος a short close-fitting undergarment with sleeves, worn by men, whereas the female garment was called *χιτώνιον*. Sometimes it had only one sleeve, leaving the other arm free; it was then called *ἐξωμίς*, and was specially the dress of slaves. All three might be described by the word *χιτών*. For the two mentioned together, see Dem. Mid. 583: *ὥστε με φοβηθέντα τὸν ὑμέτερον θόρυβον θοιμάτιον προέσθαι καὶ μικροῦ γυμνὸν ἐν τῷ χιτωνίσκῳ γενέσθαι.* See Becker's Charicles, pp. 415 *sq.*

ἀνδραποδιστής [*ἀνδράποδον* slave, factitive termination—*ιζειν*].

64-5. Another instance. The law punishes an **ἀνδραποδιστής**, *i.e.* one who carries off a man into slavery. If he carried off a *boy*, of course he would be equally guilty. For **ἐξαγαγὼν**, see * vi. l. 472.

67. **ὧν ἕνεκα** 'to express which.' The end of speech is not words, but the conveying of ideas.

70. **οὐδ' εἰς Ἄρειον πάγον ἀναβεβηκέναι** 'never to have taken the trouble to go to the Areopagus when the court was sitting.' A curious instance of a peculiarly Greek idea, that it was somewhat disgraceful in a citizen not to be interested in and acquainted with the processes in the law courts, assemblies, * etc. Cp. viii. l. 170; Plutarch Sol. 11, 20. **ῥᾳθυμίας καὶ μαλακίας** 'indifference and unmanliness,' lack of energy.

72. **φόνου** 'murder.' The court of Areopagus had special jurisdiction in cases of homicide.

73. **διωμοσίας** 'the sworn depositions;' properly, 'the cross depositions from either side (*διά*).'

74. **κακῶς ἀκήκοα** 'have been abused,' l. 141.

77. **φάσκοντα** 'to acquit one who pleads that he is a homicide, because the prosecutor swore that "he killed."' See on l. 56.

79. **καὶ αὐτὸς** 'why, you, your very self.'

86. **οὕτω . . λαμβάνειν** 'that you should interpret the laws just as I am now doing.' Cf. Dem. 805, *παρὰ τὴν ὀργὴν ὑμῶν βουλήματα λαβών* 'interpreting your wishes by your moments of anger.'

89. **ὅπως ἂν βούλῃ** 'in whatever sense you please.'

93-5. **ὥστε . . πλεονεκτεῖν** 'that you ought to claim advantages, not in proportion to your services, but in proportion to the injustice you have been able to do without being punished.'

99. **μαθεῖν** 'understand.'

101. **ἀλλὰ νῦν** 'even at this late hour,' even though he has never learnt it before. **ἐπὶ τοῦ βήματος** 'while he is actually on the bema,' though of course he ought to have learnt it before coming to court. *βῆμα* 'suggestus' = (1) the raised dais in the Pnyx in which public speakers stood, called also *ὁ λίθος* [Arist. Pax, 680, or *ἡ πέτρα* Eq. 956]. (2) In a law court there were two furnished with seats, one for the prosecutor, and one for

the defendant; hence Demosthenes (in Olympiod. 1176, 31) says, *σιωπῇ ἐκαθήμην ἐπὶ τοῦ ἑτέρου βήματος*. Aesch. in Ctes. § 207. This also is called *ὁ λίθος*, Ar. Ach. 683.

102. **πράγματα**. See on ii. l. 3.

103. **Σόλωνος**; for the *κύρβεις* on which these laws of Solon were written, see xv. 133, 'The laws written on wooden rollers (*ἄξονες*) and triangular tablets (*κύρβεις*) preserved in the Prytaneion, were known as the laws of Solon,' R. C. J. These were written *βουστροφηδὸν*, *i.e.* the lines continued from left to right, and from right to left.

104. **δέδεσθαι**, infinitive as imperative. **ποδοκάκκῃ** 'stocks.' Suidas gives two derivations of the word—(1) *πούς . . κακῶσις* (2) *πούς . . κατοχή*. Hesychius notices both forms, *ποδοκάκη* and *ποδοκάκκη*. See Harpocr. The law from which this is an extract is given in Demosth. Tim. 733, 105. The wooden stocks (*τὸ ξύλον*) had a hole for the neck and hands and feet. Aristoph. Lys. 680, *ἀλλὰ τούτων χρῆν ἁπασῶν ἐς τετρημμένον ξύλον Ἐγκαθαρμόσαι λαβόντας τουτονὶ τὸν αὐχένα*. See also Equit. 367.

105. **προστιμήσῃ** have awarded it *in addition*, *i.e.* to a fine.

109. **ἐν ταῖς . . ἕνδεκα** 'when the eleven were undergoing their audit.' See on iii. l. 69.

113. **ἐπεγγυᾶν** 'let him give security.' This quotation must consist of two separate phrases, quoted for the sake merely of the obsolete word in each. **ἐπιορκήσαντα**, which in Lysias's day would mean 'having sworn falsely,' is here used for the simple *ὀμόσαντα* 'having sworn by.' *δρασκάζειν* is used for the common *ἀποδιδράσκειν*. [Hesychius explains it by *κρύπτεσθαι ἀποδιδράσκειν*; the former word indicating some confusion between *δρασκάζειν* and *δασκάζειν* (?), or arising from some notion of secrecy in *δρασκάζειν* 'to effect one's escape like a runaway slave.' Cf. *φάσκω*.]

117. **ἀπίλλει** 'excludes by (shutting) the door' ['*ἀπίλλω*, better *ἀπείλλω* from root *Fελ*, whence *εἴλω εἰλέω ἅλ-υ-σι-ς*, a chain—*ἀλ-έ-σκ-ομαι*, etc. Curt. Gr. Et., § 656.' R. C. Jebb]. This fragment again is quoted without its context merely for the sake of the obsolete word *ἀπίλλειν*. It seems to be referring to the crime of 'aiding and abetting' a thief. 'Whoever shuts to the door when a thief is inside,' *i.e.* to protect him by keeping off help from without. Cf. *ἢν δ' ἀποκλείῃ τῇ θύρᾳ*, Arist. Eccl. 420.

121. **ἐπανάγνωθι** W. *ἔτι δ' ἀνάγνωθι*. **στάσιμον** 'may be put out to interest.' [Hesych. explains *στασάμενον* by *δανεισάμενον*.]

And. de Red. § 11, ὅσον γε μοὶ κατέστησαν, quanti mihi steterunt, 'cost.' For στάσιμον 'weighable,' see L. and Sc.

126-32. ὅσαι . . θεράποντος. These fragments of laws seem to refer to assaults on women and slaves; see Plut. *Sol.* 23. '[Except] those females who walk about openly,' *i.e.* for prostitution. 'Let a man be accountable for damage done to a domestic or female slave.' The εἶναι seems to be unaccountable without the context. Of the obsolete words πεφασμένως is from the perf. part. of φαίνω, of which we have πέφανται, Æsch. Ag. 374; πέφασμαι, Soph. O. C. 1543, etc. And the participle πεφασμένος in Solon's Poems, xiii. 71: see Veitch. πολοῦνται, survived in poetical language, Æsch. P. V. 645, as also the active πολέω, Eur. Alc. 291. In prose the compound περιπολέω was still in use, and is found in Plato, Xenophon, etc., and περίπολος a patrol, in Thucydides, etc. οἰκῆος (οἰκεύς) equivalent to οἰκέτου, is often found in Homer, and οἰκεὺς once in Sophocles (O. T. 756).

133-5. σιδηροῦς 'stupid.' Rare, in an intellectual sense; in Aesch. in Ctes. 166 it means 'cold,' 'unimpassioned.' In Plut. Cic. 26 'hard-hearted.' νῦν τε καὶ πάλαι 'perpetual' or 'common to antiquity and to ourselves.'

138. τοῦ βήματος 'the platform of the defendant.' See on l. 101.

141. ἀκοῦσαί τινα 'that one should be said,' l. 74.

143. γοῦν 'at least.' γοῦν introduces a reason for thinking that what has been said is true, or at least reasonable.

144. τοιαύτην γνώμην ἔχειν 'to have such an idea current about me.' γνώμη here stands for the opinion, not of the speaker, but that held about him, his 'reputation.' Cf. the use of *opinio*.

146. τῆς συμφορᾶς, the consequences of a conviction, *i.e.* ἀτιμία. [Cf. Demosth. Mid. 533: οὗτος ἀστρατείας ἑάλω καὶ κέχρηται συμφορᾷ. The Latin *calamitas* is used in the same sense]; whereas if the speaker could be shown to deserve the imputation of parricide the penalty would be death.

147. ἀλλὰ . . ἠτίμωσεν 'nay, he even secured the disfranchisement of the man who gave evidence against him,' *i.e.* for perjury.

148. ἐκεῖνο, *i.e.* the throwing away of his shield.

152-3. οὐδενὸς . . ἁλώσεται 'whereas his penalty, if convicted of slander, would be not at all equal to his deserts.'

154. **τίνος . . ἐγκλήματος** 'what charge have you against me that should prevent it?' For constr. and meaning see viii. l. 78. But Francken would read *πρὸς ὑμῶν*, I think unnecessarily.

155. **πότερον—ἀκήκοα** 'can it be because I have deserved the imputation?'

156. **βελτίων καὶ ἐκ βελτιόνων** 'a better man and of better extraction.' Dem. de Cor. § 10. For the importance attached to family, see vi. § 64, and cf. Arist. Eq. 185; Ran. 727 *sq.* The opposite would be *πονηρὸς καὶ ἐκ πονηρῶν*.

159. **ἀλλ' . . κατεσκέδασται** 'well, this is not the story which has been spread broadcast through the city.' There is a notion of hostility in the word,—'against him or me,' cf. Plat. Apol. 18 C, *οἱ ταύτην τὴν φήμην κατεσκεδάσαντες*.

ἐν ᾗ sc. *δωρέᾳ*, but *ἐν ᾧ* 'in which matter' would be much more usual.

163. **Διονύσιον** the witness who had been disfranchised for perjury. **συμφορᾷ** *i.e. ἀτιμίᾳ*. See *supra*, l. 146.

166-171. **εἴημεν . . χρῆσθαι.** The words of Dionysius are given first as indirect speech, and the perfect optative is used; and then, as often in Greek, the very words are given with the verbs in the indicative, *ἀπέθανον . . ἑαλώκασι . . ἦν*. Goodwin, § 242 b. **στρατείαν** cogn. accus., Goodwin, § 158. **κρεῖττον—ἦν αὐτῷ** 'it had been better for him.' For the omission of **ἂν** see Goodwin, § 222, note 1.

172. **τὰ προσήκοντα** sc. *ἀκούειν*, 'as he deserves.'

173. **παρὰ τοὺς νόμους**, joined with *ὑβρ.* and *λέγοντι*, 'using words forbidden by the laws.'

178. **οὔτε τοῖς πολεμίοις κ.τ.λ.** *i.e.* was never taken prisoner.

180. **ὦφλεν εὐθύνην** 'was cast in a suit on his audit,' *i.e.* so conducted every office he held as never to lose a suit brought against him when he stood his examination after it. **εὐθύνη** is here used not for the audit itself, but for a suit in regard to it. *ὀφλεῖν εὐθύνην* as *ὀφλεῖν δίκην*, Andoc. i. § 73. [Li. and Sc. would alter the form *εὐθύνην* to *εὔθυναν* here and in other places.]

181. **ἐν ὀλιγαρχίᾳ** *i.e.* during the reign of the Thirty. **ἀπέθανεν** 'he was put to death,' vi. l. 474.

183. **ἐκείνου** sc. the father. 'As though it were his father and not himself who had been slandered.' He argues that to be said to have been murdered by his son was an insult to the father's memory.

184-186. **ἀνιαρότερον** 'more distressing.' **αἰτίαν** 'reproach,' 'slur on his memory.' **ἀνῄρησθαι**, *ἀναιρέω*, 'to be made away with.'

186-90. **οὐ ἔτι . . δειλία.** He means that his father, having brought home his own arms and trophies taken from the enemy, has dedicated them in temples at Athens, whereas the defendant's shield, having been thrown away, is hung up as a trophy in an enemy's temple. **πρὸς** 'at,' not inside, but either on the walls or near the temple. **ἀνάκειται** 'are dedicated,' 'laid up.' For such a dedication of spoils taken in war, see Thucyd. 3, 114, *τὰ δὲ νῦν ἀνακείμενα σκῦλα ἐν τοῖς Ἀττικοῖς ἱεροῖς.* **σύμφυτος** 'inborn,' 'hereditary.'

192. **τὰς ὄψεις** 'outward appearance.' **νεανίαι** 'gallant.' Cf. Dem. de Cor. § 313, *ἐν τίσιν οὖν σὺ νεανίας καὶ πηνίκα λαμπρός;* hence the verb *νεανιεύεσθαι*, 'to swagger like a youth,' and in later Gk. to 'act with spirit.'

196. **ὀργισθεὶς** 'in a moment of anger.' Obs. the aorist of a momentary effect.

199. **οὐδεμίαν . . δίδωσι** 'makes no allowance for.'

202-3. **οὐ γάρ πω ᾔδειν** 'for I had yet to learn.' 'I did not know then, nor do I think now.' **τοὺς μὲν ἰδόντας** 'those who saw the shield thrown away.'

206. **καταψηφίσασθαι** 'condemn,' 'to give votes *against*.' *κατὰ* in composition with a verb takes a genitive when its sense is *adverse* or *hostile*; when its sense is *completion*, it takes the accusative. The opposite 'to acquit' is *ἀποψηφίζεσθαι*. Each dicast had two *ψῆφοι* given him, one for acquittal, the other for condemnation, distinguished either by colour, or by being pierced; and he put into a voting box whichever he pleased. For various methods of doing this, see Dict. of Ant., Article
* *ψῆφος*, and cf. Orat. vi. § 37.

209. **ὃς μόνος . . πάγῳ.** 'I, who all by myself, as soon as I had come of age, indicted the Thirty (for murder) before the court of the Areopagus.' The time of the *δοκιμασία* of an Athenian youth, about which some doubt and confusion have existed, is clearly stated in the newly-found treatise of Aristotle, Rep. Ath. 42, agreeing substantially with Pollux, 8, 105. When he was eighteen his demesmen formally verified his age, his freedom, and his legal parentage, and entered him on the list [*ἐγγράφειν*]. The Boulê revised this entry [*δοκιμάζει τοὺς ἐγγραφέντας*], demanding proof of the youth's age, and fining the demesmen if it appeared that it was less than the law required. Having passed this *δοκιμασία* the boy became *ἔφηβος* and was a citizen, and could marry. But his citizen rights were still incomplete. He could not sue or be sued except in regard to his inheritance, or that of his mother if an heiress; nor speak or vote in the ecclesia; though it appears he could bring a charge before the

Areopagus, that is, for murder or sacrilege. Two more years had to elapse before he was fully on a footing with the other citizens. This was expressed by the phrase *ἐπὶ διετὲς ἡβᾶν*. During the first year he was under the direction of special officers called *σωφρονισταί* and *ἐπιμεληταὶ* and did military duty in the Peiraeus. He then appeared before the people in the theatre, went through certain military manœuvres, was publicly armed, and did frontier duty as *περίπολος* for a year. At the end of the two years he took the citizen oath in the temple of Agraulos, and was entered on the deme-register of those capable of drawing lots for office [*τὸ ληξιαρχικὸν γραμματεῖον*]. This completed his citizenship, of which he could not be deprived except by a *δίκη ξενίας* or some legal sentence of disfranchisement.

He says 'directly I came of age': we know from § 4 that in 404-3 B.C. he was thirteen; since the *δοκιμασία* is to be taken as in the eighteenth year, this would date his indictment of the Thirty as taking place 399-8; 'of the Thirty only Pheidon and Eratosthenes stayed at Athens; and we may gather from this that Eratosthenes probably escaped the penalty of death when impeached by Lysias in 403.' R. C. Jebb, *Attic. Or.*, i. 296.

213. **τοῖς ὅρκοις οἷς** 'the oaths which you have taken;' *οἷς* is attracted into the case of its antecedent. Goodwin, § 153.

ORATION V. [12].

[This Oration possesses unique historical value, as being an exposition, though from a partisan point of view, of the conduct and policy of the Thirty Tyrants, composed immediately after their expulsion by one who had had personal experience of their rule, and who from his own sufferings would be likely to put every point against them with the most telling force. At the same time we must remember that it was addressed to an audience who also knew accurately the facts of the case, which would be a check on excessive exaggeration or directly false statement.

Athens is taken by Lysander in the spring of B.C. 404 [17th of Munychion (3d April), Plut. Lysand. 15: see Clinton], and the Thirty are soon after established, and retain power till November (Poseideon).

Early in their career they began to feel the want of money, and having exhausted the gains to be made by the death and confiscation of certain notorious characters, they resolve on using a similar severity towards certain rich resident aliens, who were known to be disinclined to the Revolution.

Ten are first selected, including two of small means to elude the imputation of interested motives; and among the first to be attacked were Lysias and his brother Polemarchus, who were carrying on a prosperous trade as armourers. Polemarchus is seized and put to death. But Lysias managed by liberal bribes to secure the connivance of his captors in his flight. He escaped to Megara, and shared in the subsequent return of the popular party, giving them such substantial assistance that he was at once granted citizenship, though this grant was immediately cancelled as illegal, and he subsequently resided in Athens as an Isoteles.

In November-December, 404 B.C., those of the Thirty who were still alive retreated from Athens to Eleusis, with the exception of two, Pheidon and Eratosthenes. Their government was replaced by a board of Ten, of which Pheidon was one.

Thrasybulus establishes himself in Phylè in September, and afterwards in the Peiraeus, in November-December (Poseideon), B.C. 404, and in the early months of the following year, B.C. 403, carried on war against the Ten who succeeded the Thirty.

This eventually resulted in the victory of the popular party, the deposition of the Ten, and the return of the fugitives to Athens, about June B.C. 403; and by August of that year the old constitution was completely restored. Almost immediately after this Lysias impeached Eratosthenes, as the member of the Thirty who had arrested him, for the murder of Polemarchus, and for his general conduct as one of the Thirty;—probably on his giving an account of his office (εὔθυναι), and before the expedition which took place later in the year to drive the Thirty from Eleusis, § 80. [See Professor Jebb, *Attic Orat.*, vol. i. pp. 261-4.] If this supposition be right, the trial would be before an ordinary Heliastic Court.

This account of the Thirty should be compared with that of Xenophon [Hell. ii. 3-4]. See also Appendix, 'The Thirty.'

Lysias was able to impeach Eratosthenes, because the members of the Thirty, the Ten, and the Eleven, who served the Thirty, were expressly exempted from the amnesty (Hell. 2, 4, 38); unless they would submit to a scrutiny (Andoc. i. § 90). See on iv. l. 209. But whether the speech was ever delivered seems uncertain. Very soon after the full citizenship was conferred on Lysias the decree was reversed on the γραφὴ παρανόμων brought in by Archinus against Thrasybulus, and Lysias may have had no opportunity of delivering it, and at any rate he failed to convict.]

4. **μήτ' ἂν ψευδόμενον . . . κατηγορῆσαι** 'not even if he took to lying could a man make his accusations worse than the facts.'

7. **ἀπειπεῖν** 'to give in,' 'to be tired.' **τὸν χρόνον.** The reference seems general, not to any particular time allowed for his speech.

9. **πρὸ τοῦ** 'before this.' Goodwin, § 143, 2.

15. **οἰκείας** 'personal,' because the accused had been the cause of the death of his brother.

16. **ἀφθονίας . . ὀργίζεσθαι** 'infinite motives for anger.'

18. **οὔτ' ἐμαυτοῦ πώποτε . . κατηγορεῖν.** This speech of Lysias (B.C. 403, soon after the final defeat of the oligarchs) was his first. Perhaps the reputation it gained him suggested to him professional speech-writing as a means of repairing the losses he had suffered under the Thirty.

22-25. **μὴ . . ποιήσωμαι,** for subj. after the historic tense *κατέστην* see Goodwin, § 216, 2. **δι' ἐλαχίστων** 'in the fewest words possible.'

27. **ἐπείσθη ὑπὸ Περικλέους.** He was persuaded by Pericles to come to Athens from Syracuse. See Life, § 1.

29. **δίκην οὔτε . . ἐφύγομεν** 'we were never prosecutors or defendants on any private suit whatever.'

33-5. **συκοφάνται** v. l. 149. **φάσκοντες** 'pretending,' iv. l. 56. *μὲν . . δὲ* after *πονηροί* and *φάσκοντες* are omitted by W. and R. I do not think emendation is required, though Cobet proposes *καίτοι ταῦτα* for *τοιαῦτα*, the MSS. having *καὶ τοιαῦτα.* 'But when the Thirty had come to power,—being unprincipled and vexatious, while pretending that their object was to clear the city of bad men,—though they used arguments of this kind, the actions they ventured upon were quite in a different spirit.'

40-1. **Θέογνις—καὶ Πείσων.** These two names are in the list of the Thirty given by Xenophon (Hell. 2, 3, 2). We do not hear of them again. The proposal here attributed to them was, that each of the Thirty should select one Metic for confiscation. This detail,—the selection first of ten, among whom were to be two poor men to avoid the scandal of interested motives,—we owe to Lysias. **τῇ πολιτείᾳ ἀχθόμενοι** 'disaffected to the constitution,' *i.e.* to the government of the Thirty.

43-4. **τῷ δ' ἔργῳ** 'but in reality,' answering to *δοκεῖν*, [equivalent to the usual opposite of *ἔργῳ*, *i.e.* *λόγῳ*] 'an excellent pretext for *pretending* to punish, but in reality for making money.' For **δοκεῖν** = 'pretend,' cf. Arist. Ran. 564 ; Nub. 1174 ; Eur. Med. 79. **τὴν—ἀρχὴν** 'the government.'

47. **περὶ οὐδενὸς ἡγοῦντο** 'they made no scruple,' 'they cared nothing at all.'

48. **ἔδοξεν . . δέκα.** Xenophon [Hell. 2, 3, 21] says that the Thirty agreed to take one each. But the number seems too large to have been at once arrested. And probably Lysias, giving more full details, is right in saying that they began with ten. Bremi supposes the number to have been reduced in deference to the vehement remonstrances of Theramenes. Others would alter *δέκα* to *τριάκοντα*, but see on l. 76.

50. **πρὸς τοὺς ἄλλους** 'in the case of the others,' *i.e.* the rich ones.

52-3. **ὥσπερ τι . . πεποιηκότες** 'as they might have defended themselves (ἀπελογήσαντο ἄν) if they had carried out any other reasonable measure.' **εὐλόγως** in a good sense opposed to εὐπρεπῶς. **διαλαβόντες** 'having distributed the houses to be visited between them.' For **ἐβάδιζον** cp. Dem. de Cor. § 132.

56. **εἰς τὸ ἐργαστήριον** 'to the workshop.' Lysias had in partnership with his brother a manufactory of arms (§ 19). His stock does not seem to have been all within reach of the tyrants, as we find him afterwards supplying the Demus with 200 shields. *Vide* Life, § 8.

ἀνδράποδα . . ἀπεγράφοντο 'began having a list of the slaves made,' *i.e.* by their clerk. This is the force of the middle, the clerk ἀπέγραψε. See Herod. 7, 100. For the employment of slaves in manufactories, see Dem. Aph. 816, where he says that his father had two workshops, one of the same kind as this of Lysias, where he had thirty-two or thirty-three slaves, and one upholsterer's workshop, where he had twenty slaves at work. See Becker's *Charicles*, p. 303.

59. **ἔφασκεν** 'said yes.'

62. **νομίζει** 'believed in.' 'I knew that he regarded nothing human or divine, but believed neither in gods nor men,' *i.e.* that from fear neither of gods nor men would he feel bound by an oath. νομίζει would properly apply only to θεούς. Cf. Arist. Nub. 818, etc. The expression is almost proverbial, and made more forcible by the zeugma. It is put more fully in regard to the unjust judge (S. Luke xviii. 2), τὸν θεὸν μὴ φοβούμενος καὶ ἄνθρωπον μὴ ἐντρεπόμενος.

67. **τὴν κιβωτὸν** 'my money chest,' *arca* ('*posita nunc luditur arca*'). It seems generally used for 'desk' or 'box' for documents.' Ar. Eq. 1000. To which meaning there is also a reference in Vesp. 1056. Demosthenes uses the diminutive form κιβώτιον (788 *fin.*) It was of wood, Arist. Pl. 710-11. **δωμάτιον** *cubiculum*.

72. **κυζικηνοὺς . . δαρεικοὺς**. The Kyzikene *Stater* was a gold coin equivalent to 28 Attic drachmæ. Boeckh, p. 23; Dem. 914. See Append. III. The *Daric*, a Persian gold coin circulating in Greece, as equivalent to 20 drachmæ. Boeckh, p. 21.

φιάλας *pateræ*, 'flat cups,' used especially for libations.

76. **Μηλόβιός τε καὶ Μνησιθείδης** two of the Thirty. There therefore appear to have been three in each party, which would account for the number ten mentioned by Lysias as that selected for the first raid on the Metics. *Supra*, l. 48.

82. **εἰς Δαμνίππου** 'to the house of Damnippus,' as above *εἰς τοῦ ἀδελφοῦ τοῦ ἐμοῦ.* Damnippus was apparently trusted by the Thirty, but we know nothing more of him.

85. **ἑτέρους** another party of Metics, who had been arrested.

87. **ὡς . . ἤδη** 'for in any case I should have to die.' **ὑπάρχοντος** 'there was death for me to start with whatever I did.'

92. **τὴν σεαυτοῦ δύναμιν** 'everything in your power,' 'all the assistance you can give.' Here the singular *δύναμις* = *δυνάμεις* '*opes.*'

98. **ἀμφίθυρος** *i.e.* with a back door as well as a front door.

104. **ἔφευγον**, notice tense, 'I attempted to escape.'

104-6. **αὐλείῳ θύρᾳ . . τριῶν δὲ θυρῶν.** The arrangement most common in a Greek house of any size was an entrance from the street by the *αὔλειος θύρα* into a court (*αὐλή*), round which the various rooms were arranged, the whole forming the part of the house reserved for men (*ἀνδρωνῖτις*). This was separated by a door (*θύρα μέσαυλος*) from another court, which, with its surrounding rooms, was reserved for the women (*γυναικονῖτις*). Some houses would have only one entrance, while others, if their position allowed it, would have another called the *κηπαία θύρα*, because it would often open into a garden. Here Lysias has to pass (1) the *μέσαυλος θύρα*, (2) the *κηπαία θύρα* ; but what is the third? Becker suggests a door from the garden into the street. It may possibly be that the passage leading from the *ἀνδρωνῖτις* to the *γυναικονῖτις* had two doors, one at each end. See Becker's *Charicles*, pp. 251 to 271.

107. **εἰς Ἀρχένεω** 'to the house of Archeneos the ship captain.' *Ἀρχένεως-ω-ῳ.*

111. **διέπλευσα** '*effected* a passage to Megara.' Obs. the aorist compared with the imperf. in l. 104.

112-113. **παρήγγειλαν . . παράγγελμα** 'gave their usual order.' A word of military origin, from passing the word *along* the ranks, l. 311. The Thirty had the right of putting any to death who were not in the *κατάλογος* of the Three Thousand. See Appendix, 'The Thirty.'

118. **ἐξενεχθῆναι** 'to be carried out for burial.' *efferri.* **κλεισίον** a small mean hut or bedroom. In Demosth. Mid. 270 it means a brothel. Some write *κλισίον* root *κλι*, *κλι-ν-ω*, *κλί-νη*, etc. See

Curtius, 150. It seems rather connected with κλει-, κλεί-ω, κλεί-ς. See Meisterh. *Gramm. Att. Insch.* pp. 28, 40.

129. **εἰς τὸ δημόσιον** 'to the treasury,' which would either use them as δημόσιοι 'public slaves' or sell them. For the word see i. l. 33.

132. **ἑλικτῆρας** 'earrings of twisted gold.' Rt. Ϝελ expanded to ἑλικ (ἕλιξ, ἑλίσσω). Curtius, 361. They are enumerated among the ornaments of women in a fragment of Aristophanes, 309. Hesychius has ἑλικτῆρες ἐνώτια.

140. **χορηγίας . . εἰσφορὰς** for χορηγία, the expenses of equipping a chorus, see Dict. of Ant. The εἰσφορὰ was an extraordinary property tax, levied generally in war-time. We hear of it for the first time during the siege of Mytilene B.C. 428. See Thucyd. 3, 19. Boeckh. p. 471. Lysias and his brother, as Metics, would, unless specially exempt, pay their εἰσφορὰ like the rest; but the χορηγία of a Metic (though not of an Isoteles) was, it appears, confined to the Lenean festival; the Scholiast on Arist. Plut. 954 (quoted by Boeckh), says that consequently others than citizens were then only allowed to take part in the choruses.

142. **πᾶν τὸ προσταττόμενον** 'all the legal obligations of a Metic.' See i. l. 9.

144. **λυσαμένους** 'though we had ransomed.' λύειν 'to release on ransom,' λύεσθαι 'to obtain the release of a man by paying the ransom.'

145. **οὐχ . . ἐπολιτεύοντο** 'though our conduct, Metics as we were, was so much superior to theirs, though they were citizens.' **οὐχ ὁμοίως** 'better,' an instance of a phrase arising from a desire to avoid overstatement, called by grammarians *litotes* or *miosis*.

146. **πολλοὺς . . ἐξήλασαν** *i.e.* by their tyranny they drove many good men to take refuge with the enemies of Athens, and so became hostile to their own city. This is what Theramenes urges also in his speech in the defence against Critias, Xen. Hell. 2, 3, 42-3.

149. **ἀτίμους τῆς πόλεως** 'deprived of their citizenship.' The genitive of the part following verbs of sharing, etc., because ἀτίμους εἶναι = στερηθῆναι. Goodwin, § 170, 2. This ἀτιμία does not include confiscation of property. [τῆς πόλεως is omitted in Rauch. 9th ed. Weidner reads τῇ πόλει.]

153. **εἰργασμένοι εἰσίν.** Indirect quotations after **ὅτι** and **ὡς**—(1) *after primary tense the verb retains mood and tense of direct discourse*; (2) after secondary tenses the verb either is changed to same tense of opt. or retains its original mood or tense. Goodwin, § 242. Here in direct speech the verb would have been *οὐδὲν εἰργάσμεθα.*

154. **ἐβουλόμην ἄν** 'I could have wished'; implying that it is vain to wish it now. *Infra*, 600.

156. **οὔτε αὐτοῖς τοιαῦτα ὑπάρχει** 'neither have they any such conduct to plead.'

161. **ἐξυπηρετῶν** 'gratifying to the full.' Like the Latin *obsequens.*

164-7. **καὶ πρὸς . . αὐτὸν τοῦτον** 'if with him himself, wretch as he is.' **διαλέγεσθαι** 'to hold a conversation.' **ἐπὶ—τῇ—ὠφελείᾳ . . βλάβῃ** 'for his good,' 'for his hurt.' *ἐπί* with dative showing the attending circumstances of an action, l. 327. **ὅσιον καὶ εὐσεβές.** The former refers to the avoidance of contamination of the person, the latter to his duty to the gods: 'consistent with self-respect and piety.'

167. **ἀνάβηθι** 'mount up on the *βῆμα*,' *i.e.* the tribune or platform of the prosecutor. See iv. l. 101. The evidence was taken at a preliminary trial (*ἀνάκρισις*), and was read over to the witness in court, who was required to signify his assent by bowing his head or speaking. Thus Lysias may in writing his speech introduce this examination as though it actually took place in court. Cf. a similar examination in xi. § 5.

173-7. **ἵνα μὴ ἀποθάνωμεν . . σώσειας . . ἀποκτείναις.** Goodwin, § 216, 2. [Weidn. Rauch. omit *μή*.]

180. **ἐπὶ σοὶ μόνῳ ἐγένετο** 'it depended entirely on you.'

186-7. **καὶ μὴν** 'nay more.' **εἴπερ** 'admitting that.' **ὡς αὐτῷ προσετάχθη** is the object of *πιστεύειν* in apposition to *τοῦτο*, 'the fact that he was ordered to do so.'

188-9. **οὐ γὰρ . . ἐλάμβανον** 'for he will not say, I presume, that in the matter of the *Metics* they took security of him.' **οὐ—δήπου**, like *nisi forte*, introduces an absurd or impossible supposition. Dem. de Cor. § 13. **ἐπεί τοι τῷ** 'for who, pray, was less likely to have been so charged than one who.' **τοι** introduces what the speaker thinks a self-evident truth. [Weidn. Rauch. *ἔπειτα* for *ἐπεί τοι.*] *ὅστις*=*qui* with subj.

191. **ἀποδεδειγμένος** pass. part. with middle sense. **γνώμην** *i.e.* his opinion *against* the murders; the sense is quite clear without the addition of *ἐναντίαν* which some editors have made.

192. **ταῦτα** cognate accusative sc. *ταῦτα τὰ ὑπηρετήματα.* **οἷς** attracted to the case of the antecedent understood after *ἀντειπόντα.* Goodwin, § 153, 1. The attraction rarely occurs except into genitive and dative. *Ib.* Note 2.

198. **ἀποδέχεσθαι** 'to accept the excuse.'

201. **ἴσως ἂν . . εἴχετε** 'perhaps you might now pardon him with some reason.'

* 202. **νῦν δέ.** Orat. i. l. 3. **παρὰ τοῦ ποτε καὶ** 'from whom in the world *are* you to exact punishment at all?'

204. **καὶ μὲν δή** 'now again,' introduces a new point, the *μέν* is an emphatic particle, cf. l. 240. 'Again, whereas his crime is that he arrested my brother, not in his house but in the street (where he might have let him escape without breaking their orders), *you* are angry even with those who entered your houses in search of any one of you or yours.' The point is that it was much more difficult for an emissary of the Thirty to connive at an escape of a victim if actually found in his house, and yet such agents incurred the popular wrath; whereas Eratosthenes found Polemarchus in the street, and might have let him go without direct breach of orders, and yet did not do
* so. **παρὸν** acc. neut. absol. See ii. l. 98.

211-13. **ἐκείνοις,** *i.e.* those who found their victims at home, and could not therefore easily connive at their escape. **καταλαβοῦσιν ἐξάρνοις γενέσθαι** 'to deny having found them though they had caught them.'

214. **ἔπειτα κ.τ.λ.** 'or at any rate that he did not see him.'

215. **οὔτ' . . εἶχεν** 'did not involve or admit of refutation or examination by torture.'

218. **εἴπερ** 'if as you say.'

223. **τούσδε** 'these judges here in court.'

224. **ἃ ἴσασι . . λαμβάνοντας** 'using the facts which they know to have actually happened as sure proofs of what was then said,' *i.e.* by you when you pretend that you spoke against this murder. No witnesses can be brought forward, for the debate was a secret one among the Thirty.

227-8. **παρεῖναι** sc. in the senate house when the Thirty were debating. **παρ' αὐτοῖς εἶναι** 'to be at home,' *apud nos esse*, so *παρ' ἐμοί, παρ' ὑμῖν*, etc. **αὐτοῖς** = *ἡμῖν αὐτοῖς*.

233. **ὁπότε** 'seeing that,' see on ll. 285 and 619. **φάσκων** see on iv. l. 56, 'what would you have done if you had spoken *against* the victims, seeing that when you allege that you spoke *for* them you killed Polemarchus?'

234-5. **τί ἂν** sc. *ἐποιήσατε*, which is equivalent to *κατεψηφίσασθε ἢ ἀπεψηφίσασθε*, and therefore the **ἂν** really belongs to *ἀπεψηφίσασθε* 'what would you judices have done if you had been Polemarchus' sons or brothers?' **ἀπεψηφίσασθε** 'would you have voted for his acquittal.'

238-9. **ὡμολόγηκεν**, *i.e.* by alleging that he spoke against it. See l. 175. **τὴν διαψήφισιν** 'the decision,' *i.e.* by a division of votes on the preliminary question as to his guilt or innocence. **καὶ μὴν δὴ** see on l. 204.

246. **τὸ ἴσον ὑμῖν ἕξουσιν** 'will be no worse off than you are,' *i.e.* will enjoy equal rights with you. See l. 647.

248. **ἐκκηρύττουσιν** 'banish by proclamation.' The subject of the verb is the government of the various towns in which the Thirty had taken refuge. The Thirty and their agents, the Eleven, were expressly excepted from the amnesty. Xen. Hell. 2, 4, 38.

250. **ἦ που** 'of course they will consider that they are giving themselves superfluous trouble in avenging you' (the actual sufferers).

252-256. Referring of course to the condemnation of the generals after the battle of Arginusæ, B.C. 406. For the hasty and illegal condemnation of these generals, see Xen. Hell. 1, 8, 1-38; and also the rapid repentance of the people, *ib.* 39-40.

256. **τούτους δέ** sc. *οὐκ ἄρα χρὴ κολάζεσθαι*; but by what is called a *rhetorical anacoluthon* the subject of *χρὴ κολάζεσθαι* is repeated—*αὐτοὺς καὶ τοὺς παῖδας*.

266. **τῷ φεύγοντι** 'by the defendant': dat. of the agent, used especially with perf. and pluperf. tenses of passive verbs. Goodwin, § 188, 3. See Wayte on Dem. Timor. 759.

* 268-9. **τοιούτων . . οἱ.** See on ii. l. 270.

271. **αὐτῷ προσήκει** 'is it open to him.'

274. **ἐξαπατῶσιν**, irregularly put for *ἐξαπατᾶν*, which we should

expect to answer to *μηδὲ ἀπολογεῖσθαι*. The speaker having a somewhat extended description to give, insensibly adopts the indicative as the proper mood for a narrative. Markland wished to read *ἐξαπατῆσαι*.

278. **ἐπεὶ** explains *οὐδὲ τοῦτο . . προσήκει*, 'it is not open to him to advance this plea, for just bid him state,' etc.

280. **αὐτοι**, *i.e.* the Thirty and their party.

281-2. **ἢ πόλιν ἥν τινα τοιαύτην . . κατεδουλώσαντο** 'or what city they ever gained of such magnitude as yours which they enslaved.'

282. **ἀλλὰ γάρ** 'but did they, in point of fact?' *denique*, introducing a clinching question. W. and Fuhr. om. sign of interrog.

285. **οἵτινες** 'seeing that they actually,' etc. 'men that actually,' etc. *Qui dejicerent.*

288. **περιεῖλον** 'dismantled,' *i.e.* took down the walls round the Peiraeus ; one of the conditions enforced by Lysander. He here attributes it to the action of the Thirty, though they were not officially appointed until afterwards ; but it was their party who made the terms with Lysander, and he insinuates that it was not from obedience to the orders of Lysander that they carried out the work, but for their own party ends.

295. **ἐπὶ τῶν τετρακοσίων** 'at the time of the four hundred,' B.C. 411. During the years 412-411 (immediately after the Sicilian disaster) the Athenians were making a gallant struggle to retain their supremacy over the Islands, everywhere instigated by Alcibiades to revolt. The only one which remained faithful to them was Samos, in which the democratical party succeeded in ousting the oligarchical party ; and there the Athenians had for a time a secure base of operations. Meanwhile, Alcibiades, wishing to return to Athens, professed to have persuaded Tissaphernes to offer the Athenian generals at Samos an alliance and assistance against Sparta, if only an oligarchical form of government were set up in Athens. The army was opposed to this, but some of the generals accepted the proposal, and Pisander was sent to Athens to propose it. The oligarchical clubs were worked by Pisander, Theramenes, and Phrynichus (Thucyd. viii. 54, 3) ; and the change to a government of 400, with a select ecclesia of 5000 (Thucyd. viii. 67, 3), was voted. The 400, however, tried for some time to carry on the government without the existence of the 5000. The revolution was frustrated by several circumstances :—(1) The Persians, by making a new treaty with

Sparta, showed that the professions of Alcibiades were false. Thucyd. viii. 57, 9, cf. 88. (2) The army at Samos, led by Thrasybulus and Thrasyllus, declared for the democracy. (Thucyd. viii. 75-6.) (3) Dissensions arose in the 400 themselves, the philosophical Theramenes insisting on the 5000 being really called into existence. (Thucyd. viii. 89.) (4) The Spartans delayed helping the oligarchs. (Thucyd. viii. 90-1.) (5) The Spartans freed Euboea, thus thoroughly alarming the people, who turned upon the pro-Spartan or oligarchical party. Phrynichus was assassinated, and Antiphon and Archiptolemus impeached and executed. (Thucyd. viii. 90-8). The only part of the revolutionary programme left was, that the franchise was nominally confined to the 5000 (though this was not kept to in practice), and that certain official pay was discontinued.

At the first flush, however, all those who sympathised with the oligarchical movement would be anxious to be at Athens to take part in it, and Lysias charges Eratosthenes with having actually deserted his post in order to be at Athens and share in the revolution. IATROCLES is not known from any other source.

300-1. **τἀναντία . . ἔπραττε** 'he was engaged in intrigues against the democratical party.'

302. **τὸν . . μεταξὺ βίον,** *i.e.* his life between 411 B.C. and 405 B.C., in which year the battle of Ægospotami, **ἡ ναυμαχία,** took place.

305. **πέντε ἄνδρες ἔφοροι.** This committee of five, appointed by the oligarchical clubs, was the first step towards the revolution of the Thirty. (See Appendix 'The Thirty'). They called them 'Ephors,' probably in compliment to the Spartans. **ὑπὸ τῶν καλουμένων ἑταίρων** 'by those who were styled their clubsmen.' The influence of the party clubs is noticed by Thucydides (3, 82, 11) as one of the effects of the bitter party spirit generated by the Peloponnesian war; originally, however, though formed for party purposes (*ἐπὶ δίκαις καὶ ἀρχαῖς*, 8, 51, 4), they were within the lines of the constitution.

308. **ὧν . . ἦσαν** we do not know the names of the other three. Probably Theramenes was one.

309. **οὗτοι δὲ φυλάρχους . . φυλακάς** 'and these appointed phylarchs over the city pickets.' *φυλακή* for *φύλακες*. It seems that the ephors got their own partisans appointed phylarchs (ordinarily ten, in command of the tribal cavalry) and gave them the superintendence of the posts of the city guard, usually performed by officers called *φρούραρχοι* (Xen. Œcon. 9, 15), to keep in their own hands the control of the egress and ingress through

the city gates. I do not therefore accept the emendation adopted by a large number of scholars from Taylor to Weidner of *φυλάς* for *φυλακάς*.

311-12. **παρήγγελλον** 'always passed the word.' See on l. 112, *i.e.* they sent orders by their clubsmen to see that the votes of the ecclesia were such as they required (the ecclesia being still nominally supreme). **κύριοι ἦσαν** 'they (these 'Ephors') had unlimited powers.'

314. **ἐπεβουλεύεσθε** 'you were having plots laid against you'

315-6. **ψηφιεῖσθε . . ἔσεσθε.** For these tenses, see Goodwin, § 217. **πολλῶν . . ἐνδεεῖς,** *i.e.* of provisions. For the distress of Athens at this time, see Xen. Hell. 2, 2, 11, *ἐπεὶ παντελῶς ἤδη ὁ σῖτος ἐπιλελοίπει, κ.τ.λ.*

316-8. **ὅτι . . ἔσονται . . συνήσονται.** For the tenses, see Goodwin, § 243. The original mood and tense is retained, for they would have said, *ἐσόμεθα—συνησόμεθα.*

321-4. **τῶν ἐφόρων** 'one of the Ephors,' see l. 305. **τοὺς . . ἀκούσαντας** 'those who heard it from Eratosthenes himself.' He could not bring as witnesses those actually engaged with him, because they were all either banished or killed, or were prevented by their oaths from coming forward.

324. **ἐσωφρόνουν** 'were in a right frame of mind.'

327-8. **οὐκ ἂν ἐπὶ μὲν . . ἐπὶ δὲ τοῖς . .** In English *μὲν* may be left untranslated, and *δὲ* translated by 'while.' **ἐπὶ . . κακοῖς,** cf. l. 164-6.

331. **ἀνάβητε.** Cf. l. 168.

334-6. **ἄλλων δὲ πολλῶν** 'but of many measures of a different character,' *i.e.* bad. **μὴ . . παρανόμως** 'to refuse to hold office at all unconstitutionally.' **ἔπειτα** 'but if he did do so.'

337-8. **εἶεν . . μηνύουσιν.** Note the variation of mood. Some read *εἰσι.* **Βάτραχος καὶ Αἰσχυλίδης** two informers employed by the Thirty, whose names we only learn from Lysias. The former is mentioned in the *κατ' Ἀνδοκίδου*, § 45. (Lysias (?) 6.)

341-7. **καὶ μὲν δή . . ἀποτρέποντες.** His argument is: 'he showed his ill-will to the Demus by his silence; for a hater of the Demus lost nothing by saying nothing, as there were plenty to do the damage; while a lover of the Demus could have had no fairer opportunity of showing his goodwill by speaking in its defence.' **ἐνταῦθα** 'at that crisis,' 'in those circumstances.' **πῶς οὐκ . . ἔδειξαν** 'of course they could have shown.'

349-55. ὅπως . . φανήσεται . . ἐναντιούμενος 'let him, however, take care not to be shown to have opposed the Thirty in open speech.' The pres. *ἐναντιούμενος* is historic. The argument is: if he could safely speak against the wishes of the other members of the Thirty, it is plain that he had great influence, and was not held back from fear at any rate from opposing their tyrannical measures. It was not fear but hatred of his country. **ἀλλὰ μὴ ὑπὲρ Θηραμένους.** We do not hear of Eratosthenes' defence of Theramenes, but we know generally that he was of his party, and was one of the two moderates who afterwards remained in Athens when the rest of the Thirty retired to Eleusis.

359. ὡς . . παραστήσω 'as I will in both points establish by many proofs.' *παραστησω* 'I will bring it before you.' Cf. the use of the intrans. tenses, *infra* l. 429.

361. ταῦτα *i.e.* the confiscations, murders, etc., which the Thirty were carrying out. **ὁπότεροι** 'which of the two parties in the Thirty,' *i.e.* the extreme party, headed by Critias and Charicles; or the moderate party, headed by Theramenes and Pheidon.

364. Θρασυβούλου. See Appendix, 'The Thirty.' Thrasybulus seized Phylè in September and held it through the winter of B.C. 404, as is evident from the storm of snow mentioned both by Xenophon (Hell. 2, 4, 3) and Diodorus (14, 32). PHYLÈ was a strong post commanding the pass over Mt. Parnes, by which the road from Thebes to Athens lay, and was 100 stades (about 12 miles) from Athens. Thrasybulus had before shown his devotion to the democracy, see note on l. 295.

367-70. ἐλθὼν . . κατεψηφίσατο 'he went with his colleagues (the Thirty) to Salamis and Eleusis, and haled to prison three hundred of the citizens, and voted for their death—one vote being passed upon them in a mass.' This took place after Thrasybulus, in Sept. 404, had occupied Phylè. The Thirty determined to secure Eleusis as a place of retreat; and in order to do this, under pretext of taking a list of citizens in Eleusis fit to act as guards, etc., got all suspected of being opposed to them into their hands; and, next day, summoning a meeting of the Hoplites included in the 'Catalogue,' and the Knights in the Odeon, they secured a vote condemning them all to death (Xen. Hell. 2, 4, 8-10). Xenophon only mentions Eleusinians, but Diodorus (14, 32) adds also Salaminians. See Appendix, 'The Thirty.' Lysias is careful to say, **μιᾷ ψήφῳ**; for it was against the law to condemn a number of citizens by one vote of the ecclesia. Each should be subjected to a vote individually, in accordance with the *ψήφισμα Καννώνου*; a constitutional principle violated in the condemnation of the generals after Arginusæ (Xen. 1, 7, 21-37). Hesychius gives the decree thus (s.v. *Καννώνου*) *διειλημμένους τοὺς κρινομένους ἑκατέρωθεν ἀπολογεῖσθαι.* Of Cannonus we know nothing else.

371. **ἐπειδὴ . . ἤλθομεν.** Late in the year 404 Thrasybulus succeeding in entering the Peiræus and occupying the eastern elevation Munychia, the party of the Thirty occupied the Agora of the western town; and after a battle in which Critias and Hippomachus were killed, the party of Thrasybulus occupied the entire Peiræus, and to them flowed in from all sides members of the democratical party from their places of exile, or escaping from the city (*ἄστυ*) itself.

372-3. **διαλλαγῶν** 'there followed attempts at coming to terms.' The remaining members of the Thirty (except Pheidon and Eratosthenes) retired to Eleusis, and Ten were elected to conduct the government. Diodorus (14, 33) says that they were simply elected as ambassadors with full powers to make the peace. They, however, acted much in the spirit of the Thirty. **πρὸς ἀλλήλους ἔσεσθαι** 'that we should behave to each other,'—but some adjective seems wanting.

375. **κρείττους ὄντες** 'having got the upper hand,' *i.e.* in the fight between the party of the City and that of the Peiræus. **αὐτούς** the remains of the army of the City who stayed for a time to try and make terms. Nep. Thrasyb. 2, 6.

376. **οἱ δὲ εἰς τὸ ἄστυ ἐλθόντες** 'but they went to the upper city and expelled.' **ἄστυ** Athens proper is so called, as distinguished from the lower town or Peiræus. Thus the Thirty had immediately after the death of Theramenes forbidden all whom they did not trust to enter *τὸ ἄστυ*, confining them to the Peiræus. Xen. Hell. 2, 4, 1. The meaning of *ἄστυ* as a general term for what we should call 'the capital' is illustrated by Isocr. xvi. § 27, where the speaker says that some called Athens *ἄστυ τῆς Ἑλλάδος* 'the capital of Hellas.'

381-3. **Φείδων . . Ἱπποκλῆς . . Ἐπιχάρης.** These are the only names of the Ten elected after the expulsion of the Thirty which we know. **ὁ Λαμπτρεὺς** 'of the deme Lamptra,' a deme of the tribe Erectheis.

385-7. **ἑταιρείᾳ.** See on l. 305-6. **πολὺ μεῖζον** 'they embittered the party-feeling, and the war waged by the City party against the party of the Peiræus.'

390. **ἐστασίαζον** 'they were splitting into parties,' *i.e.* in the Thirty.

393. **τὰς ἀρχὰς** 'their offices.' The Ten would have all the power of supreme government, each in equal degree.

396-7. **ἐκεῖνοι** 'the Thirty.' **ὑμεῖς** he always addresses the judges as though they were identified with the popular party.

401. **καταγαγεῖν** 'to bring home from exile.'

405. **ἐλθὼν εἰς Λακεδαίμονα.** When the first attempts at coming to terms failed, the Ten, and the remains of the Thirty at Eleusis, seem to have made great efforts to induce the Spartans to interfere; and eventually, though direct help is refused, Lysander obtains them a loan of a hundred talents, and gets himself appointed harmost, and his brother Libys admiral (Xen. 2, 4, 28; Diod. 14, 30): and he would have interfered with crushing effect, had it not been for the jealousy or corruption of King Pausanias.

* 407. **Βοιωτῶν.** See on xv. l. 175. This was skilfully contrived to arouse Spartan jealousy, and was plausibly supported by the fact that the exiled Democrats had been eagerly received by various Bœotian towns, and that Thrasybulus had set out from Thebes on his expedition to seize Phylè, with the secret help, Diodorus (14, 32) assures us, of the Thebans themselves.

408. **οὐ δυνάμενος.** Xenophon says nothing about this failure to obtain help, but he implies that there were difficulties; for he says that Lysander *managed* in their behalf (*συνέπραξεν*) to get them a loan, and have himself appointed harmost. So that the most that Sparta did was to appoint a harmost known to be hostile to the Democrats, and leave him to do what he liked.

412. **ἄρχοντα,** *i.e.* a harmost, or Spartan 'resident.'

419. **εἰ μὴ δι' ἄνδρας ἀγαθούς** 'and they would have done so if it had not been for some good loyal men.' For this compressed use of *εἰ μή*, cf. Dem. 680, **ἐξ οὗ κυρωθέντες ἄν, εἰ μὴ** *δι' ἡμᾶς, ἠδίκηντο οἱ δύο τῶν βασιλέων.* **δηλώσατε** 'make it clear once for all.' The aor. imperative is used as referring to one particular act, *i.e.* the punishment of Eratosthenes.

423-4. **ὅμως δέ** sc. *παρέξομαι.* **ἀναπαύσασθαι** the speaker would sit down and rest, while the clerk read over the depositions to the witness, requiring his consent to them by word or sign. See on iv. l. 101. **ὡς πλείστων** 'from as many mouths as possible.'

426. **Θηραμένους.** For an account of the part played by

Theramenes in the Revolution, see Appendix. It may be allowed to add here that this account of him is from a thoroughly unfriendly point of view. I think it is clear, from a careful review of our authorities, that Theramenes was an honest man. But he was a philosopher and a doctrinaire, and had a Socratic ideal of a perfect state which, both in the time of the Four Hundred and in that of the Thirty, he thought he saw his way to realise, but was quickly undeceived by the development of selfish aims in his colleagues. As, therefore, he sympathised neither with the prejudices of the Democrats, nor the self-seeking of the Oligarchs, he came to be trusted by neither.

429-30. **παραστῇ** '*in mentem veniat.*' Cf. ii. l. 112. **Θηραμένους κατηγορῶ** 'I am really accusing Theramenes.'

433. **καίτοι σφόδρ' ἂν κ.τ.λ.** The irony amounts to a negative. 'He shields himself under the name of Theramenes, he would not have pretended that he took measures for building the walls as a mere member of Themistocles' party, though *for pulling them* down he gladly avails himself of the plea of being one of Theramenes' party.'

436. **οὐ γάρ.** No! for these two men (Themist. and Theram.) have rendered services of quite a different sort.

437-9. **ὁ μὲν γὰρ . . ᾠκοδόμησεν.** For the ruse by which Themistocles secured time to build the walls, see Thucyd. 1, 90-2. **περιέστηκεν** 'what has happened to the State is exactly the reverse of what one might have expected.'

440-6. **ἄξιον . . γάρ.** In spite of this unfriendly criticism the party of Theramenes were the moderate party in the Thirty, and might justly appeal to that fact in mitigating the anger of the Democracy. **ἀναφερομένας** 'resting on an appeal to his name.' Sandys on Eur. Bacch. 29. **αἰτίου** sc. *Θηραμένους*.

447. **τῆς προτέρας ὀλιγαρχίας**, *i.e.* of the Four Hundred. See on l. 295. B.C. 411.

449-51. **τῶν προβούλων ὢν** 'one of the (Ten) commissioners,' *i.e.* the Ten originally appointed (B.C. 411) to propose the revision of the constitution to the ecclesia, which they did in the temple of Poseidon at Colonus, a mile outside the city. Thucyd. 8, 87, calls them *συγγραφεῖς αὐτοκράτορες*. Harpocration (s.v. *συγγραφεῖς*) asserts that thirty were elected. **ταῦτ' ἔπραττεν** 'was abetting this policy.' **τοῖς πράγμασι** 'this policy.'

453. **Πείσανδρον . . καὶ Κάλλαισχρον.** For the former, see on l. 295. Of the latter nothing seems known beyond the fact that he was one of the Four Hundred.

457. **μετέσχε τῶν 'Αριστοκράτους ἔργων** 'joined the intrigues of Aristocrates.' According to Thucydides (8, 90), Theramenes broke off from the violent faction of the Four Hundred

on the subject of their great submission to the Spartans, and especially in regard to a fort to be built at the entrance of the harbour of Peiræus, which he and his party alleged was to facilitate the entrance of the Spartans. For the name of Aristocrates as a leader of the moderates we are indebted to Lysias, not Thucydides.

460. **κατηγορῶν ἀπέκτεινεν** 'accused and caused their death.' Antiphon, the famous orator (some of whose speeches are preserved), of whom Thucydides (8, 68, 2) says that on this occasion he made the best speech in defence within his memory. For the joining of Archiptolemus in his condemnation our authority is Lysias. The rest of the extreme party escaped mostly to Decelea, and one Aristarchus to Œnoe (Thucyd. 8, 98).

461. **ὥστε ἅμα . . ἀπώλεσε.** He was base in both cases; his loyalty to the Oligarchs enslaved Athens, his loyalty to Athens was the death of his friends.

464-70. **τιμώμενος . . πιστεύειν.** The speaker now goes on to consider the conduct of Theramenes in the negotiations with Lysander after the battle of Ægospotami. See Appendix, 'The Thirty.'

465. **αὐτὸς** 'of his own accord.'

471-2. **πραττούσης . . σωτήρια** 'when the Council of the Areopagus were engaged in measures for saving the city.' The Council of the Areopagus had no legislative or political functions; but in this time of extreme distress, *i.e.* when the city was awaiting its fate at the hands of Lysander, it seems to have temporarily taken the conduct of affairs into its hands. Compare the decree passed afterwards for the restitution of the constitution, which contained this clause: *ἐπιμελείσθω ἡ βούλη ἡ ἐξ Ἀρείου πάγου τῶν νόμων ὅπως ἂν αἱ ἀρχαὶ τοῖς κειμένοις νόμοις χρῶνται.* Andoc. Myst. § 84.

474-5. **τῶν πολεμίων . . ποιοῦνται** 'preserve secrets on the enemies' account,' *i.e.* lest the enemy should learn them.

482-4. **ἤλπισε** 'expected.' **οὐχ ὑπὸ Λακεδαιμονίων . . ἐπαγγελλόμενος** 'not acting under compulsion from the Spartans, but making them voluntary proposals.' An entirely groundless charge against Theramenes. The Spartan Government all along refused to listen to less terms (Xen. Hell. 2, 2, 13-14), though Xenophon does also insinuate that his long delay with Lysander was not loyal (*ib.* 16). The fact seems to be that he thought submission necessary, and that he was justified therefore in securing it.

491-2. **ὁ λεγόμενος . . ἐτηρήθη** 'until the expiration of the time mentioned by him had been awaited.' **ἐκείνου** seems to be Lysander, and the time 'mentioned' to be that fixed by Lysander for the Athenians to make peace. Xenophon says nothing of this. Weidn. reads *ὁ ὡμολογημένος ὑπ' ἐκείνων*.

492-3. **καὶ μετεπέμψατο, κ.τ.λ.** 'and he sent for the Spartan ships from Samos.' This really refers to a later period after the peace was made, and Lysander had sailed to Samos. The Oligarchs sent for Lysander to overawe the assembly into electing the Thirty. **ἐπεδήμησε** 'settled in the town.' The Spartan garrison occupied the Acropolis (*infra*, l. 663) and also the Odeum at its foot (Xen. Hell. 2, 4, 10), with a Spartan harmost Kallibius. The change of nominative is awkward, but *ἐπιδημέω* must be intransitive.

496. **Φιλοχάρους καὶ Μιλτιάδου.** Philochares and Miltiades were joint-commanders of the Spartan fleet with Lysander. **περὶ τῆς πολιτείας** 'about the reform of the constitution.'

502-3. **Δρακοντίδης** appears in the list of the Thirty, and was probably one of the five 'Ephors' also. See Appendix, 'The Thirty.' **ἀπέφαινεν** 'was declaring.'

503-6. **ὅμως** 'in spite of all the force brought to bear on you.' **ἐξεκλησιάζετε** 'you were deciding in solemn assembly.' For the form, see Veitch. The more correct form would be *ἠκκλησιάζετε*, as being derived from compound substantive, and some would thus write it. For analogous form, see on *ἐγκωμιάζω*, Rutherford's *New Phrynichus*, p. 82.

510-11. **τοὺς τὰ ὅμοια . . αὐτῷ** 'were for the same policy as he was.'

513-15. **παρασπόνδους** 'guilty of breaking the terms of the truce.' The breach of the treaty consisted in the failure of the Athenians to pull down the specified length of the long walls * within the required time. See vi. l. 61. **σωτηρίας** 'bare existence.'

517. **τὴν παρασκευὴν** 'the elaborate nature of the plot.' By * *παρασκευὴν* (see ii. l. 122) he means to infer that the question was not an open one, but had been prearranged.

519-20. **τοῦτο γοῦν . . συνειδότες** 'having *at least this* to comfort their consciences.'

522-5. **παρήγγελτο** 'orders had been passed round to them.' See *supra*, l. 311. **ἔφοροι** see on l. 305. **ἐκ τῶν παρόντων** 'of those actually in the assembly.'

530-1. **ἐκείνῳ**, *i.e.* Theramenes. **ἐν τῇ βουλῇ ἀπολογούμενος** 'when defending himself in the Boulè against Critias.' The speech, as given by Xenophon (Hell. 2, 3, 35-49), contains no such admissions. Theramenes details the points on which he split with his colleagues. (1) When they began to arrest good and innocent men instead of the sycophants and other ill-disposed people whom they first attacked. (2) When they decided on the attack upon the Metics. (3) When they disarmed the people. (4) When they hired the Spartan guard.

531-2. **ὀνειδίζων . . κατέλθοιεν** 'reproaching the exiles with the fact that they had been restored by his means.'

535-6. **τοῖς εἰρημένοις . . ἐμοῦ** 'exactly in way just stated by me.' **τοιούτων** 'with such a return,' *i.e.* condemnation and death.

540-1. **τολμήσουσιν . . ἀποφαίνειν** 'they (*i.e.* those who speak for him now) will have the hardihood to proclaim themselves Theramenes' friends.'

544. **δικαίως δ' ἂν** 'as he would with equal justice have done in a democracy.' The phrase is elliptical for *δικαίως δ' ἂν δόντος*. For *ἂν* with participle, see Goodwin, § 211. For elliptical use of *ἂν*, *ib.* § 212.

545-7. **δὶς**, *i.e.* at the time of the Four Hundred and of the Thirty. **παρόντων . . ἀπόντων** 'democratical and oligarchical constitutions.' **τῷ καλλίστῳ ὀνόματι** 'the fairest pretext.' Theramenes consistently maintained that the end of his policy was that the 'best men,' *τοὺς βελτίστους*, should possess the supreme power (Xen. Hell. 2, 3, 19-22).

553. **τουτουί** 'that man before you,' *i.e.* the defendant Eratosthenes.

554-6. **μηδὲ μαχομένους . . ἐχθρῶν** 'and not to show yourselves superior to the national enemy when in arms, while you allow yourselves to be beaten by your opponents when you come to votes.'

558. **ἀποῦσι . . τοῖς τριάκοντα** 'those of the Thirty who are away from Athens.' The remaining members of the Thirty, after their defeat in the Peiræus, retired to Eleusis, except Eratosthenes and Pheidon, who stayed at Athens. The party thus at Eleusis was further defeated and scattered a few months

later (Xen. Hell. 2, 4, 43). **ἐπιβουλεύετε** 'concert measures against.' The moderation, however, of the popular party towards the Oligarchs was remarked by Plato (Menex. 234 E). See also Grote's Hist. ch. 66.

561-7. **δὲ καὶ** 'may even.' **οὗτος μὲν . . καθέσταμεν** 'he was then at once prosecutor and judge; in the present state of things he and I are in the ordinary position of prosecutors and defendants.' **τῶν γινομένων** joined with **δικαστής**.

568. **ἀκρίτους.** One of the articles of the constitution under the Thirty was that they should on their own authority be capable of condemning to death any persons not on the 'roll,' *κατάλογος* (Xen. Hell. 2, 3, 51).

569. **κατὰ τὸν . . κρίνειν** 'you think it right to let them have a trial according to law.'

570-2. **ἂν** observe its place in the sentence, drawing especially attention and emphasis on **παρανόμως**, though it belongs to **λάβοιτε**.

573. **εἴησαν . . δεδωκότες** 'will they have fully paid the penalty they deserve?' For this periphrasis for a perfect optative, see Madv. § 180 d. It refers to a future supposition as to things that would *then* be past. *Supra*, l. 315.

578. **καλῶς ἂν ἔχοι** 'would full reparation be made?'

582. **ἡντινοῦν,** sc. *δίκην* 'any possible satisfaction which you could get.' **ἥντινα** 'of the sort which.'

587-8. **τούτου** 'the defendant.' **καταπεφρόνηκεν** 'has conceived an utter contempt for.'

592-6. **οἳ οὐ τούτοις . . ἀφήσετε** 'who have come here not so much with a view of defending these men, as from the idea that they will secure complete indemnity for their past actions, and, for the future, license to do as they please, if when you have once got them you let go the men who have been the causes of your greatest evils.'

598. **ὡς καλοὶ κἀγαθοὶ** 'on the ground of their *own* high character.'

600. **ἐβουλόμην . . ἂν** 'I could have wished.' Cf. *supra*, 154. From *ἐβουλόμην* to *ἀπολλύναι* is parenthetical.

605. **οὐδὲ τὰ δίκαια** 'not even bare justice,' *i.e.* to say nothing of special indulgence, which they now ask for these men.'

609-12. **διὰ . . τὸ ὑμέτερον πλῆθος** 'owing to' or 'by means of you the people,' *i.e.* by your votes of acquittal. **δεινὸν ἦν** 'it was dangerous.' **ἐπ' ἐκφορὰν ἐλθεῖν** 'to undertake the burial.' **ἐπί** 'for the purpose of.' See Aesch. in Ctes. § 235.

619. **ὁπότε** 'since we see that.' Cf. *supra*, l. 233.

621-3. **ἀντειπεῖν** 'to speak in condemnation.' **Ἐρατοσθένει.** Dative of agent with passive verb. See *supra*, l. 266.

625. **τῶν ἄλλων Ἑλλήνων**, *i.e.* of all other Greeks besides the Thirty.

629-31. **δῆλοι . . ὀργιζόμενοι.** See on iii. l. 56. 'You will make it plain that you are angry.' So **ὀφθήσεσθε . . ὄντες** 'you will be seen to be.'

632. **οὐχ ἕξετε, κ.τ.λ.** This was one of the pleas of Eratosthenes. See *supra*, l. 188.

640. **τοὺς . . ἐξ ἄστεος καὶ τοὺς ἐκ Πειραιῶς** 'the party of the city and the party of the Peiræus,' referring to the time of Thrasybulus' occupation of the Peiræus. **ἄστυ** is used as before for the upper city or Athens proper. See *supra*, ll. 375-7.

647. **τοιοῦτον . . ἐν ᾧ.** See on ii. l. 270.

647-8. **ἡττηθέντες** 'being worsted as you have been,' *i.e.* the city party. **τὸ ἴσον** cf. 246, for a complete amnesty and restitution were the terms. **ἂν . . ἐδουλεύετε** 'you would now have been slaves to these men,' *i.e.* the Oligarchs.

652-3. **συνωφελεῖσθαι μὲν γάρ, κ.τ.λ.** 'For they did not think it right that you should share their advantages, though they were trying to make you share their discredit.' **συνδιαβάλλεσθαι** 'to lose credit along with them.' Cf. ii. l. 181, and Thucyd. 4, 22, 3, *μὴ ἐς τοὺς συμμαχους διαβληθῶσιν εἰπόντες καὶ οὐ τυχόντες*. His charge is that they wished as many citizens as possible to be involved in their own guilt, and that was the reason they caused the Three Thousand to vote for the condemnation of the persons they put to death. See on viii. l. 32.

657. **ἐν τῷ θαρραλέῳ ὄντες.** Thucyd. 2, 51, 8.

662. **τοῖς πολεμίοις** 'your foreign foes.'

663-7. **τῶν ἐπικούρων** 'the foreign mercenaries.' Referring to the guard of Spartans and others brought in by the Thirty. See on l. 493. **εἰς τὴν ἀκρόπολιν κατέστησαν** 'they were brought and stationed on the Acropolis.' **ἔτι πολλῶν ὄντων** 'though there is much more I might say.'

671. **ἀφῃρέθητε τὰ ὅπλα** 'you were deprived of your arms,' *i.e.* shields and spears. This was one of the first acts of the Thirty after forming the 'catalogue;' all others were deprived of their arms (Xen. Hell. 2, 3, 20), which were stored on the Acropolis. For the passive construction 'where the nearer object becomes the nominative, and the accus. of the remoter object remains,' see Madv. § 25.

672. **ἐξεκηρύχθητε . . ἐκ τῆς πόλεως** 'you were banished by public proclamation from the city.' This was immediately after the death of Theramenes. See Xen. Hell. 2, 4, 1. Diodorus (14, 5) asserts that more than half the citizens were banished; they were, however, allowed to stay in the Peiræus.

674. **ἐξῃτοῦντο** 'they demanded your extradition.' The fugitives had taken refuge chiefly at Megara and Thebes, besides the Peiræus and Oropus. The Lacedæmonians decreed that the Athenian refugees might be arrested wherever they were; but the Thebans retaliated by a decree that 'every house and town should be open to them' (Plut. Lys. 27). The Argives also, in whose town some of the fugitives took refuge, answered the demand by the Spartan Commissioners for their extradition by an order to quit the town before sunset or be treated as enemies (Demos. 197).

680. **ταφῆς τῆς νομιζομένης** 'the customary rites of burial.' See *supra*, 116-8, 148, x. l. 40. For the horror with which this additional cruelty was regarded by the Greeks, see passages adduced by Becker, *Charicles*, pp. 383-4; especially a passage in the Supplices of Euripides (524) which has been supposed to refer to some similar conduct of the Argives, but which, if delivered at this time, would have come home to the people with a special force:—

> *νεκροὺς δὲ τοὺς θανόντας, οὐ βλάπτων πόλιν,*
> *οὐδ' ἀνδροκμῆτας προσφέρων ἀγωνίας,*
> *θάψαι δικαιῶ, τὸν Πανελλήνων νόμον*
> *σώζων, τί τούτων ἐστὶν οὐ καλῶς ἔχον;*

682-3. **βεβαιοτέραν . . τιμωρίας** 'too firmly established to be touched by the vengeance of heaven.'

686. **ἐν πολεμίᾳ τῇ πατρίδι** 'in their own country, which was now become an enemy's land to them.'

688-9. **ἤλθετε . . Πειραιᾶ**, *i.e.* under Thrasybulus from Phylè. See l. 371.

690. **τοὺς μὲν ἠλευθερώσατε,** *i.e.* the citizens in the Asty who were still under the oligarchical Ten.

699. **μικρῶν . . ἕνεκα συμβολαίων** 'in liquidation of small debts.' See on i. l. 6. **ἂν ἐδούλευον** 'would now be serving as slaves.' Cf. l. 648.

706. **ἀπέδοντο** 'sold.' He does not mean the temples, but the sacred objects of value in them. Most temples had treasuries of money attached to them, besides rich offerings and works of art.

715. **πεποιημένους** 'exacting.' Perf. pass. as a middle.

716. **ἀκηκόατε, κ.τ.λ.** 'you have heard with your own ears; seen with your own eyes; experienced in your own persons; you are in possession of the facts;—Record your verdict!'

* * * * * *

ORATION VII. [14].

[' Though,' says Plutarch, ' we have no account from any writer concerning the mother of Nicias or Demosthenes, of Lamachus or Phormion, of Thrasybulus or Theramenes, notwithstanding that these were all illustrious men of the same period, yet we know even the nurse and paedagogus of Alcibiades.' Doubtless the curiosity and interest felt in the career of Alcibiades was out of proportion to his actual achievements. His beauty, his lavish expenditure, his eccentric wilfulness, his accomplishments, his personal daring, his extraordinary political career,—all made him a favourite object of gossip and amused or malevolent anecdote. But though the people might talk of him with that mixture of admiration and disapproval which is apt to follow the lawless daring of a highborn reprobate, yet he had injured or offended too many individuals to escape the punishment which rhetoricians can inflict. Accordingly we find more than one elaborately worked-up indictment against his memory.

The first is that usually attributed to Andocides (Orat. 4), which at any rate is by some contemporary speech-writer. Another is the one now before us, professedly delivered in a prosecution of his son for a breach of military law, yet quite half devoted to an attack upon the career of the father. We find, too, in the speech written in the defence of this same young man by Isocrates[1] (xvi. περὶ τοῦ ζεύγους), that the career of the father is the one object of the defence, and we may presume, therefore, was the chief subject of the attack. After reading these speeches, and deducting the most glaring falsehoods, one is surprised to find how weak in some respects the case against him is, and how easy it would be to adopt the more indulgent view of him which Plutarch seems to have entertained.

As for the son, if we may trust the account here given of him, he had all the vices of his father, without his power; and led a roving, almost piratical, life, without any compensation in the way of public services or private magnificence. Nor has he shared with his father the honour of being remembered. Hardly any particulars of his life are attainable. He tells us (Isocr. xvi. § 45-6) that when he was quite an infant his mother died, and his father was banished (B.C. 415); that before he was four years old

[1] *Francken* (Commentationes Lysiacæ, p. 108) argues that this speech of Isocrates was written for Hipponicus, the younger son of Alcibiades, whom Francken has himself invented to explain § 28 of this speech. The fact on which he relies is that the speaker of the Isocratean speech says that he was born about 415 (§ 45), whereas in our speech Alcibiades is said to be ὡραῖος (l. 204) before his father's death, B.C. 404.

he was in danger of being put to death, being held as a hostage for his father, who failed to appear to answer the charges against him; that he was banished by the Thirty when he was still a child (παῖς) B.C. 404-3; that on the restoration of the Demus he did not get the grant of land which others did, in compensation for his property confiscated by the Thirty; and was, moreover, defendant in a suit, the damages in which were laid at five talents. He seems to have inherited the personal peculiarities of his father, and Plutarch (Alcib. I.) quotes Archippus the comic poet's description of him: βαδίζει διακεχλιδὼς θοιμάτιον ἕλκων, ὅπως ἐμφερὴς τῷ πατρὶ μάλιστα δόξειεν εἶναι, κλασαυχενεύεταί τε καὶ τραυλίζεται. And this, together with the vituperation of our speech, is all that we know of him.

The present charge against him (γραφὴ λιποταξίου) arose from the fact of his having served in the cavalry in a certain campaign; whereas the speaker asserts that (1) he had been put in the list of hoplites by the strategi, and (2) that he had not passed the scrutiny (δοκιμασία) which every one by law had to pass before serving in the cavalry. The contention is that the offence of λιποταξία may be committed in two ways:—

(1) not appearing in the army when put in the list (ἀστρατεία);

(2) falling to the rear on the advance of the enemy (δειλία);

and that the defendant is guilty on the first count, because he did not appear, as he should, among the hoplites; and guilty on the second, because his serving in the cavalry instead of the infantry was really δειλίας ἕνεκα. And that if his appearing among the knights acquits him of ἀστρατεία, he is still liable for serving among the knights without having passed his scrutiny. The penalty in either case is ἀτιμία. The trial is before a panel of soldiers, presided over by the Strategi.

The question remains as to what campaign it was in which this happened. There are two indications in the speech,—(1) there was no battle fought (§ 5); (2) this was the first trial of the sort since the Peace, *i.e.* the pacification after the Revolution, B.C. 403 (§ 4). Professor Jebb concludes from these and other considerations, that the expedition meant was that sent out to assist the Thebans and relieve Haliartus, besieged by Lysander, B.C. 395. Before the Athenians arrived, however, Lysander had been defeated and killed, and the Lacedæmonians had to submit to be led back by Pausanias. See note on l. 32, and *Attic Orators*, vol. i. p. 257. Francken, on the other hand, would refer it to the blockade of Ægina by the Spartans in 388 B.C. See Xen. H. v. 1, 1.]

4-6. καὶ εἰ μή τις . . τυγχάνει. The clause takes the place of an accusative after προσήκει, 'It is every one's duty, even if he do not chance to be personally wronged by him, to regard him as an enemy as much as if he had been, because of the other actions of his life.' **ἄλλων**, *i.e.* other than the personal wrongs of each individual.

9. **τοῦ λοιποῦ** 'in the future,' genitive of 'the time within which.' Goodwin, § 179. Cp. *νυκτός, ἡμέρας, κ.τ.λ.*

10. **πεπραγμένα**, sc. *ἁμαρτήματα*. *ὧν* attracted into the case of an antecedent pronoun understood after *ἐνίοις*. Goodwin, § 153, note 1.

13. **πρὸς τοὺς πατέρας**, *i.e.* the speaker's father, and the elder Alcibiades.

16-17. **μεθ' ὑμῶν** 'with your countenance and assistance.' **αὐτὸν τιμωρήσασθαι** 'to get *full* vengeance on him,' 'punish him once for all.' Notice the force of the aorist.

21. **καθ' ἕκαστον** 'in detail'.

22-5. **εἰκὸς τοίνυν . . γενέσθαι** 'Now it is reasonable, gentlemen jurors, that men acting as jurors for the first time since the peace in a trial of this sort should be regarded not as merely jurors, but as law-makers themselves.' **νομοθέτας αὐτοὺς** the Nomothetae were a select committee of the Jurors for the year appointed to revise the laws but not to make new ones. Poll. 8, 101, Hermann, § 131. He of course here means not that the jurymen were technically Nomothetae, but that they should regard themselves as practically law-makers; insomuch that now, deciding on a case for the first time under the new *régime*, they would be setting a precedent which would be really a law.

29. **διαλαμβάνειν** 'define.' The sense of the word may be seen by Demosth. 278, *στήλαις διαλαβὼν τοὺς ὅρους*, 'having marked out the boundaries by pillars.'

★ 30. **μέλλει συνοίσειν.** See ii. l. 164.

32. **ἔνοχός ἐστι λειποταξίου**, sc. *γραφῆς* 'liable to the charge of desertion.' In l. 353 we have *ἔνοχος τῇ γραφῇ*; cf. l. 44: the dative is the more natural construction, but it admits of the genitive on the analogy of other *verba accusandi*. Madv. § 61.

32-3. **μάχην γὰρ οὐδεμίαν γεγονέναι.** No direct indication of the campaign referred to is given; but the facts correspond to that of 395 B.C., in which the Athenians sent a force to Haliartus, before the arrival of which the Spartans were defeated and Lysander killed. Jebb, *Att. Or.* vol. i. pp. 257-8; Xen. Hell. 3, 5, 16. **τὸν δὲ νόμον κελεύειν** 'whereas the regulations of the law are.'

35-6. **περὶ τούτου . . δικάζειν** 'that the soldiers should try such an one.' The court that tried military offences was composed of soldiers presided over by the Strategi.

37-8. **ὁπόσοι ἂν . . στρατίᾳ** 'such as fail to appear in the ranks,' *i.e.* as opposed to those who, though appearing, show cowardice in the battle. This offence, he contends, has nothing to do with a battle; it consists in a non-attendance on parade.

43. **τὴν ἡλικίαν ταύτην** 'either the age of the defendant,' or (more generally) 'the military age': he says *ταύτην* as being well known to his hearers, and naturally suggested by the subject. The younger Alcibiades, according to Isocrates de big., § 45, was born in the year of or just before the banishment of his father, B.C. 415. He would therefore be in B.C. 395 about twenty. The military age was from the time a man became ephebus (see iv. l. 209) to sixty.

* 44. **καταλέξωσιν.** See on iii. l. 18.

45. **ὅλῳ τῷ νόμῳ** *i.e.* to both provisions of the law,—that against cowardice on the field as well as that which regarded non-appearance.

49-50. **παρέσχε . . τάξαι** 'submitted to be placed in his proper place in the ranks with the rest.' After *παρέσχε* must be understood *ταξιάρχοις* or *στρατηγοῖς*. For the use of *παρέχειν* 'to place oneself at the disposal of,' followed by active infin., see *τοῖς ἰατροῖς παρέχουσι . . ἀποτέμνειν καὶ ἀποκάειν*, Xen. * Mem. 1, 2, 54 (L. and Sc.) **δέον** acc. abs. See ii. l. 98, etc.

55. **ἐάν τις ἀδοκίμαστος ἱππεύῃ** 'if any one serve in the cavalry without passing his scrutiny.' The cavalry was under the special charge of the Boulè, under whose auspices the scrutiny would take place. The object of it would probably be to secure that only those of the right class (*τίμημα*) served in it. This appropriation of cavalry service dates from the time of Solon, but seems to have been loosely observed since Pericles introduced military pay. The Knights received pay even in time of peace, which would partly account for the endeavour of men, not qualified, to be put in their ranks, as we have seen did take place [on iii. l. 18]. See Hermann, § 152. According to * Lycurgus (*apud* Harpocr. s.v. *δοκιμασία*) there were three classes of officials who had to pass the scrutiny, viz. Archons, Strategi. Rhetores,—and besides them the Knights.

60-4. **οὕτως . . τοὺς πολεμίους ἔδεισε** 'he so feared the enemy.' Besides the social and pecuniary motives for wishing to serve in the cavalry, the less dangerous nature of the service would influence many. **τὰ χρήματα αὑτοῦ** not *αὐτοῦ*. Lysias uses *αὑτοῦ* where no ambiguity is caused thereby nor emphasis required. Cf. l. 235, and for *αὐτοῦ* l. 177 (Francken). So perhaps *αὑτῷ* in x. 142.

66. **ἢ μετὰ τῶν πολιτῶν εἶναι** 'rather than take up his position in the ranks with his fellow citizens.' This of course does not imply that the cavalry were not fellow citizens. The speaker is thinking of the many citizens as good as Alcibiades who were performing the duty which he shirked.

71-4. **οὕτω γὰρ . . ἀδικοῦντας** 'for they had laid their plans not on the supposition that the city would perish, but that it would survive and be powerful, and exact punishments from those who broke its laws.' By using *παρεσκευασμένοι* he means to imply that Alcibiades deliberately and with treasonable

* design broke the laws (see on ii. l. 122).

76. **ἐπιστάμενος** sc. *ἱππεῦσαι* 'without having learnt the cavalry drill.'

77. **ὡς οὐκ ἐξεσόμενον** 'as though it would never be in the power of the State.' The accusative (?) abs. following a clause with genitive (*ὡς ἀπολουμένης*, etc.) is to be remarked. Cf. Thucyd. vii. 25, 9. Plat. Rep. 604 B.

79-81. **εἰ ἐξέσται . . αἱρεῖσθαι.** He is speaking especially of military subordination. **ὑμᾶς συλλέγεσθαι** 'that you soldiers should be empanelled.' See *supra*, l. 36.

82-6. **ἐὰν—γένηται** 'if a man as the enemy are coming on, having been stationed in the front rank, is found in the second.' The genitive *τῆς πρώτης τάξεως* may perhaps be regarded as a partitive genitive, 'being appointed to form part of the front rank'; or it may be looked upon as a genitive of place like *ἀριστερῆς χειρὸς* in Herodotus, see Goodwin, § 179, 2. **τούτου . . δειλίαν καταψηφίζεσθαι** 'to vote such a man guilty of cowardice'; a common construction with verbs compounded with *κατά*, cf. for instance *τῶν ἄλλων μωρίαν κατηγόρει*, Xen. Mem. 1, 3, 4. **ἀναφανῇ** 'suddenly turns up'; *ἀναφαίνεσθαι* conveys an idea of suddenness or unexpectedness, like *repente.* Cf. Dem. Cor. 328, *ῥήτωρ ἐξαίφνης ἐκ τῆς ἡσυχίας ὥσπερ πνεῦμα ἀνεφάνη.*

88-90. **ἡγοῦμαι . . ποιῆτε** 'I imagine that you are empanelled not only to punish actual offenders, but also to reduce all other offenders against discipline to a better mind,' *i.e.* the object of legal penalties is not penal only, but deterrent also. Cf. Plat. Prot. 324 B, *ὁ μετὰ λόγου ἐπιχειρῶν κολάζειν οὐ παρεληλυθότος ἕνεκα ἀδικήματος τιμωρεῖται . . ἀλλὰ τοῦ μέλλοντος χάριν, ἵνα μὴ* *αὖθις ἀδικήσῃ μήτε αὐτὸς οὗτος μήτε ἄλλος ὁ τοῦτον ἰδὼν κολασθέντα.*

102. **ἀκοσμοῦντας** used here and above, l. 90, in a military sense, 'offenders against discipline.'

108-9. **οἱ δὲ ψιλοὶ ἐστρατεύοντο** understand *ἡδέως ἄν*, 'while others would have been glad enough to have served as light-armed troops,' *i.e.* as archers, slingers, javelin men, etc., who had not to carry the heavy shield and thorax; who were therefore less exposed in battle, and had less exhausting duties to perform. **ψιλοί** is a certain emendation for *φίλοι*. **ἐκινδύνευον** sc. *ἡδέως ἂν* 'would have been glad to run their risk whatever it was.'

120-1. **οὐκ ἀξιοῦντες . . καταγνῶναι** 'demanding that you should not condemn.' The negative is joined with *ἀξιόω* as with *φημί* and *ἐάω*, see on iv. l. 39. **ὡς ἐκεῖνον** 'on the ground that he,' etc.

123. **ὃν εἰ τηλικοῦτον** 'whom (*i.e.* the elder Alcibiades) if you had put to death at the age of this young man.' We are reminded of Aristophanes' comment on the policy of the Athenians towards Alcibiades, Ran. 1432, *μάλιστα μὲν λέοντα μὴ 'ν πόλει τρέφειν | ἣν δ' ἐκτρέφῃ τις τοῖς τρόποις ὑπηρετεῖν.*

127. **εἰ αὐτοῦ μὲν ἐκείνου** 'if while you passed sentence of death upon that personage himself, you shall for his sake acquit his son when he commits a crime.' Alcibiades was sentenced to death in 415 B.C. as contumacious for not appearing to answer the charge of having profaned the Mysteries. Plut. Alcib. 22.

130. **μετὰ τῶν πολεμίων** *i.e.* with the Spartans, and especially in the matter of Decelea, Plut. Alc. 23.

131-3. **καὶ ὅτε . . ἔσται** 'nay, when as a child he had not as yet shown what he was going to be.' The young Alcibiades, we learn from Isocr. de big. § 47, was in his fourth year when he was thus seized as a hostage for his father. He was not put to death, I suppose, because such a cruelty was a freak of freedom beyond even an Athenian demus. For the tense **ἔσται** retained from the direct speech, see Goodwin, 242 b. **ὀλίγου** 'within a little.' Goodwin, § 172 b. **τοῖς ἕνδεκα παρεδόθη** 'was delivered to the Eleven,' *i.e.* for execution, see iv. l. 60.

140-2. 'The great deeds of our ancestors will not help us to recover from the enemy what *their* ill discipline loses us, and therefore it is not fair they should escape punishment for the sake of these ancestral achievements.' **τὰς . . ἀρετάς** 'the noble deeds.' Cf. Andoc., Or. i. p. 18, *ἀξιῶ κἀμοὶ διὰ τὰς τῶν προγόνων ἀρετὰς σωτηρίαν γενέσθαι.*

148-51. **ἐξαιτῶνται** 'try to beg him off.' **ἀξιῶ—ὀργίζεσθαι** 'I think one ought to be angry.' **εὑρέσθαι** 'to obtain what they sought'.

156-7. **φιλοτιμούμενοι . . δύνανται** 'pluming themselves on their influence in being able to get off even those who have been notoriously guilty of illegal conduct.'

158. **πρῶτον μὲν** answered by **ἔπειτα** in l. 161, without **δέ**. Cf. v. l. 355.

165. **αὐτοὶ οὗτοι** 'these very men,' *i.e.* the Strategi, or men in equivalent positions.

170. **μηδὲν ἔχοντες δίκαιον** 'without having any justificatory plea to offer.'

172. **ἐπιορκεῖν** 'to break your oath,' *i.e.* the oath you took as jurors. The oath is given in full in Demosth. 746, if it is genuine. See Append. V. There is no special clause which an acquittal in this case could be said to violate, except the general one, *ψηφιοῦμαι κατὰ τοὺς νόμους, κ.τ.λ.*

178. **ἧς . . ἀκοῦσαι** 'which (baseness) it is right that you should hear described.' The thing heard is usually in the accusative, the person in the genitive. We have *φθογγῆς κτύπου ἀκούειν* in the Odyssey (12, 198), but this usage is wholly Epic. The genitive here is justified by the fact of *πονηρία* not being *heard*, but *heard about*; he might have written *περὶ ἧς*. So in Arist. Ach. 306, *τῶν ἐμῶν σπονδῶν ἀκούσατε.* Clyde, § 72 f.

180-1. **ὡς ταῦτα . . γεγενημένου** 'on the plea that although he had committed this fault, yet in other respects he had been a good citizen.'

184-6. **τῶν ἀπολογουμένων ἀποδέχεσθε . . ἀρετὰς** 'you allow of defendants quoting their own good deeds.' See Madv. § 60, 1; Goodwin, § 171, note 1.

188. **τοὺς φεύγοντας** 'defendants,' not this particular defendant, but defendants as a class.

191. **παρ' Ἀρχεδήμῳ τῷ γλάμωνι** 'at the house of Archedemus the Blear-eyed.' Archedemus was a demagogue who took a prominent part in the prosecution of the generals after the battle of Arginusæ. He held some official position as *τῆς Δεκελείας ἐπιμελούμενος*, *i.e.* demarchus of the deme Decelea, Xen. Hell. 1, 7, 1, and was attacked by the Comedians as an alien and a vexatious person, see Arist. Ran. 416 :—

βούλεσθε δῆτα κοινῇ
σκώψωμεν Ἀρχέδημον
ὃς ἑπτέτης ὢν οὐκ ἔφυσε φράτορας
νυνὶ δὲ δημαγωγεῖ
ἐν τοῖς ἄνω νεκροῖσι
κἄστιν τὰ πρῶτα τῆς ἐκεῖ μοχθηρίας.

To which passage the scholiast quotes a line of Eupolis as referring to the same person, *ἐπιχώριος δέ ἐστι καὶ ξένης ἀπὸ χθονός.* His personal defect of 'sore eyes' is also alluded to in the Ranæ, 588. For the word **γλάμων** and its equivalent *γλαμυρός* (quoted by the scholiast to Arist., from Sophocles), and connected with *λημᾶν*, *λήμη*, and the Latin *gramiæ*, *gramiosus*, see Curtius, 541.

191-2. **οὐκ ὀλίγα . . ὑφῃρημένῳ** 'who had been guilty of much peculation of public money.' This was a common accusation to bring against public men, sometimes no doubt deserved, but, as is shown in x. § 48-9, often ill grounded.

193. **κατακείμενος** 'lying down at full length ;' the proper word to express the position of a person lying at table is *ἀνακείμενος*. For the **ἱμάτιον**, 'large outer robe,' see 4, 61. It would be taken off and used as a rug. For the meaning of **ἐκώμαζε** cf. Aristoph. *Plut.* 1040—

Γραῦς. *ἔοικε δ' ἐπὶ κῶμον βαδίζειν.*
Χρεμ. *φαίνεται·*
στεφάνους γέ τοι καὶ δᾷδ' ἔχων πορεύεται.

198. **ἐπειδὴ φανερῶς ἐξημάρτανε** 'upon his conduct getting beyond bounds and beginning to be notorious.' Notice the tense and the force of *ἐκ*.

200. **ὅστις . . διεβέβλητο** 'if he lived such a life as to have become scandalous even to that man who used to be the instructor of others in such things,' *i.e.* how bad he must be to shock such a man as the elder Alcibiades !

* For **διαβάλλεσθαι** 'to lose credit with,' see ii. l. 181.

201. **μετὰ Θεοτίμου . . προὔδωκεν** 'having conspired with Theotimus against his father, he betrayed Oreus to him.' We know neither the circumstances nor anything of Theotimus. Oreus or Histiæa is a town in Eubœa, and if the reading is

right the elder Alcibiades must have had a castle there. Scheibe reads 'Ὀρνεάς. Orneæ was a town in Argolis, destroyed in B.C. 416 (Thucyd. 6, 7, 2), and it is perhaps more probable that Alcibiades had a castle there than at Oreus; but it is a matter of guess work altogether, and with neither town do we know Alcibiades to have been connected. Moreover, he appears to have been in Thrace at the time. Probably we should read χωρίον, or some such word, instead of 'Ὠρεόν.

202-3. **ὁ δέ** *i.e.* Theotimus. **τὸ χωρίον** 'the fortified place'

205-6. **εἰσεπράττετο** 'tried to exact money,' *i.e.* as ransom from his father, as though he had taken the boy prisoner. **ἔφασκε** 'used to say'; a very characteristic remark.

207. **ἐκείνου**, *i.e.* the elder Alcibiades, who was murdered in B.C. 404.

208. **'Αρχεβιάδης** was one of those declared to be present in the house of Polytion at the desecration of the Mysteries by Alcibiades. Andoc. 1, 13.

209. **κατακυβεύσας τὰ ὄντα** 'having gambled away all his property.' So Æschines speaks of money: *ἐπειδὴ ταῦτα ἀπολώλει καὶ κατακεκύβευτο καὶ κατωψοφάγητο* (Timarch. § 95). *κύβοι* are dice, the game is *κυβεία*, the gambling house *κυβεῖα* or *σκιράφεια*, see Becker's *Charicles*, pp. 354-5.

210. **ἐκ Λευκῆς ἀκτῆς . . κατεπόντιζεν** 'setting sail from Leukè Aktè (white headland), he tried to drown his friends,' *i.e.* he acted as a *καταποντίστης* 'a pirate.' Harpocr. tells us that there were many places called *Λευκαί*, and that this one was probably in the Propontis. [But if 'Ὠρεόν in l. 202 is right, it would seem more naturally to be the Leukè Aktè in Eubœa, which was about thirty-five miles from Sunium, Strab. 343, 10.] Strabo mentions two other places called *Λευκὴ ἀκτή*, one in Thrace in the Propontis, and another in Libya (284, 11; 679, 11).

214. **'Ιππόνικος.** We do not know the man nor whether he had married Alcibiades' sister, or as Francken supposes was his younger brother (of whom we hear nowhere else), except from this passage; but we know that Alcibiades the elder married a daughter of this family, one of the oldest and wealthiest of Athens, whose representatives were called Callias and Hipponicus alternately. See Dicty. of Biography and Plut. Alc. 8.

215. **ἐξέπεμψε** 'divorced,' said of the man; the woman was said *ἀπολείπειν*. **πολλοὺς παρακαλέσας** 'having called many persons to witness it.' No further formality seems to have been required, but a check upon many capricious divorces was secured by the fact that the husband had to restore the dowry to the woman's *κύριος*, a very ancient custom as it seems from Hom. Odyss. 2, 132-3. Such a divorce, however, was disgraceful to

the woman. Becker (*Char.* p. 497) refers to Stobæus, 74, 1, who gives a fragment of Anaxandrides—

> χαλεπὴ, λέγω σοι, καὶ προσάντης, ὦ τέκνον
> ὁδός ἐστιν, ὡς τὸν πατέρ' ἀπελθεῖν οἴκαδε
> παρὰ τἀνδρὸς, ἢ τις ἐστὶ κοσμία γυνή.
> ὁ γὰρ δίαυλός ἐστιν αἰσχύνην ἔχων.

222. **ἀπολογίαν . . ἁμαρτημάτων** 'regulating his own life so as to make it a standing defence for his father's misdemeanours.' *ἀπολογία* is here used metaphorically in a sense nearly equivalent to our 'apology.'

224-6. **ὥσπερ δυνάμενος κ.τ.λ.** 'as though he would be likely to succeed in transferring to others the very smallest share of the disgraces which belong to himself.' **πολλοστὸν** 'the many-eth part,' 'one of an indefinitely large number,' just as *χιλιοστὸς* = 'the last of a series of 1000.' **καὶ ταῦθ'** 'and that too.'

227-30. Here follows an enumeration of the public crimes of Alcibiades; the chief of which, and the one least forgotten, was the part he took in advising the occupation and fortification of Decelea by the Spartans in B.C. 414-3, 'which above everything reduced and wasted the substance of the Athenians.' Plutarch, Alc. 23.

233-5. **τούτων** 'of this family.' **κατελθόντα** 'having returned * from exile.' see on vi. l. 444. He refers to the return of Alcibiades in 407 B.C. The people met him at the harbour and presented him with garlands, and afterwards voted him garlands of gold and the restoration of his estates. Plut. Alcib. 32-3.

234. **εἴθισται** 'he has been much accustomed,'—who? *αὐτοῦ* and *τοῦτον* prevent us from taking Alcibiades as the subject of the verb. As there is no authority for the use of *εἴθισται* as passive impersonal, we must suppose the subject to be the advocate of Alcibiades.

237. **διαβεβλῆσθαι** 'should be prejudiced in his reputation.' See *supra*, l. 200.

238. **δωρεὰς . . ἀφείλεσθε.** The second disgrace of Alcibiades followed the battle of Notium B.C. 407 (September–October).

244. **χρῆται παραδείγματι** 'he quotes as a precedent.'

245. **περὶ τῆς ἑαυτοῦ πονηρίας** 'in support of his own baseness.'

247-9. **καὶ γὰρ . . προσβαλεῖν** referring to the occupation of Phylè and then of Peiræus by Thrasybulus and the popular party in B.C. 404-3. See Appendix 'The Thirty.' **δένδρα τεμεῖν** they would have to cut down trees for use in fortifications, and also for fire. This was one of the chief mischiefs caused to Attica by the frequent invasions during the Peloponnesian war, see on ii. l. 37. **πρὸς τὰ τείχη προσβαλεῖν** 'made assaults on the city walls,' *i.e.* from the Peiræus.

251-4. **ὡς τῶν αὐτῶν . . τὴν πόλιν** 'as though, forsooth, men who being in exile invaded their country in alliance with her enemies, were in no worse a position than those who effected their own restoration, when the Spartans were in occupation of the city.' The popular party, he says, certainly made an invasion, but it was when the enemy were in possession. Whereas Alcibiades—when legally an exile—joined these very same enemies in their attacks.

255. **οὗτοι μὲν**, sc. Alcibiades and his friends.

259-60. **καὶ τοὺς βουλομένους δουλεύειν** 'even those of them who wished to be slaves,' *i.e.* the party who were content with the rule of the Thirty, and the practical subjection to the Spartans.

260-1. **ὥστ' . . ποιεῖται** 'So that he uses similar language about the two parties, while the facts are not at all similar.' With **τοὺς λόγους** supply *ὁμοίους*.

266-272. Any one knows enough of politics to be able to tell the enemy what strongholds they should seize, what forts are ill guarded, what are his country's weak points, which of her allies are ready to revolt. To do this only requires a man to be base: it does not show that he is powerful. **βουλόμενος εἶναι πονηρὸς** 'provided he is willing to play the traitor.'

272-9. 'How can it be said that the damage he did us was a sign of his *power;* when on his recall he had no *power* to carry out the war against the enemy, or undo the mischief he had done?'

The cause of Alcibiades' second disgrace was his failure to effect the reduction of Chios and Miletus, which the people confidently expected of him. Plut. Alc. 35. This disappointment was completed by the unfortunate affair of Notium, which, however, was not the fault of Alcibiades (B.C. 407, Sept.–Oct.) **πολλῶν ἦρξε τριήρων** on his return he was put in chief command of the Athenian fleet as one of the ten Strategi, in which office, after his disgrace, he was succeeded by Conon.

285-6. ὑποσχόμενος . . χρήματα this promise was one which Alcibiades had made before, at the time of the 400, see v. l. 295. He found himself baffled in his attempt to obtain Persian money by the friendship formed between Lysander and Cyrus; and was much put to it to find the funds he wanted for his fleet. Plut. Alcib. 35.

287-292. Alcibiades, upon being superseded after the battle of Notium, did not return to Athens, the speaker insinuates, for fear of his εὔθυναι, and doubtless he knew that his life would not be safe. Plutarch (ch. 36) says, 'As soon as Alcibiades heard of this (*i.e.* that he was superseded) he immediately quitted the army altogether, afraid of what might follow; and collecting a body of mercenaries, he made war upon his own account against those Thracians who called themselves free and acknowledged no king; by which means he amassed to himself a considerable treasure, and at the same time secured the bordering Greeks from the incursions of the Barbarians.' If this is a true representation it will be seen that the expression Θρᾴκης . . ἐβούλετο πολίτης γενέσθαι is a mere rhetorical flourish.

293-6. καὶ τὸ τελευταῖον . . προδοῦναι 'and finally, to cap all his former baseness, he had the hardihood along with Adeimantus to betray the ships to Lysander,' *i.e.* at Ægospotami. Adeimantus was spared by Lysander after the battle, while his colleague Philocles was killed, and he was vehemently suspected of having held treasonable correspondence with Lysander. Xen. 2, 1, 32. Demosthenes (F. L. 211) refers to a prosecution of Adeimantus by Conon, probably on this charge. The allegation that Alcibiades was involved in the same treason is not supported by Plutarch and Xenophon, who expressly say that he tried to rouse the Athenians to a sense of the danger of their position, and the advisability of removing to Sestos, but was received with anger and contempt, see ch. 36-7,—a statement also confirmed by Nepos, Alc. ch. 8. It was, moreover, against his interest that the Spartans should crush the Athenians, for he had mortally offended the Spartans, and could not be safe if they were supreme. But nothing is too bad for an Attic orator to throw at a political opponent.

302. τὸν πρόπαππον αὐτοῦ 'his (the elder Alcibiades') great-grandfather.' He is mentioned in Is. de big. 10, as taking a leading part in expelling the Peisistratids. Alcibiades the younger there calls him πρόπαππος τοῦ πατρὸς τοὐμοῦ. Herod. 8, 17.

303-5. τὸν πατρὸς πρὸς μητρὸς πάππον 'his great-great-grandfather on his mother's side.' The pedigree is this, Megacles (who opposed Peisistratus)—Cleisthenes (the Reformer)—Megacles (Pind. Pyth. vii. 15)—Deinomache married to Clinias, father of Alcibiades. δὶς ἀμφοτέρους ἐξωστράκισαν it seems doubtful whether the word is not here an anachronism.

Diodorus (xi. 55) supposes ostracism to have been introduced by Cleisthenes after the expulsion of the Peisistratids. See Hermann, § 111. But at any rate, as both this ancestral Alcibiades and Megacles were in leading opposition to Peisistratus or his sons, there is no difficulty in accounting for their being twice banished. See Herod. 6, 123. 'Αθην. πολ. c. 22.

306. **οἱ πρεσβύτεροι ὑμῶν** 'the older men of the present generation.' This refers to the condemnation of Alcibiades for contumacy. See *supra*, l. 127.

311. **τῶν ὅρκων**, see *supra*, l. 172.

314. **πρὸς μὲν . . ἄλλως δὲ** 'should he do so on the ground that while in their public life they have been unfortunate, yet in other respects they are orderly?'

318-19. **οἱ δὲ μυστήρια . . περικεκόφασι.** This was the common accusation against Alcibiades, see Plut. Alc. 18-19; Andok. *de Myst.* 62; Thucyd. 6, 27-29. Andocides says that all the Hermæ were so mutilated, except one, that one being close to his (Andocides') father's house. Jowett, Thucyd. l. c.

321-3. **ἀδίκως . . πολιτευόμενοι** 'without regard to law or justice in their behaviour to the rest of the world, or their political conduct towards each other.' **σφᾶς αὐτοὺς** 'their own partizans,' nearly equivalent to ἀλλήλους.

327-8. **καὶ μὲν δὴ** 'now it is true enough.' **ἤδη** 'before now.'

332. **οὐδενὸς ἄξιός ἐστιν** 'has no ability.' **ἐπειδὰν ἀπολογῆται** 'the moment he begins his defence.'

334. **ἀλλὰ μὲν δὴ** 'nay, to go on to another point.' ἀλλὰ shows that a possible objection is being anticipated.

336. **πράττειν ἀδύνατος** 'without any faculty for negotiation.'

339. **αὐτὸν . . φυλάττεσθαι** 'to avoid provoking him.'

345. **κατηγόρηκα** *peroravi*, 'I have made my accusation.'

349. **πολλοστὸν μέρος**. see *supra*, l. 224.

350-3. 'Having taken into account what has been omitted as well as what has been said.' **ἔνοχος . . τῇ γραφῇ**, *i.e.* *ἀστρατείας*. For *ἔνοχος*, see *supra*, l. 32.

355. **τοὺς ὅρκους**. See *supra*, l. 172.

NOTES.

ORATION X. [19.]

[This speech relates to events which happened in the period of the gradual revival of Athens, and the struggle to put an end to Spartan supremacy in the Islands and Greek cities of Asia, B.C. 398–B.C. 387.

When Conon took refuge with Evagoras in Cyprus in B.C. 405, he appears to have had with him other Athenian refugees looking up to him as their leader. One of these was Nikophemus. While Nikophemus resided at Cyprus, his son Aristophanes (like Conon's son Timotheus) remained at Athens. Nikophemus served as a Trierarch in the fleet, of which Conon took command in B.C. 396-5, and was by him appointed Harmost of Cythera in B.C. 393, and soon afterwards returned apparently to reside in Cyprus.

Meanwhile Aristophanes remained at Athens, and had married a sister of the speaker of this speech. He appears to have been a man of restless activity and great energy. His two public services mentioned here are—(1) An embassy to Dionysius of Syracuse to endeavour to detach that monarch from the Spartans, and persuade him to make an alliance with Evagoras; we do not know the date of this embassy, but it was prior to 390 B.C. [§ 19-20]: (2) A mission to the aid of Evagoras, sent in 389-8 B.C., in answer to a request of Evagoras. He went officially as *πρεσβευτὴς* (l. 151); but he seems, at the request of his father, to have made great exertions in organising a military force of *πελτασταί* (l. 145). From this time we lose sight of him and his father. For some unexplained reason both Nikophemus and his son Aristophanes were put to death without trial (l. 7), and their property confiscated.

This being done, a suspicion seems to have arisen that the State had not got all the property left by Aristophanes, and that the person who was possessed of it was the speaker's father. He is accordingly summoned for illegal possession of public money before a court presided over by the *σύνδικοι* or revenue commissioners. Before the trial however he died, and his son, the speaker, has to defend the action.

From Harpocration (s. v. *χύτροι*) we gather that Lysias had written a speech on another trial on the subject of the property, when the confiscation was proposed, which apparently was done by one Æschines, as Harpocr. calls it *τῷ κατ' Αἰσχίνου*.

The date of the speech is not accurately ascertainable, but from l. 329 (see note) we may gather that it was not long after B.C. 388-7.

The defence is necessarily founded mainly on probabilities. He argues—

(1.) That his father was not likely, from his general character, to have kept money unfairly.

(2.) That Aristophanes spent so much on public services that he was not likely to have left much.

(3.) That he was not likely ever to have had much, as his father occupied only a subordinate post, had nothing before the battle of Cnidus, and no doubt kept the bulk of what he had at Cyprus, where he had a wife and daughter.

(4.) It is not the first time that the public have been astonished to find at a man's death that he was less rich than common fame gave out. In fact it generally is so.

So far from having any of Aristophanes' money, the speaker asserts that his sister and children have been thrown on his hands, having lost even her dowry in the general wreck.

The speech is made the more interesting by lengthened allusion to the remarkable career of Conon, one of the ablest and most honest men produced by Athens at this period.]

6. **δεινός** 'clever'; *δεινὸς λέγειν* is the common phrase in Demosthenes. Plato says of Lysias (Phædr. 228 A) that he was *δεινότατος τῶν νῦν γράφειν*.

7. **οὕτως ὅπως ἂν δύνωμαι** 'to the best of my ability.' *οὕτως ὅπως* is little more than *ὡς*; Xen. Cyr. 1, 1, 2, *χρῆσθαι οὕτως*
* *ὅπως ἂν βούλωνται.* **παρασκευήν** 'preparation,' see on ii. l. 122.

17. **διαβολῆς** *invidiæ*, 'with prejudice and popular opinion against him.'

20-6. Both clauses, **πολλοὶ ἤδη—ἀπελθεῖν** and **οἱ δ' αὖ . . πεπονθόσιν**, are to illustrate the frequency with which accusations turn out to be false; 'some,' he says, 'are detected on the spot, while others are only found to be false when too late to save their victims.' The deduction is that no one ought to trust a *διαβολή* until he has heard the other side. **ὑπὲρ πάντων τῶν πεπραγμένων** 'in the whole affair,' *i.e.* not only so far as they have really lied; being convicted of one lie, they are discredited altogether. **μαρτυρήσαντες . . ἑάλωσαν** 'have been convicted of false witness. **μαρτυρήσαντες τὰ ψευδῆ** '(were convicted) of having given false evidence,' *τὰ ψευδῆ = ψεῦδος*.

29-31. **πρὶν ἂν κ.τ.λ.** 'until you shall have heard us,' *i.e.* the defence. Goodwin, § 240. **ἀκούω** 'I hear it said,' affecting a kind of simple ignorance, cf. Demosth. Con. § 18, *infra*, ll. 91, 293. **δεινότατον** 'most difficult to deal with,' *i.e.* because, as he explains, it acts unevenly; so that what is a sufficient defence at one time is not so at another.

36. **τοὺς ἐλέγχους . . ἀποδέχεσθε** 'you admit the arguments in refutation.' **ἀποδέχεσθαι** takes gen. of person and accus. of thing admitted, on the analogy of verbs of hearing. Goodwin, § 171, note 1. Cf. vii. l. 184.

37-8. **Νικόφημος καὶ Ἀριστοφάνης . . ἀπέθανον.** Nicophemus was a friend of Conon, and was left by him in command of Cythera in B.C. 393, with the title of Harmost,—either as the name to which this Spartan island was accustomed, or because the Spartans had now made that term usual for such an officer [Xen. Hell. 4, 8, 8]. As to his name, the MSS. in Xenophon give it as Νικόφηβος, and in Diod. Sic. xiv. 81, Νικόδημον. Of his son Aristophanes we only know what we learn here. As to their death 'without trial,' we can only guess that it was on suspicion of treachery or embezzlement (Jebb, *Att. Or.* i. 236); and at Cyprus, where (as Conon, since 405) Nikophemus had been living. **ἀπέθανον** 'were put to death,' iv. l. 181.

38-9. **πρὶν . . ἠδίκουν** 'before any one could arrive to hear them proved guilty.' The ἠδίκουν suggests embezzlement rather than treachery; but ll. 80-1 point to treachery.

41-3. **ἀπέδωκαν** the subject is the commanders who ordered the execution, and who would be well known to the hearers. For the outrage to Greek feeling in thus denying burial, see on v. l. 680.

47-8. **παρὰ τοὺς νόμους τοὺς ὑμετέρους** 'contrary to your laws.' The breach of the law was not in the children being deprived of a father's property which had been confiscated, but in the fact that the confiscation was carried out in the case of men who had had no trial (ἄκριτοι).

50-1. **κηδεστῶν** see below, l. 74. **προικός** his sister's dowry, which, being included in the confiscation of Aristophanes' goods, was not available for the support of the children.

52. **συκοφαντούμεθα** 'I am having vexatious charges brought against me.' Fragm. 18, διασώζοντες τὰς τῶν φίλων οὐσίας συκοφαντοῦνται ὑπὸ τῶν ὀρφανῶν πολλοί.

54. **ἐκ τοῦ δικαίου** = δικαίως 'legally and honourably.'

57. **τετραπλάσια** the calculation will be found below, ll. 401 *sq.*

58. **λογιζομένῳ . . παρεγενόμην** 'I heard him reckoning.'

61-2. **ἀλλ' ὅσοι** sc. ἀλλὰ καταγινώσκετε ἀδικίαν τούτων ὅσοι κ.τ.λ. For construction, see Goodwin, § 173, 2, note.

64-6. **πρὸς δόξαν . . καὶ σπάνιν** 'in view of an idea entertained by some of the amount of Nikophemus' property, and in view of a scarcity of money now existing in the city.' Cf. Dem. 230, *ἵνα πρὸς τὸν ὑπάρχοντα χρόνον ἕκαστα θεωρῆτε*, 'in view of the existing circumstances.' **σπάνιν ἀργυρίου**, see *infra*, l. 332.

68-9. **καὶ τούτων ὑπαρχόντων** 'even in these disadvantageous circumstances.' **τὰ κατηγορημένα** 'the allegations made by the
* prosecution,' see on ii. l. 145.

72. **εὐορκότατον** 'most strictly consistent with your oaths as dicasts.' See on vii. l. 172.

74. **ᾧ τρόπῳ . . ἐγένοντο** 'the circumstances of their becoming connections of mine.' Aristophanes being his brother-in-law, the father of Aristophanes would also be his *κηδεστής*, see
* vi. l. 4.

75-6. **στρατηγῶν γὰρ Κόνων περὶ Πελοπόννησον.** This probably refers to the spring of 393 B.C., when Conon, being then commander of the Greek contingent of the fleet collected by Pharnabazus, was engaged in ravaging the coast of Sparta, and when he appointed Nikophemus harmost of Cythera. *Supra*, l. 37. Diodorus (xiv. 81) calls him *ὁ τῶν Περσῶν ναύαρχος*, but this is no doubt inaccurate: Xenophon (Hell. 4, 3, 12) calls Pharnabazus *ναύαρχος*, and describes Conon as *τὸ Ἑλληνικὸν ἔχοντα*.

Conon. We first hear of Conon as governor of Naupactus in B.C. 411 [Thuc. 7, 31, 4]. In B.C. 408-7, being at Athens, he was elected Strategus in conjunction with Alcibiades and Thrasybulus [Xen. Hell. 1, 4, 10]. In the autumn of 407 B.C. and spring of 406 B.C. he was doing excellent service among the islands of the Ægean, and being blockaded at Mytilene escaped the fate of the other generals after Arginusæ [Xen. Hell. 1, 6-7]. In June of B.C. 405 he was still in the Ægean, and at Ægospotami managed to escape with seven or eight ships to Cyprus, where he was entertained by Evagoras. From that time till B.C. 397 he remained in retirement in Cyprus [*οὐ τὴν ἀσφάλειαν ἀγαπῶν ἀλλὰ τὴν τῶν πραγμάτων μεταβολὴν περιμένων*, Plut. Artax. 21, see also Isocr. 5, § 62, 9, 51-8]. During this time the Spartans had been often brought into collision with the Persians; the campaigns of

Dercyllidas had ended in a short armistice, B.C. 398; Agesilaus was about to invade Asia, and Pharnabazus, on the advice of Evagoras and Conon [Isocr. Evag. 54], set about collecting a large fleet in Phœnicia of 300 triremes [Xen. Hell. 3, 4, 1]; Conon, at the suggestion of Evagoras, obtained the command of the Greek part of it [B.C. 397-6]. In the years 396-5, while Agesilaus was prosecuting his successful campaign in Asia, Conon was steadily working to overthrow the Spartan naval supremacy; his achievements may be said to have begun with the revolt of Rhodes and been consummated by the battle of Cnidus [August 394 B.C.]. After this he carried the war to the coasts of Lacedæmonia, and restored the fortifications of Athens [B.C. 393], Xen. Hell. 4, 8, 9. These successes so alarmed the Spartans that they sent Antalcidas to Tiribazus, the Satrap of Western Asia, proposing to give up to the king the Greek cities in Asia, and that the Islands should be independent; Conon resisted this, and Antalcidas persuaded Tiribazus to arrest him [*ὡς ἀδικοῦντα βασιλέα*], and he was imprisoned at Sardis [Xen. Hell. 4, 8, 16; Diodor. xiv. 85]. Isocrates insinuates that he was put to death by the Persians [Panegyr. 154], but from ll. 255-267 of this speech it seems probable that he escaped again to Cyprus, and died a natural death there. But this arrest in B.C. 393 was the end of his political life. Tiribazus was superseded in his satrapy in the following year, which perhaps may account for Conon's escape. For the doubt as to his escape, see Nepos. Con. 5, *Nonnulli eum ad regem abductum ibique periisse scriptum reliquerunt. Contra ea Dinon historicus, cui nos plurimum de Persicis rebus credimus, effugisse scripsit; illud addubitat utrum Tiribazo sciente an imprudente sit factum.*

78-9. **τὴν ἀδελφὴν** '*my* sister.' **αὐτοὺς** *i.e.* Nikophemus and his son.

80-2. **τῇ τε πόλει . . ἀρέσκοντας** 'conforming to the wishes of the State at that time at least.' He means to admit that Nikophemus and his son afterwards were guilty of disloyalty, but at the time of the marriage had shown no signs of it. **ἀρέσκοντας** conveys the idea of outside conformity rather than active loyalty.

83. **ἐπεὶ ὅτι κ.τ.λ.** 'for that my father did not make this match for the sake of money, one may easily feel sure from his whole life and actions.'

86. **ὅτ' ἦν ἐν ἡλικίᾳ** 'when he was of age,' *i.e.* for marriage. See on iv. l. 209.

88-91. **οὐδὲν ἐπιφερομένην** 'who brought no dower with her.' Cf. Aesch. in Ctes. 172. **ὅτι δέ** 'but (he did so) because she was daughter of Xenophon, son of Euripides, who was not only excellent in private life, but thought worthy by you to be Strategus, as I am told.' For another instance of *anacoluthon*, see v. l. 256. For **ἀκούω** cp. l. 29. **Xenophon, son of Euripides**, was one of the Strategi at the time of the surrender of Potidaea in B.C. 430 [Thuc. 2, 70, 1]; and again in an expedition against the revolted Chalcidians in B.C. 429, in which he and the other Strategi were defeated and killed [Thuc. 2, 79, 1, and 10].

93. **ἐδόκουν κάκιον γεγονέναι** 'they seemed to be of a somewhat inferior character.' **κάκιον** is used adverbially; but the phrase is certainly harsh as applied to *persons*. [Perhaps we should read *κακίους*.] Bremi explains **κάκιον γεγονέναι** to mean 'worse born,' *i.e.* not true-bred Athenian, comparing vi. l. 413, *καλῶς . . ὄντα*. But in that place the right reading is probably *καθαρῶς Ἀθηναῖον ὄντα*. Besides, the point of this passage is a contrast between character and wealth, not purity of blood. We must suppose, therefore, a phrase *κακῶς γίγνεσθαι* equivalent to *κακῶς ἔχειν* 'to be ill,' *i.e.* in behaviour, reputation, etc.

94-5. **Παιανιεῖ** 'of Paeania,' a deme of the tribe Pandionis. **βελτίονα . . ἢ πλουσιώτερον** 'better in character than in wealth.' For this idiomatic use of two comparatives, *when two properties of the same subject are compared*, see Clyde, § 23 d, Madvig, § 92 a.

96-7. **τὴν δὲ . . Μυρρινουσίῳ** 'and the other to a man who had become poor from no fault of his own, and who was his nephew—Phædrus, of the deme Murrhinoutè;' the arrangement of the words is somewhat unnatural. *Μυρρινούτη* was a deme of the tribe Ægeis. This is the same name and deme as that of the speaker in Plato's dialogue, Phædr. 244 A. **ἐπιδούς** see viii. l. 74.

98. **Ἀριστοφάνει τὸ ἴσον** 'an equal sum to Aristophanes.' As the speaker's father appears to have had only two daughters (l. 108), we must suppose that the wife of Phædrus made a second marriage with Aristophanes.

100-1. **ὥστε εὖ εἰδέναι** 'on condition of feeling certain.' 'If I could but feel certain.' Cf. Dem., *ἐξὸν αὐτοῖς τῶν λοιπῶν ἄρχειν Ἑλλήνων ὥστ' αὐτοὺς ὑπακούειν βασιλεῖ.* Clyde, p. 204, note. **κηδεσταῖς** *supra*, l. 74.

102-4. **καὶ νῦν** 'so now in point of fact.' **Ἀλωπεκῆθεν** 'of the

deme Alopekè,' of the tribe Antiochis. ὃς . . Ἑλλησπόντῳ.
* *i.e.* who fell at Ægospotami, see vi. l. 33.

* 107. **ἐπέδωκε** see viii. l. 74. *Supra*, 97.

111. **ὅτι πολλοῖς ἂν μᾶλλον ἐχρῆτο κ.τ.λ.** 'That there were many persons he would have selected for his confidant rather than my father.' So *οἱ χρώμενοι* for 'his friends,' in Isocr. 125 A.

113-4. **ἐκείνῳ . . πράττειν** 'his (my father's) bent was for minding his own affairs,' *i.e.* not public affairs. He was
* **ἀπράγμων**, see on viii. l. 169.

119. **πρῶτον μὲν, κ.τ.λ.** Dionysius the Elder, tyrant of Syracuse [B.C. 406-367] had been assisted by the Spartans in establishing his power in B.C. 406 [Diod. xiv. 10], and he seems always to have maintained a friendship with them, which this embassy [B.C. 393] failed to break down permanently ; for long after, in B.C. 371, we find him sending a body of auxiliaries to aid Sparta and Athens against Thebes [Xen. Hell. 7, 1, 20]. See Hicks, p. 150.

120-1. **Εὐνόμου.** This may be the same man of whom we hear as in command of thirteen ships to act against the Spartans under Gorgopax, in B.C. 388, with whom he had a naval battle by moonlight, and lost three ships [Xen. 5, 1, 5-9]. **ξένου** 'proxenus' or 'guest-friend.' Though Dionysius was so much allied with Sparta, he had yet managed so far to keep on good terms with Athens as to be honoured with the citizenship. [Dem. (?) 161, *ὑμεῖς ἔδοτε πολιτείαν Εὐαγόρᾳ τῷ Κυπρίῳ καὶ Διονυσίῳ τῷ Συρακοσίῳ*]. A fragment of the stone on which the decree was engraved has been found. See Hicks, p. 126.

123. **τῶν ἐν Πειραιεῖ** referring to the democratic exiles in the Peiræus under Thrasybulus in 404-3 B.C. See Appendix. **παραγενομένων** 'in his company.'

125. **Εὐαγόρᾳ.** Evagoras was tyrant of Salamis in Cyprus till B.C. 374, for over thirty years. His character is drawn in very attractive colours by Isocrates in a panegyric addressed to his son and successor, Nikocles (Orat. ix.) He seems always to have been devoted to the Athenians, and to have been restive under his subordination to the Persians. For the assistance he rendered to Conon, especially in the matter of the command in the Persian fleet, a statue of him was put up in the Ceramicus side by side with one of Conon, and Conon's son Timotheos, see Pausan. 1, 3, 2. Many Greeks besides Conon had found refuge under his protection [Isocr. ix. 51-57]. For his Athenian

citizenship, see *supra* on l. 120. The inscription of this decree also has been found in a broken condition. Hicks, p. 127.

129. **ἔπεισαν** 'they succeeded in persuading.' See on v. l. 112.

131-2. **μετὰ δὲ ταῦτα . . βοήθειαν.** Though Evagoras had acted with the Persians at the battle of Cnidus, it was not long before he was at war with them,—a war which was said to have lasted ten years, *i.e.* from B.C. 385 to 376 [Clint. F. H. vol. ii. p. 279]. Before this he had apparently begged help from Athens, and such help we find sent under Chabrias in B.C. 388 [Xen. Hell. 5, 1, 10]. The embassy was perhaps in the preceding year. Nepos. Chabr. 2, *publice ab Atheniensibus Evagoræ adjutor datus.*

137. **πελταστὰς** 'foreign mercenaries, light armed.' This word is not used of Athenian troops until the time of Iphicrates (circ. B.C. 391). In Thucyd. it is always used of foreign mercenaries. Yet in B.C. 409 Thrasylus made an experiment in forming a corps of such troops. Xen. *Hell.* 1, 2, 1.

139. **δ' οὖν** 'however,' 'be that as it may.' Resumes the main subject after a digression.

141-3. **καὶ τοῦ ἀδελφοῦ . . κατεχρήσατο** 'and having 40 minæ belonging to his half-brother deposited at his house, he used them all up. **παρ' αὑτῷ** 'at his own house'; *αὐτῷ* might, however, stand; see on vii. 64.

147. **ἔνδον** see *infra*, 305.

149-154. 'What man think you, gentlemen,—keen after distinction and getting letters from his father telling him that he would find no lack of anything in Cyprus; having, moreover, been elected ambassador, and being on the point of sailing to Evagoras,—would be likely to leave anything he possessed behind, and not rather gratify that monarch, if he could, by contributing everything he had, and so make a handsome profit?' **ἐκείνῳ** is Evagoras. **μὴ ἐλάττω,** *i.e. πλείω.* See on v. l. 145. The point of the argument is, that Aristophanes expected to make a great profit by anything he contributed, and therefore would contribute all he had or could get.

155. **Εὔνομον** there appears to be some mistake here, as more than one witness is called, and to some points with which Eunomus was not concerned.

159. **ἐκομίσθη . . τριήρους** 'for it was brought to them on the trireme,' *i.e.* the public trireme which took out Aristo-

phanes as ambassador, and on its return brought back the money lent.

163-4. **ὁ Πυριλάμπους** the son of Pyrilampes. **αὐτῷ** sc. Aristophanes.

164-7. **ἐδεήθη μου . . τριηραρχίας** 'begged me to go to Aristophanes (telling me that he had received a gold cup from the King of Persia as a pledge) and get for him 16 minæ on it, to spend upon his trierarchy.' There is no real difficulty in this sentence. Demus applied through his brother-in-law to Aristophanes, both as supposed to be well off, and as being ambassador, and so likely to wish the expedition to be well set out. **ἐπ' αὐτῇ** cf. *δανείζειν ἐπὶ νηΐ*, Dem. 1281. **λαβεῖν** 'to get ready money.' Cf. Arist. Nub. 1135, *ὦ δαιμόνιε, τὸ μὲν νυνὶ μὴ λαβῇς.* **ἔχοι** optat. in *oratio obliqua*, see on vi. l. 62. So also **ἀφίκοιτο.**

168. **λύσεσθαι ἀποδοὺς κ.τ.λ.** sc. *ἔφη*. 'He said that he would redeem it by a payment of twenty minæ.'

172-3. **μέλλων δ' κ.τ.λ.** 'and though he was to take with him the gold cup, and to receive four minæ as interest.' For the fut. inf. after *μέλλω*, see ii. l. 164. **τὸ χρυσίον** seems to be used, though somewhat peculiarly, for 'plate.' In Thucyd. 2, 13, 3, we have *χρυσίον ἄσημον.*

174. **καὶ προσδεδανεῖσθαι τοῖς ξένοις ἄλλοθεν** 'that he had actually had to go elsewhere to borrow besides from his friends,' *infra*, l. 371. *προσδεδανεῖσθαι τοῖς ξένοις* 'to have had lent by friends.' *τοῖς ξένοις* is the dative of the agent. See on v. l. 226. Others would tr. *τοῖς ξένοις* 'for his mercenaries.' *ἀλλόθεν* explains *τοῖς ξένοις* 'elsewhere than from his own resources.' *πρὸς* 'in addition to what he had spent of his own.'

175. **ἐπειδὴ ἥδιστ' ἂν ἀνθρώπων** 'for (he said) no one would be more glad than he either to take that pledge on the spot, or to grant my request.'

181-2. **χαλκώματα . . σύμμικτα** 'miscellaneous bronze utensils,' not of a choice or valuable description.

186-7. **πρὶν . . ἡμᾶς** 'before we won the sea-fight,' *i.e.* at Cnidus. This successful engagement paved the way for the return of Conon to Athens, and the restoration of the fortifications, and no doubt gave those engaged in it considerable spoil. See l. 233. Xen. Hell. 4, 3, 11. Diodorus (xiv. 83) gives the numbers engaged as 85 Spartan ships and 90 of the fleet under Pharnabazus and Conon. Cnidus is a town and island (joined by a causeway to the mainland) on the extremity of a peninsula in Caria, which terminates with the promontory Triopium (*Kap Krio*).

188. **Ῥαμνοῦντι** 'at Rhamnus,' a deme of the tribe Aiantis.

189. **ἐπ' Εὐβούλου ἄρχοντος** 'in the archonship of Eubulus.' He is called in the list of Eponymous Archons *Εὐβουλίδης* (Hermann, p. 403) B.C. 394.

ἐν . . τέτταρσιν ἢ πέντε ἔτεσι Aristophanes did not return from his mission to Evagoras, but was put to death for some cause, l. 38. The four or five years are reckoned from 394-3 to 389-8 B.C. See on l. 131.

* 192-4. **χορηγοῖς . . εἰσενηνοχέναι.** See on ii. l. 209. **οἰκίαν** *domum*, 'a private town house,' distinguished from *συνοικία*, 'a lodging house.' The price of houses in Attica varied from 3 to 120 minæ. See Boeckh, p. 66.

195. **γῆς τε . . πλέθρα** 'more than 300 plethra of land,' about 80 acres English. House and land together cost him 5 talents (*infra*, l. 273), *i.e.* 300 minæ. The land therefore cost 250 minæ, as the house was 50 minæ (l. 194). Land in Attica therefore cost between 3 and 4 minæ per English acre (*i.e.* from £12 to £16). But this of course would vary according to the situation and nature of the soil. See Boeckh, p. 62.

197. **ἔπιπλα** 'moveable property,' including dress, furniture, and utensils, Xen. Oecon. ix. 6-7.

199-201. **ἐξενεγκεῖν** 'produce,' cf. *δεῖγμα ἐξέφερε καθ' ἑαυτοῦ*, Dem. de Cor. 323. **ἐνίοτε γὰρ . . παρέχοι** 'for sometimes, though ever so desirous, one cannot buy things which will perpetually give pleasure ever after,' sc. and so they are dispensed with; and accordingly even rich men have seldom a great deal of such property to produce.

This is a curious remark, suggesting the poorness of the Athenian houses and their appointments, arising partly no doubt from the public and far from domestic nature of the life led by the citizens. [See Boeckh, p. 64, who says that building large and fine private houses only began about the time of
* Demosthenes.] For **τοιαῦτα ἅ**, see on ii. l. 270.

203. **σκεύη** 'furniture,' much the same as **ἔπιπλα** in l. 197, but not including like it personal ornaments, etc. Cf. Dem. 1156, *τὰ δ' ἐκ τῆς ἄλλης οἰκίας ἐξέφερον σκεύη*.

203-4. **οὐχ ὅπως . . ἀφηρπάσθησαν** 'not only did you fail

to sell their furniture, but even the very doors of the chambers were pulled off.' He means that in the case of confiscations the houses were often abandoned and plundered, so that the State got nothing. Reiske mistranslated and misunderstood the passage from wrongly taking *οὐχ ὅπως* = *non modo;* whereas it = *non modo non*, see Madvig, § 212. For damage done to
* confiscated property standing unguarded, see ii. ll. 43-5. It reminds us of the account of the general scramble for the property of the abandoned monasteries after the suppression.

208. **ἀπεφαίνετο** 'were accounted for,' *i.e.* to the treasury. Cf. Dem. 821, *λῆμμα οὐδὲν ἐμοὶ γεγενημένον ἀποφαίνουσι. Id.* 480, *πλέον ἢ δέκα καὶ ἕκατον τάλαντα ἀπέφηνεν ἀπὸ τῶν πολεμίων, in ærarium rettulit.*

210. **πρὸς τοὺς συνδίκους** 'before the revenue commissioners.'
* See ix. l. 85.

214. **ἃς ᾤχετο λαβὼν** 'which he took with him when he went off,' *i.e.* to Cyprus.

219. **μηδ' αὐτοὺς κ.τ.λ.** 'though we have nothing for ourselves even.'

223. **Τιμοθέῳ τῷ Κόνωνος** the similarity of the case consists in this, that Timotheus, like Aristophanes, resided at Athens; while his father Conon, like Nikophemus, lived and died at Cyprus. Timotheus, son of Conon, played a very conspicuous part in Athenian history, from B.C. 380-378 till his death in about 352 B.C. A speech against him on a private suit is extant, ascribed to Demosthenes. Nepos, in his life of him, says that he was *disertus impiger laboriosus rei militaris peritus neque minus civitatis regendæ* (Nep. Timoth. 1). He was a close friend of Isocrates (Isocr. xv. 101). He is said to have taken more cities than any other commander, namely, twenty-four (Isocr. xv. 107-13).

224. **ἐκείνου** sc. Conon.

229. **οὐδὲ πολλοστὸν . . ὑμῖν** 'not even a very small fraction of the expectation prevalent among you.' For **πολλοστὸν μέρος**, see vii. l. 224.

231-2. **Κόνωνα . . προστάττοι** see *supra*, ll. 75-6.

233. **ὠφελειῶν** *i.e.* the gains made in the war by prizes, etc. See *supra* on ll. 186-7.

238-9. **ἐνθάδε** sc. at Athens. **παρ' αὐτοῖς** sc. in Cyprus.

241-2. **ἡγοῦντο . . ἐνθάδε** and they thought that their property in Cyprus was equally safe as that at Athens.' **σᾶ** is the Attic contraction of *σῶα*.

243-5. **καὶ εἴ τις . . διένειμεν** 'even if a man had divided among his sons what he had not earned himself, but had inherited from his father'—much less if, as was Conon's case, it was what he had gained himself by his own exertions.

245. **οὐκ ἐλάχιστα ἂν αὐτῷ ὑπέλιπε** 'he would have reserved the greater part for himself.' **οὐκ ἐλάχιστα** = *πλεῖστα* by the *litotes* usual in Greek. See on v. l. 145. He wants to show that Conon kept the greater part of his property in Cyprus, just as he wished them to believe that Nikophemus did.

249-50. **εἰ μὴ τῇ . . πόλει** a conventional reservation, 'unless some great benefit therefrom is to arise to the State.'

258. **ἀναθήματα.** See on iv. l. 186.

260. **στατῆρας.** The Attic stater = 20 drachmæ. The Kyzikene stater = 28 drachmæ. See v. l. 81.

264-5. **τουτων δὲ κεφάλαιον . . τάλαντα** 'and the total of these sums is 40 talents' (about £9640). The calculation is not an accurate one. If the staters mentioned are Attic staters (*i.e.* 20 drachmæ), the account will stand thus:—

ἀναθήματα (5000 staters at 20 drachmæ)	16	talents	40	minæ
Legacy to nephew	1	,,	40	,,
Do. to brother	3	,,	0	,,
Remainder to son	17	,,	0	,,
	38	talents	20	minæ.

If the staters are Kyzikene staters, *i.e.* valued at 28 Attic drachmæ, 5000 of them will be 23 talents 20 minæ; and the total 45 talents. See Appendix.

266-7. **ἀπεφάνθη.** See *supra*, l. 208. **ἐν τῇ νόσῳ ὢν** 'being in his last illness,' clearly indicating, according to the speaker, that Conon died at Cyprus. See *supra*, l. 75.

272-84. The speaker then goes on to show that he can account for the expenditure of fifteen talents by Aristophanes, more than a third of the amount of Conon's property (and that excluding what his father Nikophemus kept at Cyprus), which is much more than he could have been expected to have at all, and shows that he could not have left much behind him at his death. His point is that Nikophemus, like Conon, kept the bulk of his property at Cyprus, not at Athens; and that his son Aristophanes can yet be shown to have spent at Athens more than he could reasonably be expected to have had. He reckons in this way:—

Purchase of house and land . . .	5 talents	0 minæ
spent as Choragus for self and father	0 ,,	50 ,,
spent as Trierarch	1 ,,	20 ,,
εἰσφοραὶ for self and father . . .	0 ,,	40 ,,
expedition to Sicily	1 ,,	40 ,,
mission to Cyprus	5 ,,	0 ,,
	14 talents	30 minæ

He says the whole is little less than fifteen talents, and we must observe that the price of the land is said to be *more* than five talents, but he does not say how much more. For the **κατεχορήγησε** 'used up as Choragus,' **τριηράρχων** and **εἰσενήνεκται** contributed in extraordinary taxes (*εἰσφοραί*), see *supra*, l. 191, and v. l. 140. For the expedition to Sicily, *supra*, l. 120, and the mission to Cyprus, l. 131. **ἀποφανθῆναι**, see *supra*, ll. 208, 266.

293. **ἀκήκοα**. See *supra*, ll. 29, 91. This is the third time the speaker has prefaced a general observation with this word. It seems as though he were assuming the rôle of an inexperienced and ingenuous youth,—another instance of the *dramatic* art of Lysias.

298-300. **αὐτίκα** 'for instance.' See l. 438. **Ἰσχομάχῳ**. There is a man of this name mentioned by Andoc. de Myst. § 124; and by Demosth. (?), Contra Theotim. 1331. But there is nothing to enable us to identify them. **ἐνειμάσθην** 'divided between them.'

304-6. **οἶκος** 'estate,' whereas *οἰκία* is the 'house.' *πάντα τοῦ οἴκου εἶναι ὅσα τις κέκτηται*, Xen. Œcon. 1, 5. **Νικίου** Nicias was exceedingly rich, Thucyd. 7, 86, 4, *ὅτι πλούσιος ἦν*,—as was his son Nikeratus, Xen. Hell. 2, 3, 39. **καὶ τούτων τὰ πολλὰ ἔνδον** 'and that too mostly in ready money.' **τούτων** sc. *ταλάντων*. **ἔνδον** lit. 'in the house,' as opposed to property in land or mortgages. Demosth. in Aphob. A. 816, *ἀργυρίου δ' ἔνδον ὀγδοήκοντα μνᾶς*, as opposed to money invested, *ἐνεργά*. See *supra*, l. 147.

309. **τὴν οὐσίαν** attracted into the case of its relative *ἥν*. Francken proposed to avoid this by altering *ἀξία ἐστὶν* to *ἀξίαν ἴστε*.

310-11. **Καλλίας** the third of the name (vii. l. 214) was

celebrated for his profligacy and extravagance; he was the prosecutor of Andocides for profanation, who says of him (de Myst. § 130), that common report affirmed that his father, οἰόμενος υἱὸν τρέφειν ἀλιτήριον αὐτῷ τρέφειν 'a curse.' He, however, was a great friend of the Sophists, and the scene of Xenophon's 'Banquet' and Plato's 'Protagoras' is laid at his house. He is
* said to have died in great poverty. **τοίνυν** 'again,' ii. l. 68.

313. **ἐτιμήσατο**, sc. τὴν οὐσίαν, 'he valued his own property at 200 talents.' ἐτιμήσατο is middle, as in the phrase θανάτου τιμῶμαι, 'I assess my punishment at death,' whereas the Dicasts would say τιμῶμεν. For the genitive ταλάντων, see Goodwin, § 178.

314-5. **τὸ τοίνυν . . ἐστι** 'his rateable property, you know, is assessed at not even two talents.' τίμημα is not the value of a property, but of that part of it considered subject to taxation. The proportion thus rateable varied,—in the first class it was a fifth, and less in the lower classes. Accordingly Callias' property would be at least ten talents—a sum equal to that which, according to Plutarch, his brother-in-law Alcibiades forced him to advance, in addition to his wife's original dowry, on the birth of his son (Plut. Alcib. 8).

315. **Κλεοφῶντα**. See v. l. 55.

319. **οἱ προσήκοντες καὶ οἱ κηδεσταί** 'his relations by blood
* and by marriage.' See vi. l. 4.

321. **ἀρχαιοπλούτων** 'men possessed of hereditary wealth,' opposed to νεόπλουτοι. The word seems properly to belong to poetry. See L. and Sc.

324. **ὁ δεῖνα** 'this or that man.' Goodwin, § 85.

328-30. **αὐτοὶ γὰρ κ.τ.λ.** 'for you yourselves lately heard in the assembly that Diotimus had forty talents more than he acknowledged himself from the ship captains and merchants.' **Διότιμος**. We find Diotimus in joint command with Iphicrates in B.C. 388-7 [Xen. Hell. 5, 1, 25]; the word ἔναγχος therefore may indicate a date not long after this; but that of course depends on the assumption that the money thus unaccounted for was obtained during this command. We find Diotimus also acting as a subordinate of Alcibiades in 408 B.C. [Xen. Hell. 1, 3, 12].

332-4. **ἀπογράφοντος** 'giving in an account.' **δεομένης κ.τ.λ.** 'in spite of the fact that the State was in want of money,' see *supra*, l. 66. In B.C. 387 the Persian and Spartan fleets under Tiribazus and Antalcidas, supplemented by ten ships sent by Dionysius, so blocked up the Hellespont as to prevent the supplies of corn from Pontus, on which Athens greatly depended, from reaching her; and caused great distress and loss. This, combined with the long-protracted hostilities, will well account for the poverty of the exchequer.

335-8. **λογίσασθαι** 'to give in his accounts.' **εἶτα ἔπαθέ τι** 'and then if anything had happened to him,' a common euphemism for *ἀπέθανε*.

343-5. **αἴτιοι οὖν εἰσι . . ἐπιθυμοῦντες** 'that you have ere now been deceived in regard to many persons,—yes, and that some have perished quite unjustly,—you too have to thank those men who show reckless audacity in falsehood, and are eager to bring vexatious charges against others.' **αἴτιοι ὑμῖν** (like *ἄξιοι ὑμῖν*) 'blamable by you.' Madv. § 34. Cf. Demosth. 195, *πολλῶν κακῶν ἡ ἄνοια πολλοῖς αἰτία γίγνεται.* **πολλῶν . . ψευσθῆναι** 'to be deceived *about* many.' (Cf. construction of *ἁμαρτάνω*.) Goodwin, § 171.

346-9. **τέτταρα ἢ πέντε ἔτη ἐφεξῆς ἐστρατήγει** 'was Strategus for four or five years running.' He must refer to the years from B.C. 411-10 to B.C. 407-6, a period in the life of Alcibiades including the battle of Cyzicus (in which Mindarus was killed), the sieges of Chalcedon and Byzantium, his return to Athens, and his second disgrace. Plut. Alcib. 28-36. It is not clear whether Alcibiades during all this time was technically a Strategus; but he was in command of Athenian vessels. **διπλάσια . . αἱ πόλεις . . διδόναι.** An instance of Alcibiades levying money on the subject towns occurs in Thucyd. viii. 108, 2, in the case of Halicarnassus (B.C. 411). W. condemns the whole section.

351-3. **ἀποθανών** Alcibiades was murdered in Phrygia, B.C. 404. **τῶν ἐπιτροπευσάντων** 'from his guardians,' viz. Pericles and his brother Ariphron. Plut. Alcib. 1.

366. **πιστεύετε τούτοις ἀληθῆ λέγειν οἵ, κ.τ.λ.** 'believe that they speak truth who,' etc. *ἀληθῆ λέγειν* is equivalent to a noun in the accusative case. *πιστεύειν τινί τι* (like *credo aliquid alicui*) is not common. Cf. Xen. Mem. 4, 4, 17, *τίνι δ' ἄν τις μᾶλλον πιστεύσειε παρακαταθέσθαι ἢ χρήματα ἢ υἱοὺς ἢ θυγατέρας.*

369-372. A recapitulation of § 21-3.

374-5. **οὔτε . . ἀντεῖπον** ill-behaviour to parents being a legal offence: see Appendix II.

* 376. **ἐνεκάλεσεν** for *ἐγκαλέω* and *ἔγκλημα*, see viii. l. 78.

376-8. **ἐγγὺς τε οἰκῶν . . οὐδεπώποτε.** 'And though living near the Agora, I never yet was seen in court or council chamber.' **πρὸς** 'near,' would seem to imply 'before' as a defendant or accuser; but then what could his living 'near the Agora' have to do with it? He means to claim the character of *ἀπράγμων*, one who minded his own business and was
* not perpetually haunting the law-courts, see ii. l. 1, 2; though
a want of interest in them was also considered a mark of *ῥᾳθυμία* and *μαλακία*, see iv. l. 69, 70. The Agora was the
* centre of business, see xiii. l. 150.

387. **οἱ προαναλίσκοντες** 'who advance money,' *προαναλίσκειν* is to advance money to be repaid. **οὐ—τούτου** sc. *τοῦ προαναλίσκειν* 'not simply from a desire to make a necessary advance to the State.' No holder of an office (*ἀρχή*) received a salary (though those who had special or subordinate service, *ὑπηρεσία*, did); but we have already seen that the office of Strategus brought or was expected to bring wealth [ll. 235, 346], and the same in more or less degree would be true of other offices, the Archonship, etc.

390-2. **τὰς δὲ χορηγίας . . εἰσενήνοχεν.** *Supra*, ll. 273-6.

395. **πεντήκοντα** we learn from l. 412 that he lived to seventy. His public life therefore begins at twenty. See iv. l. 209.

398-9. **ἐν οὖν . . πεφευγέναι** 'now in a public career, extending over so long a time, it is but natural to suppose that a man with the reputation for ancestral wealth should have shrunk from no kind of expense.'

The sentence is by way of introducing the witnesses who are coming to testify to the amount paid in public services by the father of the speaker. He says: 'Now you would of course feel sure that he spent a great deal, but I shall call witnesses to prove it.' The whole point of the argument is that a man who acted so liberally would not have been guilty of the meanness charged. **ἐξ ἀρχῆς** 'originally'

In spite of ll. 388-9, I feel sure that the old editors were wrong in translating **ἔχειν τι ἐξ ἀρχῆς** *magistratu suo aliquid acquisivisse*. Cf. *ἀρχαιοπλούτων*, l. 321.

401. **ἐννέα τάλαντα καὶ δισχίλιαι δραχμαί** 9 talents 20 minæ (about £2240).

403-4. **ἰδίᾳ** 'privately,' as opposed to the above-mentioned acts of munificence in *public* interests. **συνεξέδωκε . . ἀδελφάς**
* 'helped to portion daughters or sisters.' See on viii. l. 74.

τοὺς δ' ἐλύσατο 'and paid ransom for some.' This need of ransom must have often arisen at this time of continued and complicated hostilities; one such instance we have heard of in vii. l. 208.

411. **πλάσασθαι τὸν τρόπον τὸν αὑτοῦ** 'to assume a false character' (*πλάττειν fingere*). Cf. Dem. de Cer. 304, *τῆς φιλανθρωπίας, ἣν . . ἐκεῖνος ἐπλάττετο.*

413. **οὐδ' ἂν εἷς λάθοι** 'nobody in the world could continue to hide his baseness through a period of seventy years.' **ἐν** see l. 398.

418-9. **τῷ χρόνῳ ὃν . . νομίσατε** 'which be sure is the clearest test of truth.' Rauchenstein quotes Pind. Ol. xi. 53, *ὅ τ' ἐξελέγχων μόνος ἀλαθείαν ἐτήτυμον χρόνος.* Xen. Hell. 3, 2, 2, *συνεμαρτύρησεν ὁ ἀληθέστατος λεγόμενος χρόνος εἶναι.*

424-5. **εἰς χρημάτων λόγον** 'as a mere question of money.' **ἀποψηφίσασθαι** sc. *ἐμοῦ* 'to vote my acquittal.'

430-1. **ὀλίγα κατὰ μικρὸν . . ὠφελείας** 'to make the little I have gradually serve for the public advantage.'

432-4. **καὶ οὔτε . . δημεύσαιτε,** *i.e.* I shall not be suffering from a sense of injustice, and the State will really be better off than by the confiscation.'

* 437. **τοιαῦτα ὅθεν** equivalent to *ἐξ ὧν.* See on ii. l. 270.

438-40. **αὐτίκα** 'for instance,' *supra*, l. 298. **ὅτε ἵππευεν** 'when he was serving in the cavalry he purchased horses, not only fine ones (for chargers), but such as were fitted for racing.' **ἀθλητὴς** employed in the *ἆθλα*. Plat. Parm. 137 A. **ὅτε ἵππευεν** to serve in the cavalry was the duty of the richer men (see vii. l. 55), who also alone could afford to keep horses for the races (*ἱπποτροφεῖν . . ὃ τῶν εὐδαιμονεστάτων ἔργον ἐστί*, Isocr. de big. § 33); and from this passage it seems that a man would be likely to choose the time of his cavalry service if possible for keeping horses for the races, the convenience of doing the two together being obvious.

441-2. **ὥστε . . στεφανωθῆναι** 'so that the city was named in the proclamation of the victor, and he himself received the wreath.' The wreath in these two games was parsley.

τέσσαρές εἰσιν ἀγῶνες ἀν' Ἑλλάδα· τέσσαρες ἱροί.
οἱ δύο μὲν θνητῶν, οἱ δύο δ' ἀθανάτων.
Ζηνὸς Λητοΐδαο Παλαίμονος Ἀρχεμόροιο.
ἆθλα δὲ τῶν κότινος μῆλα σέλινα πίτυς.

The credit reflected on the town of the victor is continually the theme of Pindar's Odes.

ORATION XI. [22.]

['The importation of corn into Attica,' says Boeckh (p. 81), 'was equal to at least a third of the consumption.' It became therefore necessary to make careful regulations concerning it. Special officers (σιτοφύλακες) were appointed to see that these regulations were obeyed, and the penalty of death was inflicted not only on dealers who infringed the law, but sometimes even on these officers for failing to prevent it (§ 16).

The retail dealers (σιτοπῶλαι, κάπηλοι, l. 164) were forbidden to charge more than one obol per *phormus* or *medimnus* in excess of the price at which they had purchased. And as an obvious way of evading this regulation would be to purchase a large stock and wait for a rise in the market price, a further regulation forbade the purchase of more than fifty *phormi* at a time.

In this case information had been laid before the Boulè that certain corn dealers had purchased more than the legal quantity of corn. Some members of the Boulè proposed that they should forthwith be handed over to the Eleven for execution. This proposal was resisted by the present speaker, who urged that they should have a fair trial. This seems to have caused him some discredit, as though he had wished to defend their illegal conduct. Accordingly, when the preliminary investigation came on before the Boulè, as was the ordinary method in cases of impeachment, he spoke against them by way of purging himself of the imputation (§ 3). And when in due course the case was remitted to an ordinary court, he delivered this speech against them.

The speech is almost entirely an appeal to the judges to act according to the laws, to vindicate their authority, and punish the offenders for the public advantage. There is no question of guilt or innocence, for the defendants admit their breach of the law. Their only pleas were—(1) That they acted in accordance with a suggestion of the σιτοφύλακες; (2) That what they did was for the public advantage, insomuch that it secured a supply of corn. He answers—(1) By showing on evidence that no such suggestion was made by the σιτοφύλακες, and that if it had been it would not excuse a breach of a plain law; and (2) That their plea of acting for the public advantage is contradicted by the fact of their having varied the selling price by as much as a drachma in one day,—in itself a breach of the law.

There is no means of definitely settling the date of the speech;

but from § 14 we should perhaps gather that it was at any rate as late as B.C. 386-7. For the whole subject of the corn trade and laws at Athens, see Boeckh, pp. 81 *sq.*]

5. **ποιουμένους λόγους** vii. l. 260, 'making speeches,' almost equivalent to *κατηγοροῦντες*, and distinguished from λογοποιεῖν, * l. 101, which has an idea of falseness. **συκοφαντεῖν,** ii. l. 257, 'to be vexatious' or 'pettifogging.'

8. **οἱ πρυτάνεις.** The senate of 500 was divided into *Fifties*, called *πρυτάνεις*, for the management of the Ecclesia. These fifties subdivided themselves into *tens* (*πρόεδροι*), each of which took turns in that duty, and elected *one* of their number as President (*ἐπιστάτης*). **ἀπέδοσαν**, *retttulerunt*, 'they brought the case before the Boulè.

We must understand *τὸ χρῆμα* or *τὸν λόγον* after *ἀπέδοσαν*, as implied in *περὶ αὐτῶν*. Cf. Eur. Orat. 251, *λόγον ἀπόδος ἐφ' ὅτι χρέος ἐμόλετε.*

11. **τοῖς ἕνδεκα.** See iv. l. 60.

16. **ἡμῶν,** sc. *βουλευτῶν*.

18. **πεισθείσης . . ταῦτα** 'being persuaded to this.'

20-3. **τοὺς λόγους . . ἐποιούμην** here has no sense of accusing. See *infra*, 95. **πρὸς . . βουλὴν** 'before the Boulè,' cf. v. l. 36. **ὅτ' ἦν αὐτοῖς ἡ κρίσις** 'when the preliminary trial was before them.' *κρίσις* here is equivalent to *ἀνάκρισις*, the preliminary trial before a magistrate to see whether the action was maintainable (*εἰσαγώγιμος*). 'When an impeachment was preferred before the Boulè . . . if their sentence was in favour of the impeachment they passed a resolution to that effect, of which their secretary gave notice to the Thesmothetæ, and it became the duty of those magistrates to bring the case for trial before a jury'—(Kennedy). **ἔργῳ ἀπελογησάμην** 'I made a practical defence' against these charges, *i.e.* by accusing the corn dealers I showed practically that it was from no personal feeling for them that I acted as I did before. **τῶν . . ἄλλων,** sc. *ῥητόρων vel βουλευτῶν*, cf. l. 10.

25-7. **τούτων . . ἕνεκα** 'for the reasons I have described.'

27-9. **αἰσχρὸν . . ψηφίσησθε** 'I think it base to stop till you have voted.' *πρὶν ἂν* should follow a negative sentence (Goodwin, § 240-2); but *αἰσχρὸν . . παύσασθαι* may be said to contain a negative idea. M. and T. § 647.

30-9. For an examination similarly reported in the first person, see v. l. 167. One of the *σιτοπῶλαι* is called up upon the Beına, and interrogated.

31. **ὡς πεισόμενος** 'on condition of obeying.'

33-5. **ἄλλο τι . . ἤ** = *nonne?* and therefore **ἔγωγε**, sc. *ἀξιῶ*, may stand in answer.

36-8. **πλείω . . πεντήκοντα φορμῶν ὧν . . κελεύει** 'more than the fifty measures which the law provides as the limit permissible.' **φορμός**, according to Boeckh (p. 82), is about the same as the medimnus. It properly means the 'basket' to carry it in [Rt. *φερ*, *φέρω*, *φορέω*, *φορ-ό-ς*, etc. Curtius, 300]. *ὧν* is attracted into the case of *φορμῶν*. **τῶν ἀρχόντων**, sc. 'the corn inspectors,' *σιτοφύλακες*, who had especial authority in the matter of the corn trade, as the *ἀγοράνομοι* in the case of other commodities, Boeckh, p. 83, *infra* 115.

44. **παρεσχόμεθα** 'I produced,' *i.e.* when speaking in the Boulè, or in the written indictment (*γραφή*).

50. **κατὰ τοὺς νόμους ὀμωμόκατε.** See vii. l. 172, and the Dicasts' oath in Appendix V.

54. **εἰς ἐκείνους**, sc. *εἰς τοὺς σιτοφύλακας*.

55. **οἱ μὲν τέσσαρες κ.τ.λ.** Of these inspectors there were fifteen, ten in the city (*ἄστυ*) and five in the Peiræus. Harpocr. s. v. *σιτοφύλακες*; Boeckh, p. 83.

58. **ὑπερβαλλόντων** 'bidding against each other.'

61. **ὡς ἀξιώτατον** 'as cheaply as possible.' **ἄξιος** 'worth the money,' hence 'cheap.'

62. **δεῖν γὰρ κ.τ.λ.** (I say to your interest) for it made no difference to them, seeing that they were obliged to sell at only an obol's profit per *phormus*.

64. **καταθέσθαι** 'to store it up.' The breach of the law would be the storing the corn till the price was raised, and then selling it so as to get more than obol profit without its being noticed that they did so, the price paid some time before being forgotten.

66-8. **καὶ ὡς κ.τ.λ.** 'and to prove that he (Anytus) said these words last year, and that they (the defendants) are proved to be guilty of engrossing corn this year.' **ἐπὶ τῆς προτέρας βουλῆς** 'during the existence of last year's Boulè.' **ἐπὶ τῆσδε** 'during the existence of this.'

70-3. **ἡγοῦμαι δ', ἂν κ.τ.λ.** 'and I think that if they really do speak the truth about the inspectors, they will not excuse themselves, but accuse them.' 78. **ἐλεύσεσθαι** rare in Attic prose.

86-7. **νυνὶ δὲ** 'but in point of fact' **δραχμῇ** 'at a profit of a drachma per *phormus*,' *i.e.* six times the legal profit. **ὥσπερ κ.τ.λ.** 'just as though they were buying by the medimnus at a time,' *i.e.* as though they had not a large store bought at a lower rate.

* 89-90. **εἰσφοράν**, see ii. l. 299. **ἣν πάντες κ.τ.λ.** 'which all the town will needs know of.'

93-4. **ταῦτα . . παρανομῆσαι** 'this they declare that they did in defiance of the law from goodwill to you.' 'I cannot believe,' he says, 'that they would refuse such a patriotic and creditable thing as an *εἰσφορά*, and yet from sheer patriotism run the risk of death by breaking the law.'

95-6. **τοιούτους . . λόγους** to advance such pleas, *supra*, l. 21.

101. **τὰς δ' αὐτοὶ λογοποιοῦσιν** 'and some disasters they invent themselves and put about.'

100-5. These rumours, set afloat in the corn market, seem to point to the period of Antalcidas' successes in the Hellespont, B.C. 388-7. **κεκλεῖσθαι τὰ ἐμπόρια** see on x. l. 332.

110-11. **ἀλλ' ἀγαπῶμεν κ.τ.λ.** 'But may think ourselves lucky if we manage to buy from them at any price whatever.' **ἀπέλθωμεν** used with any participle gives the idea of *coming badly off*. Cf. Arist. Ach. 690, *οὔ μ' ἐχρῆν σορὸν πρίασθαι τοῦτ' ὀφλῶν ἀπέρχομαι.*

115. **ἀγορανόμους**. See *supra*, l. 36.

117-18. **ἐκείνων**, se. *σιτοφυλάκων*. They were punished for not preventing the offence. **πολιτῶν ὄντων** 'and that too though the offenders were citizens,' whereas these men are only Metics.

124-6. **ὁμολογούντων . . τοὺς ἐμπόρους** 'when they confess with their own lips to making a 'corner' against the merchants.'

The ἔμποροι are the shippers of the corn, who bring it from Pontus or elsewhere, the offenders are σιτοπῶλαι 'corn-brokers' or 'dealers,' who buy it from the ἔμποροι. τοῖς εἰσπλέουσιν = τοῖς ἐμπόροις.

127. ἄλλην τινά 'any other defence than that which they have set up,' viz. that they had broken the law, but by the advice of the corn inspectors.

137. μᾶλλον, sc. rather than those who confess to the illegal act. Weidn. inserts ἢ παρὰ τῶν ἀρνουμένων.

146-9. The punishment is not only for the sake of the past, but as a deterrent for the future. Cf. vii. l. 88. τῶν παρεληλυθότων, sc. ἀδικημάτων. οὕτω i.e. 'if you acquit them.'

151. περὶ τοῦ σώματός . . ἠγωνισμένοι 'many have been tried for their life'.

158. ἀπέθνησκον 'were dying with hunger.'

163. καπήλων 'retail dealers,' an invidious term for the σιτοπῶλαι.

167. πυθέσθαι 'to be informed' as to the merits of the case.

* * * * * *

APPENDICES.

I.

'THE THIRTY.'

June-July, 405[1] B.C.

THE disaster sustained by the Athenian fleet at Ægospotami was at once recognised at Athens as extinguishing all hope of further maintaining against Sparta her power in the Ægean and Asia. The city itself, it was at once felt, must prepare to sustain a siege. The *Paralus*, which was among the few ships that escaped, hastened to carry the tidings home. It arrived in the Peiræus after nightfall. A cry of anguish was raised when the tale was told. The cry was caught up, and passed along from mouth to mouth by those who lived along the road between the long walls, and quickly reached the city. 'That night no one slept.' Preparations for a siege were hurriedly made. The harbours were blocked, the walls repaired, the guards stationed at their posts.[2] And then followed a period of terrified expectation. What would be their fate? Would it be like that which they had inflicted on the Melians, Histiæans, Scionæans, Toronæans, and Æginetans, and others whom they had massacred or sold into slavery? When would the terrible Lysander appear? When would the Spartan Ephors send their orders? All that was certain was that the city was getting crowded with citizens sent home by Lysander, who had granted their lives on condition of returning to Athens.*

Lysander himself meanwhile was in no hurry. He sent no message home until he had reduced Lesbos, and despatched

[1] In the year of Alexias (Diodor. xiii. 104), which begins June 21, 405 B.C. For account of Ægospotami, see note on vi. 1. 33.

[2] Xen. Hell, 2, 2, 3-4.

* Lysander purposely sent them home that the city, being crowded, might the sooner suffer from starvation, *εἰδὼς ὅτι ὅσῳ ἂν πλείους συλλεγῶσιν ἐς τὸ ἄστυ καὶ τὸν Πειραιᾶ θᾶττον τῶν ἐπιτηδείων ἔνδειαν ἔσεσθαι.* Xen. Hell. 2, 2, 2.

Eteonicus with ten triremes to Thrace, and had seen all the Hellenic States, except Samos, in open revolt from Athens. Even then he did not hasten back. He sent a message to the king, Agis, who was in Decelea, and another to the other king, Pausanias, who was at home, saying that he was on his way with 200 ships. The Spartans at once marched with all their available forces (πανδημεί), and occupied the Academy, a gymnasium and gardens about a mile north-west of the city, where the two kings, Pausanias and Agis, coming respectively from Sparta and Decelea, joined each other.[3] This had not long taken place when Lysander arrived at Ægina. There he expelled the Athenian settlers, and collecting such Æginetans as he could from Thyrea, put them in possession of the city.[*] He then ravaged Salamis, and finally dropped anchor at the Peiræus.[4] His large fleet effectually prevented the ingress of corn ships, while the Spartan army in the Academy shut out all hope of relief from the land side.

The Athenians now knew their fate. They were to be starved into submission and surrender. They thought, however, that surrender meant death or slavery, and for a time they preferred to endure the pangs of hunger and the other miseries of a siege. The ordinary business of life was suspended, all political disabilities removed;[5] the Senate of the Areopagus in this crisis took the direction of affairs into its hands;[6] and though many were dying of hunger there was as yet no disposition to speak of making terms. We do not know exactly how long this state of things lasted. But perhaps we may conclude that about September the resolution of the people began to give way. They then sent commissioners to Agis in the Academy,[7] offering peace and alliance on condition that the long walls and the walls of Peiræus should be left intact. Agis referred them to the Ephors; and they accordingly set out for Sparta. The Ephors met them at Sellasia, on the frontier of Laconia, at the junction of the roads from Argos and Tegea, and promptly dismissed them with the warning that they must much improve their offers if they had any hopes of success. The demand now

[3] Diodor. xiii. 107. [*] For the Athenians in Ægina see Thucyd. 2. 27; 7, 57.

[4] Xen. Hell. 2, 2, 5-9. Xenophon says he anchored at the Peiræus with 150 ships. Diodorus (xiii. 107) says, with 'more than 200.' The difference may be accounted for by supposing Diodorus to be thinking of Lysander's whole fleet, which was 200 (Xen. 2, 2, 7), but of which he doubtless left some at Ægina, and reserved others for the expedition to Samos. He kept a strict blockade, proclaiming death to any one who brought in corn, which some nevertheless did. See Isocr. xviii. § 61.

[5] τοὺς ἀτίμους ἐπιτίμους ποιήσαντες ἐκαρτέρουν. Hell. 2, 2, 11.

[6] Lysias, Eratost. l. 472, just as it came forward with assistance on the Persian invasion. Plut. Them. x. 3.

[7] Or to Decelea, as, according to Diodorus, the Spartan army was shortly withdrawn, the blockade being left to the ships, which was sufficient, as the supplies of corn came by sea. Diod. xiii. 107.

made by the Ephors seem to have been much less severe than that actually enforced afterwards; and to have been confined to the demolition of ten stades of the long walls.[8] The answer brought by these commissioners spread despair in the city. But still they were resolved to resist this destruction of their fortifications, and Archestratus, who ventured to speak in favour of yielding, was thrown into prison.

Meanwhile Lysander, having effectually blockaded the Peiræus, appears to have gone to Samos with the view of reducing the one faithful adherent of Athens still left.[9] He probably considered that there were elements at work within the city which would attain his object without any further appeal to arms. If so, he was not mistaken. It was a chance for the Oligarchical faction, of which they could avail themselves with all the appearance, and perhaps some of the reality, of patriotism.

Of that party, worsted for a time after the temporary Revolution of the 400, no one had greater influence with the people than Theramenes. Distrusted by his own party as a *doctrinaire* and unpractical politico-philosopher, jeered at by the comic poets as a turncoat,—a *cothurnus* that would fit either foot,—the people yet recognised in him a man that could be trusted, they thought, to put the safety of his country before fidelity to party. Yet in the year 405 he had been rejected on a scrutiny for the office of Strategus.[*]

This man persuaded the people to send him not to Sparta, but to Lysander, that he might ascertain whether the Spartans really meant to enslave them, or only wished the long walls down as a security for their good faith.[10] He promised to obtain a peace for them without loss of walls or ships.[11] The people, believing his assurances, and thinking that if any one could do so he would be able to make good terms for them, gave him the authority he asked. He went, leaving the people in misery and painful expectation. But instead of returning quickly with good news he spent three months with Lysander, waiting (Lysias bitterly affirms) till the people were so starved as to be willing to accept any terms.[12] Nor were the Oligarchical party idle during his absence. They were busy in persuading everybody to give in to the Spartan proposals, and in getting out of the way those who were prominent for their resistance to them.

[8] Lys. Agoratus, § 14; Xen. Hell. 2, 2, 15.

[9] Plutarch (Lysand. 14) says he was in 'Asia,' but that seems to be a loose expression for the coast and islands.

[*] Lys. Agor. § 10. The nickname κόθορνος is found in Xen. Hell. 2, 3, 31 (Critias' speech), Plutarch, Republ. 277; Nic. 2; the Scholiast on Aristophanes, Ran. 541, 964-8. The Ranæ was exhibited in B.C. 405.

[10] πίστεως ἕνεκα. Xen. Hell. 2, 2, 16.

[11] Lys. Eratosth. § 68, l. 467.

[12] Lys. l. c. Xen. Hell. 2, 2, 16.

Thus the demagogue Cleophon, who had been most strenuous in his opposition, was put to death on some frivolous accusation; and this specimen of the spirit in which the Oligarchs acted was further illustrated by the fall of others in a similar manner.[13] On his returning to Athens Theramenes found, not only that the people were so reduced by misery that they were willing to submit to any terms, but that the party which had been loudest for resistance were frightened into silence. Even then he brought no satisfactory answer from Lysander. He was referred, he said, to the Ephors and must go to them. He was sent with nine others to Sparta, with full powers to treat for peace. When the ten ambassadors returned they were met by an anxious crowd, eager for peace and for the power of leaving the hunger-stricken city. Theramenes had a heavy tale to tell. There had been solemn deliberations at Sparta, and envoys from Corinth and Thebes had urged the entire destruction of Athens; but the Spartans had refused to listen to such a proposition in regard to a city which had done such service to Hellas; and they now granted a peace on these terms:—

(1.) Long walls, and walls of Peiræus, to be pulled down.

(2.) All ships, except twelve, to be given up.

(3.) Exiles (*i.e.* of the Oligarchical party) to be recalled, and an offensive and defensive alliance to be made with Sparta: Athens acknowledging her supremacy and serving under her by land and sea.[14]

The terms were dreadful, and Lysias accuses Theramenes of being the willing proposer of them, and that he did not merely accept them under compulsion.[15] But hard as the terms were, they fell short of the worst,—destruction and slavery. They were brought before an assembly and accepted with only a few dissentients. It was now the spring of the year B.C. 404, and after the sufferings of the winter it must have been with comparative indifference that the citizens saw Lysander sail into the Peiræus, and watched him inaugurating the destruction of the long walls to the music of flute girls, and with every sign of eagerness and joy. The exiled Oligarchs had hastened back, and loudly declared that it was the birthday of liberty for Hellas.

March–April 404.

The destruction of the long walls does not seem to have proceeded very fast or very far,[16] and Lysander soon returned to

13 Lys. Agorat. § 12, x. l. 315 *sq.*; Demosth. 238.

14 A last condition is added by Diodorus, xiii. 107, viz., 'Athens to abandon all towns of which she had taken possession.' Xenophon (Hell. 2, 2. 20) only mentions the first three.

15 Lys. vi. § 70.

16 Lys. v. l. 513. For we find that Lysander in the autumn declared that the Athenians had not fulfilled their part in the terms.

his operations in Samos. But though the formal conditions of the peace were such as we have seen, there was another one, well understood, though not publicly professed. It was the abolition of the democratical form of government, and the substitution of an oligarchy.[17]

The end of the Attic year was now fast approaching [the year of *Alexias*, ending June 21, B.C. 404], when a new Boulè, new Archons, Phylarchs, and other officers, would have to be appointed. The Oligarchical party, now in the ascendant, were resolved to seize this opportunity of consummating the Revolution they had long wished for. The existing Boulè was oligarchical in tone, and lent itself readily to their schemes;[18] nor had the people perhaps after their long months of suffering sufficient spirit for effectual resistance,—the returned exiles no doubt helping to silence the murmurs of those who were still loyal to the Constitution.

The movement was begun by the political clubs. Five men were appointed by their fellow clubsmen, called in compliment to Sparta *Ephors*. These men, without having official rank, were to dictate generally to the Ecclesia, and to cause Phylarchs to be appointed who were favourable to the Oligarchical party.[19] The name of Theramenes is not mentioned among these Ephors, of whom Critias and Eratosthenes were two, but he seems to have acted with authority throughout these months. He would not allow any assembly to be held until he had again sent for Lysander.[20] Then in an assembly, at which the Spartan commanders, Lysander, Philochares, and Miltiades, were present, he proposed the appointment of Thirty men to draw up a code of laws,[21] and meanwhile to carry on the government. The proposal was received with disapproving shouts, but Lysander himself spoke, and hinted broadly that the people had rendered themselves liable to be sold into slavery for transgressing the terms of the peace, and had better look to their safety first.[22] Theramenes also spoke with energy, declaring that he cared nothing for the clamour, and that not only had he at his back the Spartan power, but a large number of citizens.[23] The result was that the opposers were silent, and either voted for the Thirty or left without

17 Lysias affirms that this was one of the voluntary offers made by Theramenes to Sparta. v. § 70.

* 18 Lysias, vi. § 20. 19 Lysias, v. § 43-4.

20 Lys. v. § 71.

* 21 Xen. Hell. 2, 3, 2. Diod. xiv. 3. Lys. xiv. 103. The γραφὴ παρανόμων was first abolished, Aeschin. iii. § 191. 22 Lys. v. § 74.

23 *Ibid.* But Diodorus (xiv. 3) represents Theramenes as resisting the proposal, and being silenced by a threat of death: a confusion apparently arising from his view of Theramenes as a friend of the Demus.

voting,[24] and the assembly voted for the appointment of the Thirty, who were made up of—Ten nominated by the above-named Ephors; ten nominated by Theramenes; ten chosen from the Ecclesia then assembled.[25] Their names were:[26]—

Polychares	Hieron	Diocles	Sophocles	Æschines	Dracontides
Critias	Mnesilochus	Phædrias	Eratosthenes	Theogenes	Eumathes
Melobius	Chremon	Chæreleos	Charicles	Cleomedes	Aristoteles
Hippolochus	Theramenes	Anaetius	Onomacles	Erisistratus	Hippomachus
Euclides	Aresias	Peison	Theognis	Pheidon	Mnesithides.

These Thirty were formally appointed by a vote of the Ecclesia, and Diodorus asserts that Theramenes was especially selected by the Demus from their confidence in his integrity.[27]

Whatever misgivings were entertained by the citizens at these changes, the immediate results were calculated to dispel them. Lysander and his fleet departed to Samos, and Agis at length evacuated Decelea and disbanded the army which had occupied it.[28] The relief must have been immense. The occupation of Decelea had now lasted nine years, and had been not only the cause of great loss but of bitter humiliation to the Athenians.[29] Now, at length the country would be free for the farmer and shepherd, and the overcrowded city find some relief, and peaceable citizens might go about their ordinary business. This pleasing anticipation was soon dispelled. The Thirty, continually postponing the revision of the laws, which was the ostensible reason of their appointment, set about establishing their power. They first secured the nomination of a Boulè and various officials devoted to their interests.[30] They then immediately began the bloody work which has rendered them infamous. The first steps taken in this direction did not seriously alarm honest citizens. Their first victims were the men who had gained an evil reputation as informers under the Democracy.[31] But they were conscious that their next step would be attended with more danger. They therefore asked and obtained the presence of a Spartan guard, and a harmost, Callibius. Relying upon these supporters they began to put to death not only such wretches as they had seized at first, but all whom they believed to be disaffected to their *régime*, and whose wealth

June 21, B.C. 404, the ἀναρχία or 'year without an Archon;' though *Pythodorus* was called Archon Eponymus by the Oligarchs.

[24] Lys. v. § 75.

[25] Lys. v. § 76, *ἐκ τῶν παρόντων*.

[26] Xen. Hell. 2, 3, 2.

[27] Diodor. xiv. 4. See note 23.

[28] Xen. Hell. 2, 3, 3.

[29] Thucyd. 7, 19, 27.

* [30] *ἐκ τῶν ἰδίων φίλων*. Diod. 14, 4. Lysias, vi. § 74, asserts that the Thirty and the Boulè were members of the 400 and their partizans, who had been in banishment.

[31] Xen. Hell. 2, 3, 12. Cp. Lys. 12. § 5, *φάσκοντες δὲ χρῆναι τῶν ἀδίκων καθαρὰν ποιῆσαι τὴν πόλιν*.

made them worth attacking,[32] employing for that object the services of various spies and informers.[33]

These cruelties, however, were not equally approved of by all the Thirty. Theramenes had had no such views in promoting the Revolution. He had a dream of a model State, from which all sycophants and evildoers should be banished, and in which 'the best men' should really govern. But this merciless execution of good men, for no offence but a leaning to the Democracy under which they had been bred, was odious to him. His opposition, in which he seems to have been supported by Eratosthenes,[34] alarmed Critias and the more violent section of the Thirty. Critias proposed as a compromise that a roll of privileged persons (3000 in number) should be drawn up, and should exercise the functions of the old Ecclesia. But Theramenes objected to a definite number. 'The object,' he argued, 'of all our measures is to have the best men (*οἱ βέλτιστοι*) as governors. It is unreasonable to suppose that such persons could ever be included in a definite number. This measure is neither one thing nor the other. It tries to establish a government which in reality is arbitrary, while in form democratical.' He was, however, overborne: the catalogue of the 3000 was drawn up; all other citizens were deprived of their arms, which were stored on the Acropolis; and this was followed by the murder of many citizens, some for the sake of their property, others from motives of private enmity.[35]

Still money was urgently needed, especially for the pay of the Spartan guard and harmost, whom they had promised to support.[36] Theognis and Peison accordingly proposed that certain rich Aliens or Metics should be put to death and their property confiscated. The pretence was to be as usual 'disaffection.' Each of the Thirty was to select a victim, and they were to arrange the execution of the design with each other.[37] But Theramenes again interposed, protesting that in so acting they would be worse than ordinary 'Sycophants,' who at any rate were content with obtaining the forfeiture of their victims' goods. The violent party among the Thirty saw that Theramenes must be got rid of. A meeting of the Boulè was summoned. The tyrants attended with daggers concealed about their persons. Critias spoke, justifying bloodshed as necessary in a Revolution, and denouncing Theramenes as worse than an open

[32] Diodor. xiv. 4.
[33] Batrachus and Æschylides are named by Lys. Erat. § 48.
[34] Lys., v. § 50.
[35] Xen. Hell. 2, 3, 15-21.
[36] Xen. Hell. 2, 3, 13, *θρέψειν δὲ αὐτοὶ ὑπισχνοῦντο.*
[37] Lys., v. § 6-7.

enemy,—a traitor to his own friends as he had ever been. Theramenes replied, justifying his changes of policy as being always dictated by the public interests, and denouncing the policy of Critias as tending to weaken the State by removing its best men. The Boulè was impressed by the words of Theramenes. Critias saw this, and at once bade his partizans show their arms; and since the new law allowed the Thirty on their own responsibility to put to death all who were not on the 'Catalogue,' he erased the name of Theramenes, and exclaimed, '*καὶ τοῦτον ἡμεῖς θανατοῦμεν*.'[38] Theramenes sprang to the altar. But the herald of the Thirty summoned the Eleven. They entered, headed by the shameless Satyrus, and in spite of his protests dragged Theramenes from the altar, and led him through the Agora to the prison, where he was compelled to drink the fatal hemlock. During this scene the Boulè sat silent, awed by the daggers of the Thirty.[39]

Thus released from all control, Critias and his party pushed on in their course of murder. The resolution as to the Metics had been partially carried out. Ten had been selected, of whom two were poor men, that their object should not be too obviously plunder, and these were visited in their houses* or captured in the street and speedily executed and their property fell into the hands of the Thirty. (Lysias, Eratosth. § 7.) Thus supplied with money, the Tyrants took further measures for their own security. They forbade all persons not in the 'Catalogue' to enter the upper city (*τὸ ἄστυ*) at all. At the same time they expelled them from their lands, which they gave to their own friends. These unhappy persons crowded into the Peiræus, or fled to Megara, Thebes, Chalcis, and other towns.[40] Diodorus asserts that more than half the citizens were in exile.[41] The Tyrants regarded these refugees as the French Republican Government did the *émigrés*. They demanded from the various towns that they should be given up. But their demand seems almost universally to have been refused, in spite of the influence of Sparta; the Thebans and the Argives, mainly no doubt from jealousy of Sparta, being especially forward in protecting them.[42]

September B.C. 404. These transactions lasted through the summer months of B.C. 404. In September of that year an event occurred which showed the Tyrants that they

[38] Xen. Hell. 2, 3. 51. But see Arist. R. A. 36-7.

[39] Diodorus (xxv. 5) asserts that Socrates, with two friends, endeavoured to rescue him [*ἅτε καὶ φιλοσοφίας ἐπὶ πλεῖον μετεσχηκὼς παρὰ Σωκράτει*]. His authority, however, is of little weight.

[40] Xen. Hell. 2, 4, 1. Lysias, *περὶ τοῦ ἀδυνάτου*, § 25.

[41] xiv. 5. [42] See on v. l. 174. * An especial grievance, Dem. Androt. § 50.

were not to be allowed to pursue their course unchecked. Thrasybulus, who had shown his devotion to the cause of Democracy at the time of the Four Hundred,[43] was one of those who had taken refuge at Thebes. This man with seventy followers suddenly sallied out of Thebes and seized Phylè, a place about twelve miles from Athens, of great strength and importance, as commanding the pass over Mount Parnes.[44] This movement was secretly encouraged by the Theban authorities,[45] no doubt from jealousy of Sparta, and its success immediately attracted the exiled Democrats from all sides. The Tyrants recognised their danger. They at once mustered their forces and marched out to attack Thrasybulus. Some of the younger and rasher spirits made an attempt to carry the place by storm, but were repulsed with loss. A snowstorm coming on in the night, after a fine day, created a panic in the camp, and caused them to return hurriedly to Athens with a considerable loss of baggage.[46] Preparations for a siege, however, were made. They sent the Spartan guards and two phylæ of cavalry to do duty on the frontier to prevent Thrasybulus from plundering the country, and did establish some form of blockade. Meanwhile Thrasybulus, having command of the road towards Thebes, was collecting a considerable force, and soon had 700[47] men with him, the exiled Democrats flocking into his camp. By a bold stroke he completed the discomfiture of his assailants. He surprised their camp in the night, killed 120 hoplites, and three knights. This seems to have broken up the beleaguering force. The Tyrants in alarm determined to secure for themselves a place of retreat in the event of their being unable to retain their position in Athens. They fastened upon Eleusis, which was especially important as commanding the western pass from Attica to the north over Dryoscephale, the party of Thrasybulus holding the central pass by Phyle. Under a pretence of holding an inspection of the citizens of Eleusis capable of bearing arms, they ordered them to file out of the city gate nearest the sea. As the name of each was taken down on the register, he passed through the gate. When, however, they got to the beach they found themselves surrounded by horsemen, whose attendants arrested them and delivered them to the custody of the Eleven. Next day an assembly was held in the Odeum of the hoplites and equites in the 'Catalogue,' and at the instance of

43 Thucyd. 8, 73-5.

44 Xen. Hell. 2, 4, 2.

45 Diodor. xiv. 32, *συνεργούντων αὐτῷ λάθρα τῶν Θηβαίων.*

46 Diodorus (xiv. 32), like Xenophon (Hell. 2, 4, 3), mentions the snowstorm and the consequent panic. But his order of events differs from that of Xenophon, in that he represents the settlement of the citizens not in the 'Catalogue' in the Peiræus as subsequent to this occupation of Phylè. But of course his authority is as nothing against that of Xenophon.

47 Xen. Hell. 2, 415. Diodorus (l. c.) says 1200.

Critias, who bluntly said that he wished to involve them in the consequences with himself (see Plat. *Apol.* § 32), they were condemned to death, and by one vote, which in itself was illegal.[48]

This probably took place in November B.C. 404, and Thrasybulus, now with over 1000 men, retaliated by effecting an entrance into Peiræus by night. The Tyrants, with hoplites, Spartan guards, and knights, hurried down the road between the long walls. Thrasybulus endeavoured to prevent their entrance into the Peiræus, but without success, the space to be guarded proving too large. He therefore retired to Munychia, an elevation on the eastern part of the Peiræus,[49] where there was a temple of Artemis and a sacred enclosure called the Bendedeion. The Tyrants occupied the Agora of the main town, and the road leading from it to Munychia. They had the superiority in numbers, and their troops were massed fifty deep; but Thrasybulus had the great advantage of an elevated position, having a slope to charge down, and the enemy so thickly massed in front of them that his men could not well miss doing execution with arrows and javelins. After a short but stirring speech Thrasybulus gave the word ['Ενυάλιος] for the charge, and they rushed down the hill, turned the enemy, and pursued them to the level ground.[50] But though no great execution seems to have been done, the victory was rendered extremely valuable by the fall of Critias, who, with another of the Tyrants, Hippomachus, and about seventy men, was killed in the *mêlée*.

The result was a conference between the two parties.

November 404.

Cleocritus, occupying a peculiar and sacred position as μυστῶν κῆρυξ, urged the necessity of peace, and declared that the Tyrants in eight months[51] had killed more than the Spartans in ten years.* The Tyrants, without making any answer, returned to the city, and the next day remained in gloomy conference in their council-chamber. The Three Thousand did not at first meet in a body, but collecting in groups consulted with each other. Those of them who felt themselves deeply involved in the guilt of the Tyrants were for holding out; others were for accepting terms. Finally they met and voted the deposition of the Thirty, and the appointment of ten commissioners to treat with Thrasybu-

48 As being against the *psephisma Cannoni*, as in the case of the generals after Arginusæ. Xen. Hell. 2, 4, 9. Lysias, v. 1. 370. Lysias mentions a visit to Salamis, and Diodorus (14, 32) also mentions Salaminians. The latter were probably those expelled by Lysander.

49 λόφον ἔρημον καὶ καρτερόν. Diod. 14, 33.

50 Diodorus (xiv. 33) speaks of a long and obstinate resistance. That is not the impression to be gathered from Xenophon [Hell. 2, 4, 19].

51 Xen. Hell. 2, 4, 21. The eight months must be counted from the end of March to the end of November. * More than 1500, Aeschin. iii. § 235.

lus.[52] The Tyrants, with the exception of Pheidon and Eratosthenes, retired to Eleusis. The Ten, however, did not show any disposition to make terms with the party of the Peiræus,[53] who, growing more and more numerous, within ten days occupied the whole of Peiræus, and began a kind of siege of the Asty itself.[54]

Meanwhile pressing messages for help reached Sparta from Eleusis and from the Ten in the city.[55] Nor did Lysander fail his friends in their necessity. He obtained for them a loan of 100 talents,[56] and managed to get himself appointed harmost, and his brother Libys navarchus. The party of the Peiræus were now in great straits, being beset by sea and land. But the Spartan king, Pausanias, grudged Lysander such a triumph. He persuaded the Ephors to withdraw the Spartan 'guard,' and though he continued encamped near Peiræus he did not carry on the campaign with any serious intention of completing the business. After a sham assault, and a skirmish in which some 150 Athenians fell, he gave a hint that he was willing to receive ambassadors. They were forwarded to Sparta, and in spite of offers from the Ten to give up the city to the Spartans, an arrangement was come to, of which the following were the chief terms:—

(1.) A complete amnesty and restitution of property to all.

(2.) The only exceptions to be the Tyrants, the ten commissioners who had governed in the Peiræus,[57] and the Eleven, unless they submitted to the usual *εὔθυναι*.[58]

(3.) Any of the city party who feared to stay in Athens might reside at Eleusis.

These events had occupied some months, but Thrasybulus was in possession of Athens before the end of the year of Pythodorus (the *ἀναρχία*), *i.e.* before June 21, B.C. 403. The old Ecclesia was restored and the Boulè and archons appointed for the next year, the Archon Eponymus being Euclides. This pacification was ratified by a solemn procession open to all citizens to join in a sacrifice to Athene on the Acropolis.[59]

[52] One from each tribe. Xen. Hell. 2, 4, 24. Diodorus (xiv. 33) says that they were meant to be ambassadors only to the party in the Peiræus, but made themselves tyrants.

[53] Lysias, v. l. 387-390 *sq.* Of the Ten Lysias gives three names—Pheidon, Hippocles, and Epichares.

★ [54] Xen. Hell. 2, 4, 27. [55] *Ib.* 28. Lys. xiv. § 30.

[56] Afterwards acknowledged as a State debt and repaid. Demosth. c.
★ Lept. 46. Cf. Lysias, xv. l. 175. Aristot. R. A. 40.

[57] *τῶν ἐν Πειραιεῖ ἀρξάντων δέκα.* *Not* the ten who succeeded the Thirty in the city. Aristot. R. A. 35.

[58] This proviso is not mentioned by Xenophon (Hell. 2, 4, 38), but is added by Andocides de Myst. § 90. It made little difference, as the *εὔθυναι* would be sure to result in their condemnation.

★ [59] Lysias, vi. § 80-1. Plutarch, Glor. Ath. ch. vii. Aeschin. iii. § 187.

The Democratical party used their triumph with admirable moderation. Eratosthenes, though impeached by Lysias, does not appear to have been condemned.[60] But the party of the surviving Tyrants at Eleusis could not submit to their defeat, and were said to be hiring mercenary troops. Three years later an expedition was organised against them; their Strategi were, apparently with some treachery,[61] taken and killed, and the rest induced to swear to the terms of pacification. [Aristot. R. A. 40.]

Thus this terrible year ended. The old constitution was restored and arrangements made for drawing up an amended code of laws. The amnesty was secured by a law of Archinus that an action for an alleged offence connected with these transactions might be met by demurrer, *i.e.* that the offence, if committed, was covered by the amnesty; and the demurrer was to be first tried.[62] But though hostilities were at an end, and those who had engaged in them were protected by the amnesty from direct consequences,[63] yet the events of the year affected private interests for many years to come. Scarcely any of the extant speeches of Lysias is without reference to them. Either it is a man's character that is to be cleared or blackened, or it is the suspension of legal business that has entailed loss or given an opportunity for fraud, or the damage sustained by property during the hostilities is pleaded, or the consequence of having served in the cavalry under the Thirty is in question,—in many ways it is plain that the social effects of this year of anarchy remained long after the Revolution itself was at an end.

II.

'ATIMIA.

There is a well-known passage in Andocides (de Myst. § 74-5), which very clearly explains the principles on which this punishment was awarded. [Cf. Wayte on Dem. Androt. § 35.]

There were three kinds of *ἀτιμία*:—

(A.) Temporary *ἀτιμία*, arising from indebtedness to the State, which was terminated by a due satisfaction of such claims.

(B.) Total *ἀτιμία*, disabling a man and his descendants from all civil functions, but not touching his property.

(C.) Partial *ἀτιμία*, disabling a man from the exercise of certain defined acts.

60 See on Lys. iv. l. 209, and on v. l. 558.

61 Xenophon (Hell. 2, 4, 43) says, τοὺς μὲν στρατηγοὺς ἐς λόγους ἐλθόντας ἀπέκτειναν.

62 Isocrat. c. Callim. xviii. 3.

63 But certain persons remained under partial *ἀτιμία*. For instance, those who had served in the cavalry of the Thirty could not speak in the Ecclesia or serve in the Boulè. And. Myst. § 75. And the Demus seized every chance of getting rid of them.

(A.) A man might be indebted to the State in the following ways :—

(1.) By being cast in a suit on his audit (εὐθύνας).
(2.) Or for contempt of court (ἐξούλας).
(3.) Or in public suits (γραφάς).
(4.) Or having been summarily convicted and fined by a magistrate (ἐπιβολήν).
(5.) Or having purchased a contract for some tax and failed to pay the treasury (ὠνάς).
(6.) Or by having given bail to the State.

All such debtors were bound to pay in the ninth Prytany from the time of incurring the debt (*i.e.* in the third month), or to pay double, and to have their property confiscated for the satisfaction of the debt.

(B.) Total ἀτιμία excluded a man and his descendants from all civil functions, and was incurred by the following crimes (among others) :—

(1.) Theft, or taking bribes (κλοπῆς . . δώρων).
(2.) Military offences, leaving his proper rank (λειποταξία), not joining the army (ἀστρατεία), cowardice (δειλία), not joining his ship (ἀναυμαχίου), throwing away his shield (ἀσπίδος ἀποβολή).
(3.) Having *three times* given false evidence (ψευδομαρτυρίων).
(4.) Having *three times* made a false endorsement on a summons (ψευδοκλητείας).
(5.) Ill-treatment of parents (τοὺς γονέας κακῶς ποιεῖν).

(C.) Partial ἀτιμία, inflicted for particular reasons and consisting of definite disabilities. For instance :—

(1.) Men who had served under the Thirty were disabled *from speaking in the Ecclesia*, or being *members of the Boulè.*
(2.) Some were disabled from acting as prosecutors in public indictments.
(3.) Some from laying an information (ἔνδειξις).
(4.) Some from sailing to the Hellespont or to Ionia.
(5.) Some from entering the Agora.

This is not of course an exhaustive list either of the ways in which ἀτιμία could be incurred, or the various degrees in which it was inflicted. But an attentive study of the passage, of which a *résumé* is here given, will convey a sufficiently clear idea of the subject, and will be a great help towards understanding more than one passage in these speeches.

III.

MONEY.

For the calculation of the various sums of money mentioned in these speeches, the following simple table will perhaps be useful:—

6 obols	= 1 drachma
100 drachmæ	= 1 mina
60 minæ (6000 dr.)	= 1 talent

The talent and mina were not coins but sums, and were used as symbols in the calculation of coins. The standard coin was the drachma and was, with its multiples, silver. When a numeral like δισχίλιαι is used without any coin being added, δραχμαί is always to be understood.

Besides this we have three gold coins alluded to—(1) the daric (v. l. 72), which was reckoned as worth twenty Attic drachmæ; (2) the Kyzikene stater (*ib.*), which at any rate in the Bosporus was worth twenty-eight Attic drachmæ (Demosth. 914); whether it was of that value universally does not seem certain, though perhaps Demosthenes' words (ἐκεῖ ἐδύνατο) may imply that it was not; (3) the Attic stater was worth 20 drachmæ, or if pure gold, 28; see Head, *Hist. Num.* p. 450; Kirch. *C. I. A.*, p. 160.

The Athenian silver coinage was purer than that of most other States, though at times attempts were made to debase it. See Arist. Ran. 717 *sq.* Xen. Vect. iii. 2. Polyb. 21, 32.

Down to the half-obol it was of silver, not copper, which helps to explain that curious habit often alluded to by Aristophanes of putting small change in the mouth. See Equit. 51. Pax, 645. Vespæ, 609. Aves, 503. Eccles. 818. Theophrast. Char. vi.

IV.

Two points in connection with the life of Lysias on which my statements have been attacked may be most conveniently treated here—

I. The Chronology of Lysias' life.

The dates given in the *Vitæ X. Oratorum* are as follows:—

Birth	**Year of Philocles, B.C. 459-8.**
Departure to Thurii .	**Year of Praxiteles, B.C. 444-3, *i.e.* spring of 443.**
Return to Athens .	**Year of Callias, B.C. 410-1 [summer, for the Four Hundred were in power].**
Death	**Variously stated as in his 83d, 76th, or 80th year, *i.e.* in 375, 382, or 378 B.C.**

The author also states (1) that Lysias was fifteen when he went to Thurii; (2) that he stayed there thirty years; (3) that before his death he saw Demosthenes as a *μειράκιον* [b. B.C. 384]; (4) that his father Cephalus was dead when he went to Thurii; (5) that Cephalus had originally settled at Athens on the invitation of Pericles.

Now Lampon led the colony to Thurii in the spring of B.C. 443. If Lysias was fifteen in 443, he was born in 458. But did he go to Thurii at the first establishment of the colony? Blass and others have decided that he did not do so. On the other hand, the author of the *Lives* distinctly states that he did, and Dionysius as clearly implies it. The words of the latter are:—"When he was fifteen he went to Thurii with two brothers to share in the colony which the Athenians, in conjunction with the rest of Hellas, were sending in the twelfth year before the Peloponnesian war." The use of the imperfect ἔστελλον makes any other meaning of this sentence impossible.

If, however, he did not go then, we must reject the statement of his having stayed there thirty years, as there is no reasonable doubt of his having returned in 411.

But accepting the statement of his birth in 459-8, and the length of his life as about 83 years, the date of his death would be 375, when Demosthenes would be nine years old. The statements of our authorities then are at least consistent.

The opposite view consists in rejecting all these statements except (1) the death of Cephalus before Lysias' departure for Thurii, (2) the age of Lysias at that departure.

It is then argued that Cephalus would not have been attracted by Pericles until the latter became prominent—say about 460 B.C.; that living at Athens thirty years [Lys. Erat. 4] he must have died about 430; that if Lysias was fifteen then, the year of his birth was 445.

In confirmation of this view we have no ancient testimony except this. In Plato's *Republic* Cephalus is represented as still alive, though in extreme old age, and it is supposed that the scene of the *Republic* is meant to be laid in B.C. 430. Assuming the truth of this supposition, it is still evident that a date depending on Plato's regard for historical probabilities in the grouping of a dialogue rests on a very insecure foundation; and when Professor Mahaffy (*Hist. of Gr. Lit.* ii. p. 141), assuming that Lysias died soon after 380, proceeds to say "he does not seem to have lived to an advanced age," he is stating the exact contrary of the only authorities we have, and of universal tradition. Nevertheless it may be a true statement; and if we put aside the authority of Dionysius and of the author of the Lives of the Orators, we have no certain data for a solution of the point.

II. As to the place of residence of Polemarchus.

I have said in p. xxx, "Both brothers lived in the Peiraeus." Professor Jebb has said, "From Erat. § 16 it follows that Polemarchus lived in Athens," and a writer in the *Academy* has assumed this as an undoubted fact, and my statement to be a simple blunder.[1]

[1] So also Blass *die Attische Beredsamkeit*, p. 338, '*sie besassen drei Häuser, eins im Peiräeus, wo Lysias, und ein anderes in der Stadt, wo Polemarchos wohnte, mit dem ersteren war eine Schildfabrik verbunden.*

It certainly may have been the case that Polemarchus lived in Athens. But I think it unlikely, for it rarely happened that a metic did so [Xen. Vect. 1, 6], and it does not seem certain that the brothers were *Isoteles*, though Lysias himself became so after the restoration of the democracy. Again we know from Plato [Repub. 1, 328] that Polemarchus, at one time at any rate, possessed a house in the Peiraeus. Moreover, the wife of Polemarchus was in a house in the Peiraeus at the time of her husband's arrest [Erat. § 19]; nor does the passage relied upon from the Eratosthenes, § 16, appear on closer examination conclusive. Lysias says: "Arrived at the house of the shipmaster, Acheneos, I sent a messenger to the Asty to learn news of my brother. On his return he informed me that Eratosthenes had arrested him *in the street* [ἐν τῇ ὁδῷ] and taken him off to prison." If Eratosthenes had effected the arrest in his house the proof would have been conclusive; he did it, however, in the street [or, in the road from Athens to Peiraeus?], which gives no certain indication of his place of residence. Nor can we conclude anything from the fact of Lysias sending to the Asty for news of him. He was absent from home, probably doing business in Athens, and when he was once arrested and put in prison tidings of him would be best learnt in the Asty itself.

V.

THE OATH TAKEN BY THE ATHENIAN DICASTS. PRESERVED IN DEMOSTHENES, 746.

[Oath of Athenian Dicasts. Demosth. 746. For reasons against receiving it as the genuine oath, see Wayte's notes. For the objection to Clause 2 'as if a tyranny could be voted,' it might be alleged that 'political decisions' have never failed to bring discredit on law courts, and it is in this sense that an inequitable decision is in its nature revolutionary, that Demosth., *ib.* § 152, interprets it, cf. Aesch. iii. § 195; besides, a certain number of them annually revised the laws as Nomothetae.]

'I will vote in accordance with the laws and the decrees of the Demus of the Athenians, and of the Boulè of the Five Hundred.

'That a tyrant should be I will not vote, nor an oligarchy; nor, if any try to abolish the Demus of the Athenians, or speak or put to the vote aught contrary to these things, will I hearken to him.

'Nor a cancelling of private debts, nor a redistribution of land or houses of the Athenians.

'I will not recall those in exile, nor those on whom sentence of death has been passed. Neither those who are abiding will I banish contrary to the existing laws and the decrees of the Demus of the Athenians,—I will not do so myself, nor suffer others so to do.

'I will not confirm an office so that a man hold it before he have passed his audit for another office, whether one of the nine Archons, or sacred Recorder, or whatever offices are balloted for this day with the nine Archons,—whether herald, or ambassador, or deputies.[1]

'I will not vote that the same man hold the same office twice, nor that the same man hold two offices in the same year.

'I will receive no gifts on account of my service in court,—neither myself nor any other man or woman for me, by any means or contrivance whatsoever.

'I am not under thirty years of age.

'I will listen to the accuser and the defendant both alike.

'I will give my vote on the question at issue, and none other.

'I swear by Zeus Poseidon Demeter: I invoke utter destruction on myself and my house[2] if I transgress aught of these things, and many blessings if I keep my oath.'

[1] *σύνεδροι*, *i.e.* members of the Congress of States sitting at Athens after B.C. 377. See Dict. of Antiq., Grote, ix. p. 319.

[2] Compare the comic oath in Aristoph. Ran. 586:—

> *ἀλλ' ἤν σε τοῦ λοιποῦ ποτ' ἀφέλωμαι χρόνου*
> *πρόρριζος αὐτός, ἡ γυνή, τὰ παίδια*
> *κάκιστ' ἀπολοίμην.*

Pollux (8, 122) says that the oath was by Zeus, Demeter, and Apollo.

VI

This Appendix aims to make intelligible references given in Shuckburgh's original Introduction, Notes and Appendices (marked with an asterisk in the margin of this edition) to speeches not reprinted in this volume. It translates Shuckburgh's own system of numbering the speeches and his own line numbers into the numbering of the speeches (with paragraph numbers) normally found in editions of the Corpus Lysiacum (e.g. Oxford Classical Text). At the same time it adds the gist of Shuckburgh's note from the cross reference where it helps to explain a historical, legal or syntactical point at issue in the text of a speech printed in this edition.

INTRODUCTION

p. 2	"Preface to Second Edition"	Appendix IV
p. 8	"Preface to Second Edition"	Appendix IV
p. 9	vi. l. 48.	13.7
p. 13	Orat. xvi.	32 Κατὰ Διαγείτονος
p. 18	Oration viii.	16 Ὑπερ Μαντιθέου
	Oration xiii.	24 Ὑπὲρ τοῦ ἀδυνάτου
p. 20	xvi. ll. 165, 245.	32.20 and 28
	xvi. ll. 165, 171, 176.	32.20 and 21
	vi. l. 311.	13.45
	xvi. l. 60.	32.8
	vi. l. 276.	13.40
	vi. l. 313.	13.45
	iii. l. 29.	9.6
	xii. l. 15.	23.3
	xiii. l. 147.	24.20
	ii. § 4 - 8.	7.4 - 8
	Or. xiii.	24 Ὑπὲρ τοῦ ἀδυνάτου

NOTES

p. 104	"The last case"	9. Ὑπερ τοῦ στρατιώτου
	Orat. iii. l. 58.	9.10
p. 105	ii. l. 216.	7.32

The ἂν in the apodosis is sometimes omitted (see Goodwin, § 222, note 1); e.g. Plato, *Symposium* 190c, Thucydides 7.6.1, Herodotus 8.43, Demosthenes 870. The result is represented as all but actually happening, or as certain to happen.

p. 108	vi. § 85.	13.85
	ii. § 22 and § 20.	7.22 and 20
p. 109	vi. l. 472.	13.54 (see over)

ἀνδράποδον ἐξήγαγεν 'abducted a slave.' He would thereby incur the punishment of an ἀνδραποδιστής, whether he carried off another man's slave, or a free man into slavery. See iv. l. 64.

p. 109 vii. l. 170. 16.21
p. 110 ii. l. 3. 7.1

πράγματα 'vexatious business', especially of the legal sort.

p. 110 xv. l. 133. 30.17
iii. l. 69. 9.12

εὔθυναι = (1) the audit or account submitted by a magistrate on the expiration of his office, whether annual or extraordinary, before εὔθυνοι, who were chosen by lot from each tribe; (2) a suit brought against him in respect of such audit. Cf. Andocides 10.15, εὐθύνας ὀφλεῖν. (See also on vi. l. 180.)

p. 112 viii. l. 78. 16.10

μοι ... ἔγκλημα 'charge *against* me.' Technically ἔγκλημα is the summons to attend served on the defendant in a suit. It is here used as a general term for a 'charge', the person *against* whom it is made is in the dative. Cf. a similar meaning and construction in iv. l. 154.

p. 112 vi. § 64. 13.64
vi. l. 474. 13.67
p. 113 vi. § 37. 13.37
p. 119 i. l. 33. 5.4

τῷ δημοσίῳ βοηθοῦντες 'while assisting the treasury'. Thus Jebb translates τῷ δημοσίῳ, a sense in which Demosthenes (Mid. § 182), uses it: cf. Andocides 1.73, ὀφείλειν τῷ δημοσίῳ. Cf. also Plutarch, *Themistocles* 3 and 25, δημοσίων χρημάτων and συναχθέντων χρημάτων εἰς τὸ δημόσιον. However, τὸ κοινόν is the usual word for the treasury, and τὸ δημόσιον is also used for 'the state'. See Aeschines, *in Ctes.* § 234.

p. 119 i. l. 9. 5.2

The metics or resident aliens formed in Athens a large and industrious class (calculated as 10,000 male adults in B.C. 309. Athenaeus, vi. 272 C.). They paid a tax (μετοίκιον, 12 drachmae per ann.) for the privilege of residing in the town, and were subject to public burdens and military service, though they were not admitted to serve as hoplites. Cf. v. l. 140, and Xenophon, *de Vect.* 2.2. They were under disabilities also; they were unable to inherit landed property, and were obliged to have a regular patron (προστάτης) to appear for them on all public occasions, and were liable for any offence against the various enactments concerning them to be sold as slaves. Hence it is that our orator says of Kallias (5.1) that on his contest depends his freedom, περὶ τοῦ σώματος ἠγωνίζετο.

p. 121 i. l. 3. 5.1

See also on νυνὶ δέ, iv: l. 13 above.

p. 121 ii. l. 98. 7.15

δέον, accus. absolute of neuter participle, Goodwin, § 278, 2.

p. 122 ii. l. 270. 7.40

τοιούτους ... οἷς ... οὐκ ἂν 'men of such character as these (whom you see accusing me), to whom you cannot in fairness give credit'. For τοιούτους οὕς, which is not equivalent to τοιούτους οἵους, cf. 13.1 and 13.13. We have τοιαῦτα οἷα, v. l. 694.

p. 128 xv. l. 175. 30.22

'Boeotians' are spoken of, not 'Thebans', because Thebes was now supreme in united Boeotia, and until the peace of Antalcidas (B.C. 387). See Hicks' *Manual of Greek Inscriptions*, p. 123.

p. 129 ii. l. 112. 7.17

εἰ ... παρέστη ... μοι 'if it had entered into my head'. Cf. v. l. 429.

p. 131 vi. l. 61. 13.9

The terms finally insisted upon by the Spartans seem to have included the entire destruction of the Long Walls, and those of Peiraeus. But this does not seem ever to have been entirely carried out. The terms originally were that 10 stades of the Long Walls should come down. (See also 13.14 and on v. l. 513 above.)

p. 131 ii. l. 122. 7.18

παρεσκευασάμην 'I made a corrupt arrangement with'. This is the word specially used in such cases: cf. Demosthenes 853, τοὺς μάρτυρας οὐ παρεσκευάσμεθα. *Ib.* 852, παρεσκεύασται μάρτυρας ψευδεῖς. *Ib.* 1062, πολλὰ καὶ ἀναίσχυντα παρεσκευάσαντο πρὸς τὸν ἀγῶνα. Also Lysias 13. 12, παρασκευάσαντες δικαστήριον 'having packed a court'.

p. 134 iii. l. 56. 9.10

φανερός ... μὴ ἐλθών 'plainly shown not to have gone'. Obs. φαίνομαι ἐλθεῖν 'I appear to have gone', φαίνομαι ἐλθών 'I am shown to have gone'. Goodwin, § 280, note 1.

p. 134 ii. l. 270. 7.40 (see on p. 122 above)
ii. l. 181. 7.27 (see over)

διαβεβλημένος 'in a position of suspicion and distrust'. *Si nunc jaceam invidia et contemptu perculsus.* So in Lys. (?) 8.7, διαβεβλῆσθαι is opposed to εὐδοκιμεῖν. Cf. the use of the active in Thucydides 2.18, ἡ σχολαιότης διέβαλεν αὐτόν.

p. 134 viii. 1. 32. 16.65

The policy of the Thirty was to involve as many citizens as possible in their own guilt, whereby they hoped to be more secure. Thus Critias, when urging the assembly in the Odeum to vote the death of the Eleusinians, said bluntly, δεῖ ὑμᾶς ὥσπερ καὶ τιμῶν μεθέξετε, οὕτω καὶ τῶν κινδύνων μετέχειν. τῶν οὖν Ἐλευσινίων καταψηφιστέον ἐστὶν, ἵνα ταὐτὰ ἡμῖν καὶ θαρρῆτε καὶ φοβῆσθε - Xenophon, *Hellenica* 2.4.9. See on v.1. 652.

p. 136 i. 1. 6. 5.1

In v. 1. 98, συμβολαῖα means 'debts' and in 17.3, λαχὼν παντὸς τοῦ συμβολαίου = having obtained leave to bring a suit for the recovery of the entire debt: but συμβολαῖα stands generally for any bargain or business engagement betwen two or more persons. For the technical meaning of συμβολαῖαι δίκαι, so much disputed, see Jowett, *Thucydides* vol. ii. p. lxxxv,

p. 139 ii. 1. 164. 7.24

ἔμελλε ... ἔσεσθαι 'was plainly likely to be'; for the fut. infin. with μέλλω, see Goodwin, § 202, 3. The future and present are used indifferently. The true aorist perhaps does not occur; in such a phrase as κεἰ μέλλω θανεῖν (Euripides, *Medea* 392) the aorist of θνήσκω is a quasi-present; and in Polybius 1.19.8 ἔμελλον ἐπανελέσθαι is a mark of later Greek.

p. 140 iii. 1. 18. 9.4

κατελέγην στρατιώτης 'I was put on the list for military service'. The duty of making up the list (κατάλογος) for service on any occasion fell on the Strategi. They had the whole list of citizens of military age to choose from, and no doubt if they chose fairly they would regard service on a campaign as a reason for not putting a man's name on again for a certain period. But the list thus made out seems to have been on occasions, either from favour or by allowed substitution, altered by the admission of Metics and Thetes. Thus Thucydides speaks of lists where such substitution has not taken place as χρηστοὶ or καθαροὶ (6.13.3; 5.8.2). Another unfair advantage obtained by money or favour was the alteration of the service from the infantry to the cavalry (see Aristophanes, *Knights* 1370). The list was put up on one of the ten statues of eponymous heroes in the Agora, and each person who found his name on it had to appear at the specified time with three days' rations, σίτι' ἡμερῶν τριῶν (Aristophanes, *Peace* 1182 - 3).

p. 140 ii. l. 98. 7.8 (see on p. 121 above)
iii. l. 18. 9.4 (see on p. 140 above)
p. 141 ii. l. 122. 7.18 (see on p. 131 above)
p. 144 ii. l. 181. 7.27 (see on p. 134 above)
p. 146 vi. l. 444. 13.63

For this technical use of κατέρχομαι, see Aristophanes, *Frogs* 1165, φεύγων δ' ἀνὴρ ἥκει τε καὶ κατέρχεται.

p. 147 ii. l. 37. 7.6

The yearly raids of the Spartans, crowned by their permanent occupation of Deceleia, are detailed in Thucydides. The panic caused by them drove the country people into the city, whose estates were thus often abandoned to every kind of pillage. See vii. l. 248, and Thucydides 2.18.5; 2.19.1 - 2; 2.47.3 - 4; 3.1.1 - 2; 7.18 - 19.

p. 151 ii. l. 122. 7.18 (see on p. 131 above)
p. 153 ii. l. 145. 7.27

κατηγορεῖς 'you assert in your speech for the prosecution'. In this sense κατηγορεῖν will take the accusative of the thing charged, Demosthenes, παράνοιαν αὐτοῦ κατηγορεῖν; or accusative and infinitive, *id.* ψευδεῖς ἂν κατηγόρουν εἶναι (cf. the use of *defendere*); or, as here (7.27), a simple sentence introduced by ὡς or ὅτι, as equivalent to λέγειν.

p. 153 vi. l. 4. 13.1

κηδεστής will apply to any relation by marriage (κῆδος), like the Latin *affinis*.

p. 155 vi. l. 413. 13.59
viii. l. 74. 16.10

ἐπιδούς 'giving them as dowry', see 32.6. The word implies giving something *besides*. Thucydides 2.101, ὑποσχόμενος ἀδελφὴν ἑαυτοῦ δώσειν καὶ χρήματα ἐπ' αὐτῇ; Euripides, *Hippolytus* 628.

p. 156 vi. l. 33. 13.5

The disastrous affair of Aegospotami (a small river flowing into the the Hellespont, 15 stades above Sestus) took place in the summer of B.C. 405. It was not a sea-fight, but a successful stratagem of Lysander's, whereby he took and towed off almost without a blow 171 Athenian ships, and took 3000 prisoners (Plutarch, *Lysander* 10). Out of the whole Athenian fleet, only 7, under the leadership of Conon, could be got ready in time to escape, besides the 'Paralus', which escaped to carry the news to Athens. (Plutarch says 8 besides the 'Paralus'. In the fragment of a speech of Lysias (21.11) the number is put at 12.) The men were on shore and scattered, and could not get to their ships in time to meet Lysander, who rowed swiftly over from the opposite town, Lampsacus, summoned by a signal from his own squadron of observation; Pausanias, 4.17.3, says, by the treachery of Adeimantus, one of the Athenian commanders. Xenophon, *Hellenica* 2.1.17 - 32.

p. 156 viii. l. 74. 16.10

ἐξέδωκα 'gave them in marriage', *i.e.* with a dowry or portion. This was the duty of the κύριος of a woman, who in default of a father would be the brother, see x. l. 404.

p. 156 viii. l. 169. 16.20 - 21

For the discredit attaching to indifference to public business, see on iv. l. 70.

p. 158 vi. l. 62. 13.9

οἴοιτο for this special use of the optative in *oratio obliqua*, see Goodwin, § 247.

p. 158 ii. l. 164. 7.24 (see on p. 139 above)
p. 159 ii. l. 209. 7.31

τριηραρχῶν ... εἰσφορὰς ... χορηγῶν ... λειτουργῶν. He mentions the three most costly and best known of the public expenses borne by citizens, either singly or in partnership, - the equipping a trireme, contributing to the expenses of a war, etc., and the fitting out a chorus for the plays in the theatre. There were others of course, and the student should consult the articles λειτουργία, τριηραρχία, etc., in the Dictionary of Antiquities.

p. 159 ii. l. 270. 7.40 (see on p. 122 above)
p. 160 ii. l. 43 - 5. 7.7
ix. l. 85. 17.10

τῶν συνδίκων 'the fiscal commissioners' or 'syndics' presided at the trial; cf. 16.7.

p. 163 ii. l. 68. 7.11

τοίνυν is constantly used at the beginning of a new point in the argument.

p. 163 vi. l. 4. 13.1 (see on p. 153 above)
p. 165 viii. l. 78. 16.10 (see on p. 112 above)
ii. l. 1 - 2 (and 3) 7.1 (see on p. 110 above)
xiii. l. 150. 24.20 (see over)

The Agora was surrounded by *tabernae* or shops, and they were naturally more filled by the loungers in the Agora than others more remote. A daily visit to the Agora was a usual habit of the Athenian.

p. 165	viii. l. 74.	16.10 (see on p. 156 above)
p. 166	ii. l. 270.	7.40 (see on p. 122 above)
p. 168	ii. l. 257 (and 140).	7.38 (and 20)

συκοφάντης, whatever its derivation, came to mean not merely a man who got up charges against others, true or false, but one who did so for personal profit.

p. 170	ii. l. 209.	7.31 (see on p. 159 above)

APPENDICES

p. 173	vi. l. 33.	13.5 (see on p. 156 above)
p. 176	vi. § 70.	13.70 Κατὰ Ἀγοράτου
p. 177	vi. § 20.	13.20
	xiv. l. 103.	28.14
p. 178	vi. § 74.	13.74
p. 180	xiv. l. 5.	28.1
p. 183	xiv. § 30.	28.30
	xv. l. 175.	30.22
	vi. § 80 - 81.	13.80 - 81.